44.95

Implementing Homeland Security for Enterprise IT

Related Titles from Digital Press

Rittinghouse & Hancock, *Cybersecurity Operations Handbook*,
ISBN 1-55558-306-7, 1336pp, 2003

Speed & Ellis, *Internet Security*,
ISBN 1-55558-298-2, 398pp, 2003

Kenyon, *Implementing Network Security*,
ISBN 1-55558-291-5, 648pp, 2004

Rhoton, *Mobile Security*,
ISBN 1-55558-284-2, 288pp, 2004

XYPRO, *HP NonStop Server Security*,
ISBN 1-55558-314-8, 618pp, 2003

Casey, *Digital Evidence and Computer Crime*, Second Edition,
ISBN 0-12-163104-4, 688pp, 2004

Haddow, *Introduction to Homeland Security*,
ISBN 0-7506-7787-2, 500pp, 2004

Kovacich, *The Information Systems Security Officer's Guide*,
ISBN 0-7506-7656-6, 361pp, 2003

Casey, *Handbook of Computer Crime Investigation*,
ISBN 0-12-163103-6, 448pp, 2002

Boyce and Jennings, *Information Assurance*,
ISBN 0-7506-7327-3, 261pp, 2002

For more information or to order these and other Digital Press titles, please visit
our website at books.elsevier.com/digitalpress!
At books.elsevier.com/digitalpress you can:
• Join the Digital Press Email Service and have news about
our books delivered right to your desktop
• Find the latest news on titles
• Read sample chapters of featured titles for free
• Download free software to accompany selected texts

QA
76.9
.A25
E74
2004

Implementing Homeland Security for Enterprise IT

Michael Erbschloe

HILBERT COLLEGE
McGRATH LIBRARY
5200 SOUTH PARK AVE
HAMBURG, NY 14075

ELSEVIER
DIGITAL
PRESS

Amsterdam • Boston • Heidelberg • London • New York • Oxford
Paris • San Diego• San Francisco • Singapore • Sydney • Tokyo

Digital Press is an imprint of Elsevier
200 Wheeler Road, Burlington, MA 01803, USA
Linacre House, Jordan Hill, Oxford OX2 8DP, UK

Copyright © 2004, Elsevier Inc. All rights reserved.

No part of this publication may be reproduced, stored in a retrieval system, or transmitted in any form or by any means, electronic, mechanical, photocopying, recording, or otherwise, without the prior written permission of the publisher.

Permissions may be sought directly from Elsevier's Science & Technology Rights Department in Oxford, UK: phone: (+44) 1865 843830, fax: (+44) 1865 853333, e-mail: permissions@elsevier.com.uk. You may also complete your request on-line via the Elsevier homepage (http://elsevier.com), by selecting "Customer Support" and then "Obtaining Permissions."

∞ Recognizing the importance of preserving what has been written, Elsevier prints its books on acid-free paper whenever possible.

Library of Congress Cataloging-in-Publication Data
Application submitted.

British Library Cataloguing-in-Publication Data
A catalogue record for this book is available from the British Library.

ISBN: 1-55558-312-1

For information on all Digital Press publications
visit our website at www.digitalpress.com and www.bh.com/digitalpress

03 04 05 06 07 08 10 9 8 7 6 5 4 3 2 1

Printed in the United States of America

To my Mother

To Baley Montag

Contents

Foreword

It is human nature not to take precautions or mitigate risk until after something bad occurs. Who would choose a steady diet of celery sticks over greasy fries unless cholesterol levels prove to be life threatening? Why carry terrorist insurance or conduct airport shoe screenings in the absence of a 9/11-type event? Even in circumstances where there is no first-hand misfortune, we implement protective measures because the threat is so likely that precaution becomes a social norm—like keeping Band-Aids in the medicine chest, storing a flashlight in the car, or printing hard copies of valuable contracts created on a computer—or because legal or market forces create repercussions that outweigh our reasonable beliefs that the harm will not touch us. For instance, we are incentivized to carry auto insurance by virtue of laws that take away our money or privileges if we fail to buy coverage.

The core motivator behind any precaution and mitigation activity is the belief that we are individually or collectively more secure. Regardless of whether the measure actually decreases the risk, if we believe that we can affect our physical, social, or financial security, we will embrace those assurance mechanisms. As a wise friend once said, "I don't need to know I'm right, I just need to know I believe I'm right." Enter homeland security. . . .

The components of our national infrastructure are not new—agriculture and water, public health, emergency services, telecommunications, energy services, transportation, banking and finance, government and defense facilities, and commercial entities have existed since the origin of our country. Why is it that they are now deemed critical infrastructures and key assets that require coordination between government, private citizens, and industry? One pivotal reason is that the proliferation of computer networks and information technologies (IT) has created a cybernervous system connecting these national entities. Modern information technology advances have enhanced the individual and collective functioning of critical infrastructures, while creating a tight coupling between them that challenges our traditional security-assurance mechanisms.

This book addresses the precautions, prevention, mitigation, and recovery mechanisms that will help companies enhance IT security at an organizational level, while contributing to the security of the larger national critical infrastructure. As such, it is the first of its kind to endeavor to translate *The National Strategy to Secure Cyberspace* and *The National Strategy for the Physical Protection of Critical Infrastructures and Key Assets* into practical instructions for securing our cybernervous system. Although these authoritative documents do not have legal teeth, they nonetheless wield much influence on forthcoming requirements and incentives that target enterprise IT security. Without measurable processes, tools, and know-how to implement IT security requirements, organizations are deprived of the belief that they can affect their individual and collective physical, financial, and social security assurances. This book takes on the responsibility of bridging the gap that currently exists.

Although this book focuses primarily on the who, what, when, where, and how of implementing homeland security initiatives, it is helpful to remind ourselves why our organizations should stock our proverbial IT medicine chests with cyber-Band-Aids.

Our increasing dependence on technology has brought about enhanced business functionality and productivity, while exposing our organizations to more frequent and severe threats. Securing organizations in this Internetworked society demands better cooperation with law enforcement and national security operations, since they are uniquely positioned to provide critical and specialized information services beyond the capabilities of any single organization. Cyberattacks on businesses and communication networks can crush a company's bottom line and destabilize the commercial infrastructure. Law enforcement and homeland security agencies desire to protect companies through prevention measures and the prosecution and incapacitation of criminals committing computer crime.

For private-sector enterprises, business productivity and profitability are driving forces, and law enforcement is chartered with enforcing the laws designed to protect social interests, prevent criminal activity, and promote a sense of security assurance. Unfortunately, our rapidly evolving technosociety has not engaged law enforcement to the extent that we have when responding to traditional crimes and threats.

We need to culture the same trust and partnerships between enterprises and with law enforcement to remediate cybercrime and share information about threats and vulnerabilities. The goal is to reach a stage where reporting a hack or insider compromise of our digital assets becomes as second nature as reporting a breaking and entering of our physical buildings. We cannot expect to abate the frequency and severity of cyberthreats without more components of the infrastructure working together and with law enforcement to track down cyberthreats. In the end, this interface will enable more effective prevention of cyberthreats that impair your business functionality. This crosscutting of information will help your organization understand why sharing information and involving law enforcement to help resolve a cyberincident is not counterproductive to business goals.

This book can help advance public-private cooperation by identifying essential elements of an organization's policies and procedures, incident response plans, and IT security awareness programs, and partnerships that will further the goals of your organization, law enforcement, and homeland security.

In order to believe that we can take steps to enhance our homeland security, we must strive to live the model advocated in this book at an organizational level and to engender a social norm of sharing information and taking precautionary measures.

Erin Kenneally, M.F.S., J.D.

Forensic Analyst/Attorney

San Diego Supercomputer Center

Preface

Both *The National Strategy for the Physical Protection of Critical Infrastructures and Key Assets* and *The National Strategy to Secure Cyberspace* have many consequences as well as opportunities for IT managers. This book provides IT managers with an introduction to those national homeland security initiatives and a framework to implement and integrate into their organization's enterprise IT environment.

Security, and especially computer security, is one of the largest-growth professions of the twenty-first century. The soaring increase in the number of Internet users, combined with the constant computerization of business processes, has created new opportunities for computer criminals and terrorists. Study after study has consistently revealed that cyberattacks, hacking, and computer-based criminal activities are costing businesses and government organizations billions of dollars each year.

Just as law-enforcement agencies around the world started to fight back against computer crimes, a new element was introduced—terrorism and the threat of cyberterrorism. It has been a long, hard struggle to train law-enforcement personnel in computer crime–related issues and to recruit skilled computer professionals into law-enforcement careers. Although these efforts are far from finished, it is important for organizations of all types that depend on computers and communications networks to start working more closely with law enforcement.

How companies can benefit from using the Internet is expanding everyday. There are more new marketplaces. There are new marketing, sales, and customer-service methods. The worlds of business and consumers have rapidly become the wired and connected world. It is truly an exciting time to be in business. However, it is truly a time of opportunity for terrorists to disrupt our new world of communications and commerce easily and readily. To keep this from happening, the IT community, which now includes law-enforcement and national security operations, will need to work together.

Introduction

The September 11, 2001, terrorist attacks illustrated the immense vulnerability of the United States to terrorist threats. Since then there have been considerable efforts to develop plans and methods to protect critical infrastructures and key assets. The government at all levels, private-sector organizations, and concerned citizens have begun to establish partnerships and to develop action plans. But there are many questions yet to be answered about what organizations should actually do to protect their assets and their people, while participating in national efforts to improve security. This book, *Implementing Homeland Security Initiatives in Enterprise IT*, provides practical steps that managers in all organizations and sectors can take to move security from the planning process into practice.

The Department of Homeland Security (DHS) began formal operations in early 2003. DHS was formed as a result of the September 11, 2001, terrorist attacks on the World Trade Center, the Pentagon, and in Pennsylvania.

Physical protection of infrastructures and assets

In February 2003, DHS published *The National Strategy for the Physical Protection of Critical Infrastructures and Key Assets,* which outlines national goals, objectives, and principles to help physically secure critical infrastructures. The strategy calls for cooperation between government, industry, and private citizens and is designed to protect:

- Agriculture and food
- Water
- Public health

- Emergency services
- Defense industrial base
- Telecommunications
- Energy
- Transportation
- Banking and finance
- Chemical industry and hazardous materials
- Postal and shipping
- National monuments and icons
- Nuclear power plants
- Dams
- Government facilities
- Commercial key assets

Chapters 1 through 5 provide business planners with an analysis of the principles and call for action from *The National Strategy for the Physical Protection of Critical Infrastructures and Key Assets*. There are several points about the physical protection of computer systems and telecommunications systems that planners should address. First and foremost is that the U.S. government expects cooperation in the prevention of events that could damage the private sector's ability to function and deliver essential services[1].

One of the key steps that the U.S. government wants to accomplish is "Taking stock of our most critical facilities, systems, and functions and monitoring their preparedness across sectors and governmental jurisdictions[2]."

To participate fully in this effort, the type of exposure inventory and mitigation analysis will need to be executed for all assets owned or controlled by an organization to determine if they are critical to the national infrastructure. Federal agencies are to assist state and local governments and private companies in their efforts to

- Organize and conduct protection and continuity of operations planning and elevate awareness and understanding of threats and vulnerabilities to critical facilities, systems, and functions.

- Identify and promote effective sector-specific risk-management policies and protection practices and methodologies.
- Expand voluntary protection-related information sharing among private entities within sectors, as well as between government and private entities.

It is uncertain how government security and disaster-recovery requirements for organizations identified as holding assets considered critical to the economy and security of the United States will evolve. However, given all of the priorities and principles detailed in the strategy documents, the following steps apply:

- Conduct an exposure inventory.
- Assess mitigation and protection steps that are in place.
- Perform a risk analysis.
- Adjust mitigation and protection steps based on outcome of risk analysis.
- Maintain vigilance in monitoring and detecting incidents.
- Detect incidents and verify occurrence.
- Report to law enforcement or appropriate government agency.
- Assess damage.
- Restore systems.
- Evaluate similar systems or environments for vulnerability.
- Adjust mitigation and protection steps based on occurrence of incidents.
- Return to monitoring mode.

Cybersecurity in the age of terrorism

DHS also released *The National Strategy to Secure Cyberspace* in February 2003. It provides a framework for protecting technology assets from electronic or hacking attacks. The documents sets forth several priorities:

- Priority I: A National Cyberspace Security Response System

- Priority II: A National Cyberspace Security Threat-and-Vulnerability Reduction Program
- Priority III: A National Cyberspace Security Awareness and Training Program
- Priority IV: Securing Governments' Cyberspace
- Priority V: National Security and International Cyberspace Security Cooperation[3]

There are several steps that organizations can take to stay in sync with the national strategy to secure cyberspace. The following action steps and modifications to disaster-recovery plans (DRPs) and procedures are appropriate for each of the five priorities for securing cyberspace.

Chapters 6 through 11 provide managers with an analysis of the steps required to meet the goals of *The National Strategy to Secure Cyberspace.*

To meet the goals of priority I and participate in a national cyberspace security response system, an organization should take or be prepared to take the following steps:

- Prepare to participate in a public-private architecture for responding to national-level cyberincidents. This may mean that under certain alert conditions organizations will need to report various types of activities and intrusion attempts.
- Prepare to contribute to the development of tactical and strategic analysis of cyberattacks and vulnerability assessments. This will require more detailed reporting of activities and intrusion attempts on an ongoing basis.
- Join in a shared synoptic view of the health of cyberspace with government agencies and other organizations.
- Be a recipient of information from an expanded Cyber Warning and Information Network (CWIN) when DHS is coordinating crisis-management activities for cyberspace security, and participate in national incident-management efforts.
- Participate in the development of national public-private continuity and contingency planning efforts as well as mobilization exercises to test plans.

To meet the goals of priority II and participate in a national cyberspace security threat and vulnerability-reduction program an organization should take or be prepared to take the following steps:

- Assist in enhancing law-enforcement's capabilities for preventing and prosecuting cyberspace attacks. This will mean reporting more incidents and filing necessary complaints to support the prosecution of perpetrators.
- Be forthwith in providing information that will contribute to national vulnerability assessments so that all organizations will better understand the potential consequences of threats and vulnerabilities.
- Deploy new and more secure protocols and routing technology in order to reduce vulnerabilities. This will require upgrading or replacing less secure technology.
- Deploy and use digital control systems and supervisory control and data-acquisition systems that the government has labeled as trusted or that in some other way meets government standards.
- Deploy and upgrade software that can reduce and remediate vulnerabilities. This will mean installing patches more frequently or eliminating less secure software from the product mix used by the organization.
- Help to analyze infrastructure interdependencies and improve the physical security of cybersystems and telecommunications systems to make them meet potential government standards
- Contribute to a process that helps to prioritize federal cybersecurity research and development agendas and assess and secure emerging systems.

To meet the goals of priority III and participate in a national cyberspace security awareness and training effort, an organization should take or be prepared to take the following steps:

- Participate in a comprehensive national awareness program to help enable businesses, the general workforce, and the general population to secure their own parts of cyberspace.

- Improve in-house training and education programs to support national cybersecurity needs.
- Accept and have staff participate in private-sector-supported and widely recognized professional cybersecurity certifications.

To meet the goals of priority IV and participate in securing governments' cyberspace, an organization should take or be prepared to take the following steps:

- Provide information to the government that helps to assess continuously threats and vulnerabilities to federal cybersystems.
- Assure that all users in an organization that may need to use federal cybersystems are trustworthy individuals and are trained on security issues.
- Provide information to the government that may help to secure federal wireless local area networks and keep those networks secure.
- Assist in improving security in government outsourcing and procurement by providing information as requested about contractors, equipment, software, and services.
- Assist state and local governments in establishing information technology security programs, and encourage such entities to participate in information sharing and analysis centers with similar governments.

To meet the goals of priority V and participate in developing greater national security and international cyberspace security cooperation, an organization should take or be prepared to take the following steps:

- Help strengthen cyber-related counterintelligence efforts by providing the government with information about known activities that may be relevant to these efforts.
- Provide information to the government that can improve capabilities for attack attribution and response before, during, and after an incident.

- Assist the government in improving the coordination of responses to cyberattacks within the U.S. national security community by providing information or technical assistance.
- Assist the government to facilitate dialog and partnerships among international public and private sectors focused on protecting information infrastructures.
- Participate in the government's national and international watch-and-warning networks to detect and prevent cyberattacks as they emerge.
- Use influence to get other countries to accept the Council of Europe Convention on Cybercrime.

Chapter 12 provides a look into the future of homeland security and a road map for implementing homeland security initiatives by organization level. Appendix A covers the acronyms used in this book. Appendix B lists homeland security resources.

Endnotes

1. *The National Strategy for the Physical Protection of Critical Infrastructures and Key Assets* (February 2003).
2. Ibid.
3. *The National Strategy to Secure Cyberspace* (February 2003).

Acknowledgments

The Digital Press team that worked on this book provided outstanding comments and input. They did a great job. The technical reviewers, John Vacca and John W. Rittinghouse, were extremely helpful.

I also want to acknowledge my associate Baley Montag for his insight, support, and the summary of his novel *ExopaTerra,* which depicts how terrorist attacks will likely occur in the future. Of course, I always need to acknowledge the support of my close friends, who never cease to encourage me to analyze and write.

1

Organizing Homeland Security Efforts

In order to build and sustain a long-term homeland security effort, policy makers, planners, and managers need to agree upon a set of basic conclusions and principles that establish a foundation from which to design and implement programs that will result in improved security. This may be very difficult to achieve in a politically charged democratic environment, where various constituencies often put their needs before the needs of society. However, there has been enough consensus established to result in several actions on the part of the U.S. government.

This chapter covers the modifications of organizational structures, new laws, and expanded training and analysis activities implemented by the U.S. government to address homeland security needs. Appreciating the scope of these changes can help information technology (IT) managers, planners, and decision makers understand the seriousness of government efforts and how they may impact their organizations in the future. Understanding the impact these changes may have can also help IT managers prepare for aligning policies and practices with national priorities. This chapter provides background on the following areas:

- The scope and nature of the terrorist threat
- New laws that provide the government with broader powers to deal with terrorism
- How the government is coordinating efforts to deal with terrorism
- How the government is working to improve international cooperation to deal with terrorism
- New approaches to training that are being used for federal agents and local law enforcement
- The threat condition warning system established by the government

- Systems established by the government for citizens and organizations to report information about possible terrorist activities
- How homeland security is being funded
- What action steps IT managers should take as a result of these changes and trends

1.1 Agreeing that the threat is real

The September 11, 2001, attacks brought terrorism to the forefront of government concern. However, terrorism and political and economic threats to the United States and its industrial allies existed well before the September 11, 2001, attacks on the World Trade Center (WTC), the Pentagon, and in Pennsylvania. The bombing of the U.S. federal office building in Oklahoma City on April 19, 1995, which killed 168 people, and the 1993 bombing of the WTC were among the worst such events in the 1990s.

Two U.S. embassies in Kenya and Tanzania were bombed minutes apart on August 7, 1998, leaving at least 252 people dead (including 12 U.S. citizens) and more than 5,000 injured. Over the last three decades, terrorist attacks have become commonplace around the world, in places including Colombia, Israel, Indonesia, Lebanon, Saudi Arabia, Pakistan, the Philippines, and Yemen.

On February 11, 2003, Robert S. Mueller, director of the FBI, testified before the Select Committee on Intelligence of the U.S. Senate in Washington, DC, stating that during the prior 17 months, the FBI had charged 197 suspected terrorists with crimes (99 of whom have been convicted at the time of this writing) and that the FBI had disrupted terrorist plots across the country, including those in the following places:

- Portland, where six were charged with providing material support to terrorists
- Buffalo, where seven al-Qaida associates and sympathizers were indicted in September 2002 for providing material support to terrorism
- Seattle, where Earnest James Ujaama (a.k.a. Bilal Ahmed) was charged with conspiracy to provide material support to terrorists and suspected of establishing a terrorist training facility in Bly, Oregon
- Detroit, where four were charged with document fraud and providing material support to terrorists

- Chicago, where Benevolence International Foundation Director Enaam Arnaout was charged with funneling money to Al Qaeda
- Florida, where three U.S. citizens were arrested for acquiring weapons and explosives in a plot to blow up an Islamic Center in Pinellas County in retaliation for Palestinian bombings in Israel

In nation wide efforts the FBI successfully froze $113 million from 62 organizations and conducted 70 investigations, 23 of which resulted in convictions.

History has forced the undeniable conclusion that the threat of terrorist attacks in the United States and against properties of the U.S. government and resident corporations and individuals located around the world is indeed real.

1.2 Establishing a legal basis to pursue security

In the aftermath of the September 11, 2001, terrorist attacks the USA. Patriot Act was introduced by the Bush administration. Attorney General John Ashcroft wanted Congress to pass the bill, without modification, in a one-week period. Vermont Democrat Patrick Leahy, chairman of the Senate Judiciary Committee, did convince the Department of Justice (DOJ) to accept some changes, which may have saved the act from being completely overturned in court. Members of the House made many improvements to the act. The Senate and House versions were expediently reconciled, and President Bush signed the act into law on October 26, 2001.

According to the Congressional Research Service (CRS) Report for Congress entitled *The USA PATRIOT Act: A Sketch,* authored by Charles Doyle, senior specialist in the American Law Division, the act gives federal officials greater authority to track and intercept communications, both for law-enforcement and foreign-intelligence gathering purposes. It also vests the secretary of the treasury with regulatory powers to combat corruption of U.S. financial institutions for foreign money-laundering purposes. The act further seeks to close U.S. borders to foreign terrorists and to detain and remove those within U.S. borders. The act creates new crimes, new penalties, and new procedural efficiencies for use against domestic and international terrorists.

For the purpose of criminal investigations and the acts of tracking and gathering communications, the act modifies the procedures to do the following:

- Permit pen register and trap-and-trace orders for electronic communications such as e-mail.
- Authorize nationwide execution of court orders for pen registers, trap-and-trace devices, and access to stored e-mail or communication records.
- Treat stored voice mail like stored e-mail (rather than like telephone conversations).
- Permit authorities to intercept communications to and from a trespasser within a computer system (with the permission of the system's owner).
- Add terrorist and computer crimes to Title III's predicate offense list.
- Encourage cooperation between law enforcement and foreign-intelligence investigators.
- Establish a claim against the United States for certain communications privacy violations by government personnel.
- Terminate the authority found in many of these provisions and several of the foreign-intelligence amendments with a sunset provision (December 31, 2005).

The act eases some of the restrictions on foreign-intelligence gathering within the United States and affords the intelligence community greater access to information unearthed during a criminal investigation, while establishing and expanding safeguards against official abuse. The act also does the following:

- Permits "roving" surveillance (court orders omitting the identification of the particular instrument, facilities, or place where the surveillance is to occur when the court finds the target is likely to thwart identification with particularity)
- Increases the number of judges on the Foreign Intelligence Surveillance Act (FISA) court from 7 to 11
- Allows application for a FISA surveillance or search order when gathering foreign intelligence is a significant reason for the application rather than the reason
- Authorizes pen register and trap-and-trace device orders for e-mail as well as telephone conversations

- Sanctions court-ordered access to any tangible item, rather than only business records held by lodging, car-rental, and locker-rental businesses
- Carries a sunset provision
- Establishes a claim against the United States for certain communications privacy violations by government personnel
- Expands the prohibition against FISA orders based solely on an American's exercise of his or her First Amendment rights

Federal agencies fight against money laundering through regulations, criminal sanctions, and forfeiture. The act bolsters federal efforts in each area. The act expands the authority of the secretary of the treasury to regulate the activities of U.S. financial institutions, particularly their relations with foreign individuals and entities and requires the secretary to promulgate regulations:

- Requiring securities brokers and dealers, as well as commodity merchants, advisors, and pool operators to file suspicious activity reports (SARs)
- Requiring businesses, which were only to report cash transactions involving more than $10,000 to the IRS, to file SARs as well, imposing additional "special measures" and "due diligence" requirements to combat foreign money laundering
- Prohibiting U.S. financial institutions from maintaining correspondent accounts for foreign shell banks
- Preventing financial institutions from allowing their customers to conceal their financial activities by taking advantage of the institutions' concentration account practices
- Establishing minimum new-customer identification standards and record keeping, and recommending an effective means to verify the identity of foreign customers
- Encouraging financial institutions and law-enforcement agencies to share information concerning suspected money-laundering and terrorist activities
- Requiring financial institutions to maintain anti-money-laundering programs, which must include at least a compliance officer; an

employee-training program; the development of internal policies, procedures, and controls; and an independent audit feature

The act contains a number of new money-laundering crimes, as well as amendments and increased penalties for earlier crimes. It outlaws the following:

- Laundering (in the United States) of any of the proceeds from foreign crimes of violence or political corruption
- Prohibits laundering the proceeds from cybercrime or supporting a terrorist organization
- Increases the penalties for counterfeiting
- Seeks to overcome a Supreme Court decision finding that the confiscation of over $300,000 (for attempt to leave the country without reporting it to customs) constituted an unconstitutionally excessive fine
- Provides explicit authority to prosecute overseas fraud involving American credit cards
- Endeavors to permit prosecution of money laundering in the place where the predicate offense occurs

The act creates two types of forfeitures and modifies several confiscation-related procedures. It allows confiscation of all of the property of any individual or entity that participates in or plans an act of domestic or international terrorism, and it also permits confiscation of any property derived from or used to facilitate domestic or international terrorism. Procedurally, the act:

- Establishes a mechanism to acquire long-arm jurisdiction, for purposes of forfeiture proceedings, over individuals and entities
- Allows confiscation of property located in this country for a wider range of crimes committed in violation of foreign law
- Permits U.S. enforcement of foreign forfeiture orders

- Calls for the seizure of correspondent accounts held in U.S. financial institutions for foreign banks that are in turn holding forfeitable assets overseas
- Denies corporate entities the right to contest a confiscation if their principal shareholder is a fugitive

In addition to the above, the act creates new federal crimes for:

- Terrorist attacks on mass-transportation facilities
- Biological weapons offenses
- Harboring terrorists
- Affording terrorists material support
- Conducting the affairs of an enterprise that affects interstate or foreign commerce through the patterned commission of terrorist offenses
- Fraudulent charitable solicitation

The act increases the penalties for acts of terrorism and for crimes that terrorists might commit. It establishes an alternative maximum penalty for acts of terrorism; raises the penalties for conspiracy to commit certain terrorist offenses; envisions sentencing some terrorists to life-long parole; and increases the penalties for counterfeiting, cybercrime, and charity fraud.

In other procedural adjustments designed to facilitate criminal investigations, the act:

- Increases the rewards for information in terrorism cases
- Expands Posse Comitatus Act exceptions
- Authorizes "sneak and peek" search warrants
- Permits nationwide, and perhaps worldwide, execution of warrants in terrorism cases
- Eases government access to confidential information
- Allows the attorney general to collect DNA samples from prisoners convicted of any federal crime of violence or terrorism

- Lengthens the statute of limitations applicable to crimes of terrorism
- Clarifies the application of federal criminal law on American installations and in residences of U.S. government personnel overseas
- Adjust federal victims' compensation and assistance programs

1.3 Coordinating efforts to improve security

To enable government agencies to coordinate better all of the efforts needed to improve security, the Department of Homeland Security (DHS) was formed is the United States. Agencies from several U.S. government departments were brought together under DHS. The agencies of DHS are organized under four major directorates: Border and Transportation Security, Emergency Preparedness and Response, Science and Technology (S&T), and Information Analysis and Infrastructure Protection.

The Border and Transportation Security Directorate brings together the major border security and transportation operations, including:

- The U.S. Customs Service (from the Department of the Treasury)
- The Immigration and Naturalization Service (from the DOJ)
- The Federal Protective Service (from the GSA)
- The Transportation Security Administration (from the Department of Transportation)
- Federal Law Enforcement Training Center (from the Department of the Treasury)
- Animal and Plant Health Inspection Service (from the Department of Agriculture)
- Office for Domestic Preparedness (from the DOJ)

The Emergency Preparedness and Response Directorate oversees domestic disaster-preparedness training and coordinates government disaster-response; it includes:

- The Federal Emergency Management Agency (FEMA)
- Strategic National Stockpile and the National Disaster Medical System (from the Department of Health and Human Services)

- Nuclear Incident Response Team (from the Department of Energy)
- Domestic Emergency Support Teams (from the DOJ)
- National Domestic Preparedness Office (from the FBI)

The S&T Directorate has the mission of utilizing scientific and technological advantages to improve security and includes:

- CBRN Countermeasures Programs (from the Department of Energy)
- Environmental Measurements Laboratory (from the Department of Energy)
- National BW Defense Analysis Center (from the Department of Defense)
- Plum Island Animal Disease Center (from the Department of Agriculture)

The Information Analysis and Infrastructure Protection Directorate analyzes intelligence and information from other agencies (including the CIA, FBI, DIA, and NSA) involving security threats and evaluates vulnerabilities in the nation's infrastructure. The directorate includes:

- Critical Infrastructure Assurance Office (from the Department of Commerce)
- Federal Computer Incident Response Center (from the GSA)
- National Communications System (from the Department of Defense)
- National Infrastructure Protection Center (from the FBI)
- Energy Security and Assurance Program (from the Department of Energy)

The Secret Service and the Coast Guard will also be located in DHS. They will remain intact and report directly to the secretary of homeland security. In addition, the INS adjudications and benefits programs will report directly to the deputy secretary as the Bureau of Citizenship and Immigration Services.

1.4 International cooperation to improve security

On March 18, 2003, John S. Pistole, the deputy assistant director of the Counterterrorism Division of the FBI testified before the U.S. Senate Committee on Foreign Relations about the efforts of the FBI to coordinate antiterrorism efforts with law-enforcement organizations in other countries.

Pistole pointed out that the FBI's Office of International Operations, which oversees the Bureau's Legal Attaché (Legat) program, is a vital component in counterterrorism efforts. It is primarily through the Legat program that efforts to investigate and share information with international law-enforcement and intelligence organizations is coordinated.

With the assistance of the Department of State (DOS), the FBI established 45 Legat offices. Through a memorandum of understanding (MOU) with the DOS, FBI Legats are part of the embassy community. The MOU acknowledges the ambassador as chief of mission. In addition to investigative and host-country liaison responsibilities, Legats work with the administrative officer of the embassy regarding their needs within the embassy itself.

Legats respond to requests from other DOS employees, provide regular briefings to the ambassador and/or deputy chief of mission, and participate in all other in-house activities, such as emergency action meetings and weekly country team meetings. The Legats work in close coordination with regional security officers and other embassy staff to prevent terrorist incidents from occurring.

The FBI's 45 Legats are staffed by 126 special agents and 74 support personnel. By the end of the fiscal year, it was proposed that the staffing level increase to 145 special agents and 83 support personnel for new offices in Abu Dhabi, the United Arab Emirates (UAE); Kuala Lumpur, Malaysia; Sanaa, Yemen; Tbilisi, Georgia; and Tunis, Tunisia. In addition, there will be three suboffices created in Bonn (Berlin, Germany); Milan (Rome, Italy); and Toronto (Ottawa, Canada). Six existing Legat offices will also receive additional personnel. Those offices are Amman, Jordan; Cairo, Egypt; Islamabad, Pakistan; Manila, Philippines; Ottawa, Canada; and Riyadh, Saudi Arabia. Of the additional $44.7 million that the FBI was allotted for its counterterrorism mission overseas, approximately $23.7 million was earmarked for Legat expansion.

1.5 Improvement of security skills and efforts

On March 4, 2003, Robert S. Mueller, director of the FBI, testified before the U.S. Senate Committee on the Judiciary in Washington, DC, about what the FBI has done to improve the skills and work methods of the bureau. This includes establishing the Analysis Branch in the Counterterrorism Division to conduct strategic assessments of the terrorism threat to the United States. Since September 11, 2001, the FBI increased the number of counterterrorism analysts by 61 percent, which quadruples the number of analysts performing such work prior to September 11, 2001.

The FBI also implemented a number of initiatives aimed at enhancing training for the analytical workforce, including creating the College of Analytical Studies, which, in conjunction with the CIA, has begun training new intelligence analysts. By the end of 2003 more than 200 analysts are expected to have completed the six-week training course.

A new executive assistant director for intelligence (EAD/I) will have direct authority and responsibility for the FBI's national intelligence program. Specifically, the EAD/I will be responsible for ensuring that the FBI has the optimum strategies, structure, and policies in place, first and foremost, for the counterterrorism mission. The EAD/I will also oversee the intelligence programs for the counterintelligence, criminal, and cyberdivisions and will ensure that the FBI is sharing information with federal, state, and local agencies.

To improve the system for threat warnings, several specialized counterterrorism units were formed, including:

- CT Watch, a 24-hour counterterrorism watch center, to serve as the FBI's focal point for all incoming terrorist threats
- The Communications Analysis Section to analyze terrorist electronic and telephone communications and identify terrorist associations and networks
- The Document Exploitation Unit, which identifies and disseminates intelligence gleaned from millions of pages of documents or computers seized overseas by intelligence agencies
- The Special Technologies and Applications Section to provide technical support for FBI field office investigations requiring specialized computer technology expertise and support

- The interagency Terrorist Financing Operations Section devoted entirely to the financial aspects of terrorism investigations and liaison with the financial services industry

There are also 66 joint terrorism task forces (JTTFs) in place to enhance cooperation with federal, state, and local agencies. It was also planned that the FBI would provide 500 JTTF agents and state and local law-enforcement personnel with specialized counterterrorism training. In addition, specialized counterterrorism training will be provided to 224 agents and training technicians from every field division in the country so that they, in turn, can train an estimated 26,800 federal, state, and local law-enforcement officers in basic counterterrorism.

The Office of Law Enforcement Coordination (OLEC) was created to enhance the ability of the FBI to forge cooperation and substantive relationships with all of its state and local law-enforcement counterparts. The OLEC has liaison responsibilities with the White House Homeland Security Council.

The FBI Intelligence Bulletin, which is disseminated weekly to over 17,000 law-enforcement agencies and to 60 federal agencies, provides information about terrorism issues and threats to patrol officers and other local law-enforcement personnel who have direct daily contact with the general public, contact which could result in the discovery of critical information about those issues and threats.

To prevent terrorists from acquiring weapons of mass destruction (WMD), the FBI is coordinating with suppliers and manufacturers of WMD materials in an effort to help them voluntarily report any suspicious purchases or inquiries.

To augment local field office investigative capabilities, flying squads were established to provide for specialized personnel to respond to fast-breaking situations and provide a surge capacity in support of FBI rapid deployment teams.

Several steps are also being taken to address the shortcomings of the bureau's IT. The first major step in the right direction is the Trilogy Program. The Trilogy Program was designed as a 36-month effort to enhance effectiveness through technologies that facilitate better organization, access, and analysis of information. The overall direction of the Trilogy Program is to provide all FBI offices with improved network communications, a common and current set of office automation tools, and easy-to-use, reengineered, Web-based applications.

The original plan for Trilogy was development and deployment over 36 months from the date of the contract awards for the infrastructure and applications development, May and June 2001, respectively. The events of September 11, 2001, impacted many aspects of the FBI, including the Trilogy Program. Recognizing the urgent need for improved IT, I ordered that Trilogy implementation emphasize those capabilities most urgently needed to support the FBI's priority cases.

Director Mueller also pledged support for the president's initiative to establish a Terrorist Threat Integration Center (TTIC), which will merge and analyze terrorist-related information collected domestically and abroad. TTIC will analyze information, both foreign and domestic to provide a comprehensive threat picture. TTIC participants will continue to be bound by all applicable privacy statutes, executive orders (EOs), and other relevant legal authorities for protecting privacy and constitutional liberties. TTIC will institutionalize the process to produce the daily threat matrix. As it becomes fully operational, it will be the focal point for requests for terrorist threat analysis.

TTIC is headed by a senior U.S. government official, who will report to the director of Central Intelligence. This individual will be appointed by the director of Central Intelligence, in consultation with the director of the FBI and the attorney general, and the secretaries of homeland security and defense.

The FBI's Counterterrorism Division, the director of Central Intelligence's Counterterrorist Center, and TTIC (which will include significant participation by DHS) will relocate to a single new facility in order to improve collaboration and enhance the government's ability to thwart terrorist attacks and bring terrorists to justice. This move is designed to:

- Speed the creation of compatible information infrastructure with enhanced capabilities, expanded and more accessible databases, and greater network sharing on counterterrorism issues.
- Enhance interaction, information sharing, and synergy among U.S. officials involved in the war against terrorism.
- Potentially allow the FBI and CIA each to manage more effectively their counterterrorism resources by reducing overhead and redundant capabilities.
- Further enhance the ability of comprehensive, all-source analysis to guide collection strategies.

1.6 Creation of a threat condition system

The U.S. government established a Homeland Security Advisory System to inform organizations, businesses, and individuals about the level of perceived threat that exists, based on intelligence and analysis activities of the various departments and agencies that are responsible for monitoring threat levels. Figure 1.1 shows the graphic that is used by DHS to depict threat conditions.

The threat conditions each represent an increasing risk of terrorist attacks. Beneath each threat condition are some suggested protective measures, recognizing that the heads of federal departments and agencies are responsible for developing and implementing appropriate agency-specific protective measures:

Low condition (green). This condition is declared when there is a low risk of terrorist attacks. Federal departments and agencies should consider the following general measures, in addition to the agency-specific protective measures they develop and implement:

Figure 1.1
Threat levels for homeland security.

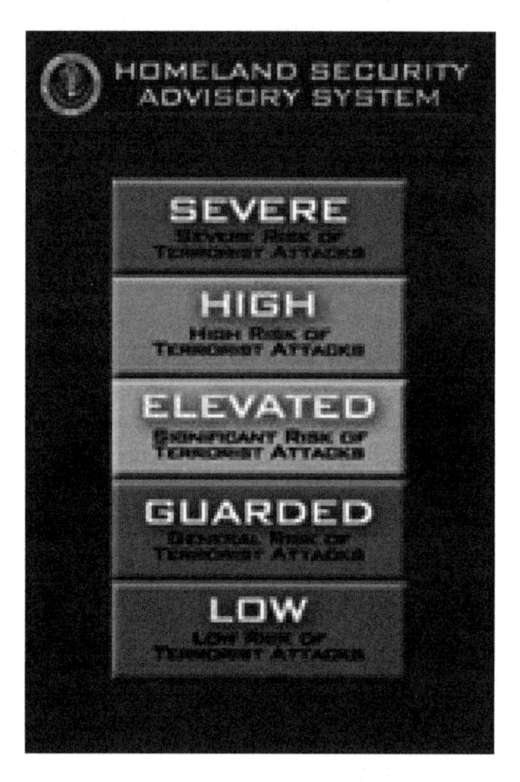

- Refining and exercising as appropriate preplanned protective measures
- Ensuring personnel receive proper training on the Homeland Security Advisory System and specific preplanned department or agency protective measures
- Institutionalizing a process to assure that all facilities and regulated sectors are regularly assessed for vulnerabilities to terrorist attacks and all reasonable measures are taken to mitigate these vulnerabilities

Guarded condition (blue). This condition is declared when there is a general risk of terrorist attacks. In addition to the protective measures taken in the previous threat condition, federal departments and agencies should consider the following general measures in addition to the agency-specific protective measures that they will develop and implement:

- Checking communications with designated emergency response or command locations
- Reviewing and updating emergency response procedures
- Providing the public with any information that would strengthen its ability to act appropriately

Elevated condition (yellow). An elevated condition is declared when there is a significant risk of terrorist attacks. In addition to the protective measures taken in the previous threat conditions, federal departments and agencies should consider the following general measures in addition to the protective measures that they will develop and implement:

- Increasing surveillance of critical locations
- Coordinating emergency plans as appropriate with nearby jurisdictions
- Assessing whether the precise characteristics of the threat require the further refinement of preplanned protective measures
- Implementing, as appropriate, contingency and emergency response plans

High condition (orange). A high condition is declared when there is a high risk of terrorist attacks. In addition to the protective measures taken in the previous threat conditions, federal departments and agencies should consider the following general measures in addition to the agency-specific protective measures that they will develop and implement:

- Coordinating necessary security efforts with federal, state, and local law-enforcement agencies or any National Guard or other appropriate armed forces organizations
- Taking additional precautions at public events and possibly considering alternative venues or even cancellation
- Preparing to execute contingency procedures, such as moving to an alternate site or dispersing their workforce
- Restricting threatened-facility access to essential personnel only

Severe condition (red). A severe condition reflects a severe risk of terrorist attacks. Under most circumstances, the protective measures for a severe condition are not intended to be sustained for substantial periods of time. In addition to the protective measures in the previous threat conditions, federal departments and agencies also should consider the following general measures in addition to the agency-specific protective measures that they will develop and implement:

- Increasing or redirecting personnel to address critical emergency needs
- Assigning emergency response personnel and prepositioning and mobilizing specially trained teams or resources
- Monitoring, redirecting, or constraining transportation systems
- Closing public and government facilities

1.7 Establishing an incident- and tip-reporting system

Several methods have been established for businesses, individuals, and government agencies to report incidents or suspicious behavior to DHS. An incident relating to computer systems is the act of violating an explicit or implied security policy. These activities include, but are not limited to:

- Attempts (either failed or successful) to gain unauthorized access to a system or its data
- Unwanted disruption or denial of service
- The unauthorized use of a system for the processing or storage of data
- Changes to system hardware, firmware, or software characteristics without the owner's knowledge, instruction, or consent

The Federal Computer Incident Response Center (FedCIRC) has developed both a short incident-reporting form and a long incident-reporting form to assist agencies in reporting incidents. The short form allows a reporting agency to quickly report an incident when detailed information regarding the incident is not available. The long form can be used by a reporting agency when more information has been gathered about the incident, and the reporter is able to provide a more detailed report.

The choice to either use the short or long form is at the discretion of the reporting agency. All submissions using either form will be considered a new incident; therefore, the form cannot be used to provide additional information for an incident that has previously been reported. If agencies want to provide additional information regarding an existing report, they need to call a hotline at 1-888-282-0870 and provide the watch analyst with the incident report number that was assigned to the report. DHS can then update the incident report record and provide further assistance if required.

Organizations that are not a component of the federal government or reporting an incident that affects a federal agency or department are directed to file incident reports with the National Infrastructure Protection Center (NIPC) and the Computer Emergency Response Team Coordination Center (CERT/CC). The Web sites are www.nipc.gov/incident/cirr.htm and https://irf.cc.cert.org, respectively. Private individuals are directed to fill out the NIPC incident form.

The FBI has also established a tip-reporting system. While the FBI continues to encourage the public to submit information regarding the September 11, 2001, terrorist attacks, the tip-reporting form can also be used to report any suspected criminal activity to the FBI. The form is located at https://tips.fbi.gov.

The Department of the Treasury has also established a system by which citizens can report activities related to the financing of terrorism. A toll-free telephone number has been set up at 1-866-867-8300. This campaign is designed to collect information on funding mechanisms that support terrorist activities, including underground financial systems, illicit charities, and corrupt financial service providers, and even crimes such as check fraud, identity fraud, and credit card fraud that may be used to support terrorists. The Department of the Treasury and of the DOS are seeking to raise public understanding of just how terrorist financing occurs. Figure 1.2 shows the brochure used to support the rewards program, and Figure 1.3 shows one of the posters used in the campaign to promote the program.

The secretary of state may offer rewards of up to $5 million for information that prevents or favorably resolves acts of international terrorism against U.S. citizens or property worldwide. Rewards also may be paid for information leading to the arrest or conviction of terrorists attempting,

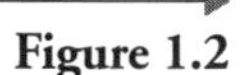

Figure 1.2

Figure 1.3

Stopping Terrorism Starts With Stopping The Money

International terrorism directed against Americans is financed by money sent to terrorists from sources around the world. The U.S. Government is offering a reward for information leading to the dismantling of any system used to finance a terrorist organization and information leading to the arrest or conviction of those who planned or aided in any act of terrorism against U.S. persons or property.

If you have ***any*** information about individuals or organizations that finance terrorists, please call 1-866-867-8300 in the U.S.; outside the U.S. contact the nearest U.S. embassy or consulate.

Illicit Sources

Profits from a variety of criminal enterprises benefit terrorist organizations. Some of the more common are:

- Drug manufacturing, smuggling, and distribution
- Identity theft for profit
- Credit-card, insurance, welfare and food-stamp fraud
- Theft, adulteration, and resale of infant formula
- Counterfeit merchandise schemes involving a host of consumer items such as designer clothing, jewelry, fashion accessories, and household products
- Interstate cigarette smuggling
- Alternative remittance systems and unlicensed currency remitters

Suspicious Transactions

- Account transactions that are inconsistent with past deposits or withdrawals (cash, check, wires, etc.).
- Transactions involving a high volume of incoming or outgoing wire transfers, with no logical or apparent purpose, that come from, go to, or transit through locations of concern (i.e., sanctioned countries, non-cooperative nations, sympathizer nations).
- Unexplainable clearing or negotiation of third party checks and their deposits in foreign bank accounts.
- Structuring at multiple branches or the same branch with multiple individuals.
- Corporate layering; that is, transfers between bank accounts of related entities or charities for no apparent reasons.
- Wire transfers by charitable organizations to companies located in countries known to be bank or tax havens.
- Lack of apparent fund-raising activity (i.e., lack of small checks or typical donations) associated with charitable bank deposits.
- Using multiple accounts to collect funds that are then transferred to the same foreign beneficiaries.
- Transactions with no logical economic purpose (i.e., no link between the activity of the organization and other parties involved in the transaction).
- Overlapping corporate officers, bank signatories, or other identifiable similarities associated with addresses, references, and financial activities.
- Cash debiting schemes in which deposits in the United States correlate directly with ATM cash withdrawals in countries of concern. Reverse transactions of this nature are also suspicious.
- Issuing checks, money orders, or other financial instruments, often numbered sequentially, to the same person or business, or to a person or business whose name is spelled similarly.

www.treas.gov/rewards www.rewardsforjustice.net

A campaign by the Departments of State and Treasury to combat terrorism financing.

Up To $5 Million Reward • Responses Kept Strictly Confidential

committing, conspiring to commit, or aiding and abetting the commission of such acts. The USA Patriot Act of 2001 authorizes the secretary of state to offer or pay rewards of greater than $5 million if he or she determines that a greater amount is necessary to combat terrorism or to defend the United States against terrorist acts. The secretary has authorized a reward of up to $25 million for information leading to the capture of Osama bin Laden and other key Al-Qaida leaders.

1.8 Funding for homeland security

A $36.2 billion fiscal year (FY) 2004 budget was requested for DHS in order to maintain funding for critical operations of each of the agencies and to expand and improve homeland security efforts. This represents a 7.4 percent increase in funding over FY2003, and a 64 percent over FY2002. The FY2004 budget highlights include the following.

1.8.1 Information analysis and infrastructure protection

This budget will support the department's ability to analyze and identify potential threats, assess vulnerabilities, map those threats to vulnerabilities, and provide the information from which to organize protective measures. A total of $829 million was requested for this initiative—an increase of $652 million (370%) over the FY2003 level. This funding includes approximately $500 million to assess critical infrastructure (nuclear power plants, water facilities, telecommunications networks, and transportation systems) and to work to ensure that the highest-priority vulnerabilities are addressed.

1.8.2 S&T

Another $803 million was requested for the department to develop new partnerships with the private sector to research, develop, and deploy homeland security technologies—an eightfold increase over 2002. The S&T Directorate's Advanced Research Project Agency will direct $350 million in new funding to address gaps in high-priority operational areas, such as protecting critical infrastructure and borders.

1.8.3 Preparing for and responding to national emergencies

The budget requests $5.9 billion for emergency preparedness and response, an increase of 16 percent ($838 million) over FY2003. The Emergency Preparedness and Response Directorate will coordinate all necessary response efforts quickly and effectively, including maintaining and strengthening the strategic national stockpile of drugs, vaccines, and equipment, with $400 million requested to continue this initiative. An additional $890 million is requested to prepurchase critically needed vaccines and medication for biodefense.

1.8.4 Borders and transportation systems

Also requested was $18.1 billion for the Border and Transportation Security Directorate to meet the strategic goals of improving border and transportation security. The budget also supports DHS's effort to restructure the border-security agencies to enhance efficiencies and create one seamless border service.

In addition, $4.8 billion was requested for the Transportation Security Administration, an increase of $160 million from FY2003 after subtracting one-time costs from its startup. The budget request also includes funding for the comprehensive entry-exit system, which will enable the DHS to track the entry and exit of visitors to the United States. Another $100 million in new resources is requested in FY2004 for a total of $480 million.

Further, $3.5 billion is requested to support the nation's first responders, including $500 million in grants for assistance to firefighters, $500 million for state and local law-enforcement terrorism-prevention initiatives, and $181 million for the Citizen Corps.

Other initiatives for Border and Transportation Security include:

- $62 million of new funding for the Container Security Initiative
- $307 million additional investment in the Automated Commercial Environment
- $119 million additional investment for nonintrusive inspection technology
- $40 million of new funding for Atlas/Chimera to address requirements in the Border Security Act
- $18 million for the Customs Trade Partnership against Terrorism initiative

1.8.5 Ports and waterways

The budget provides $6.7 billion to recapitalize the Coast Guard and an additional $615 million, which is 10 percent above the FY2003 level, to support the deployment of maritime safety and security teams, the procurement of coastal patrol boats, and continued development of the maritime 911 system. (A total of $134 million was requested for the maritime 911 system.) The budget includes $500 million to continue the Deepwater program, which is upgrading the Coast Guard's fleet of cutters, aircraft, and related systems to improve performance across DHS as the Coast Guard's activities become more integrated with other DHS components.

1.8.6 Immigration services

The FY2004 budget continues the president's $500 million initiative to reduce the backlog of applications, while at the same time ensuring that national policies for issuing visas to visitors are consistent with security and foreign-policy interests.

1.8.7 Protecting the nation's leaders and suppressing counterfeiting

The Secret Service had a $1.3 billion request in the budget, an increase of nearly 10 percent over FY2003.

1.8.8 Other essential missions

The FY2004 budget provides $12.2 billion for other essential missions not specifically related to homeland security, an increase of 5 percent, which includes an increase of:

- $83 million (6%) for Border and Transportation Security
- $18 million (1%) for Emergency Preparedness and Response
- $319 million (9%) for the Coast Guard

1.9 Preparing for the impact of change

The many changes that the U.S. government has made during the last two years are only the beginning of the efforts that will be required to deal with terrorism. These changes also represent a permanent paradigm shift in the way the government operates.

Action Checklist Number 1 (see Table 1.1) shows the steps that IT managers should take as a result of reading Chapter 1, including determining what position their organization has taken regarding the national strategies for participating in homeland security or improving internal security measures. IT managers should assure that security-planning efforts in IT are in step with those of their organization.

The next chapter examines some of the real-world conditions and challenges that the government faces in the implementation of the national strategies to improve homeland security.

Table 1.1 *Action Checklist Number 1*

Action Item	**Status (e.g., Completed, Pending, or N/A)**
Determine if the organization has taken a position on homeland security.	
Evaluate how the organization's position on homeland security impacts IT.	
Assess how the USA Patriot Act impacts IT support requirements.	
Assess if the formation of DHS impacts IT support requirements.	
Evaluate what actions the organization needs to take if the threat level is raised by the government.	
Evaluate what actions the IT department needs to take if the threat level is raised by the government.	

HILBERT COLLEGE
McGRATH LIBRARY
5200 SOUTH PARK AVE
HAMBURG, NY 14075

2

Cross-Sector Security Priorities and Issues

There are many challenges to face as the government and private-sector organizations implement new measures to improve homeland security. All organizations need to train employees on what to watch for and how to report threats or suspicious activities. This is important because, as the terrorist attacks of September 11, 2001, demonstrated, this is a new type of war in which the adversary will exploit opportunities that many citizens may consider harmless.

This chapter presents the results of a cross-sector survey of managers and IT staff across 100 name-brand organizations about the state of IT security policies, plans, and training. It also examines some perceptions of professionals that may well play a role in the implementation of the national strategies to improve homeland security. (Note: In cases where survey respondents did not answer a question, they were not included in the analysis, and to avoid repetitiveness in the text, the percentages that did not respond are not indicated.) This data will allow IT managers to compare the status of several homeland security–related issues in their organizations, including:

- Changes in IT management practices that resulted from the terrorist attacks of September 11, 2001
- Changes in IT management practices that resulted from the establishment of DHS
- Adequate and appropriate IT staffing
- The implementation of DRPs and related training
- The implementation of information systems (IS) security plans and related training
- The implementation of data privacy plans and related training

- The adequacy of end-user training
- Professional concerns about IT and society

2.1 Terrorist attacks changed IT management practices

In a survey of 100 name-brand organizations in the United States conducted for this book, 46 percent of the organizations reported that the terrorist attacks of September 2001 have not changed their IT management policies or practices at all. Another 17 percent was unsure if the attacks had led to changes in IT management practices. However, 36 percent reported that various types of changes have occurred in the way their organizations managed IT. Table 2.1 shows some of the comments made about how IT management practices were impacted by the terrorist attacks.

Table 2.1 *How IT Management Practices Changed Because of Terrorist Attacks*

Type of Change in Practices
Tighter intrusion procedures and greater checks on corporate travel.
We have tightened the firewall policies. We also look more closely at the firewall logs and reports.
Security and disaster recovery are taken more seriously. They are starting to get the attention they need.
Senior management has shown an increased interest in (and a willingness to spend money on) IT security.
Strengthened BCP and CSIRT practices.
More concerns over security. All policies were reviewed and rewritten where necessary.
IT security, physical, and personnel security measures have been strengthened and given greater emphasis.
Renewed emphasis on BCP/DR with executive mandate and direction.
Greater impetus toward physical security.
We have an ISO 17799 project actively working with a preassessment. We also participate in security roundtables facilitated by two local universities.
DR sites are at least 100 miles away from main facility.
Increased upper-management awareness.

Table 2.1 *How IT Management Practices Changed Because of Terrorist Attacks (continued)*

Type of Change in Practices
It has given senior management a better view on security practices and it makes it easier to get a security project funded.
More emphasis on disaster recovery and business continuity. IS security training has been budgeted and approved by senior management. User interest is high and training attendance is mandatory. Policies and procedures have been updated or revised and employees trained.
DR became a priority.
Increased security and awareness.
Much more physical security on IS areas, computer rooms, etc.
Tightened security, decreased bureaucracy, better security training for all employees, lockdown of many systems to prevent any unauthorized software installation.
Yes, the disaster recovery plan has been given a higher priority.
More urgency in developing needed training and policies.
Has ramped up security awareness and preemptive measures substantially.
Enforced the use of computers for work-related items only.
More security in place and more monitoring of inappropriate data transfers. Corporate-wide virus protection installed.
Heightened security awareness and caused procedures to be tightened.
Focused attention to review, enhance, and otherwise improve system security safeguards, policies, practices and procedures.
Greater regard for security policies (both physical and logical for information systems).

Survey respondents were also asked how the establishment of the DHS will change their IT management policies or practices. While 47 percent reported that the new department would not change any IT management practices, 39 percent did not know if the establishment of DHS would have any impact on IT management practices. Most of the remaining 14 percent commented that the presence of DHS would have a positive impact on their organizations' IT management practices. This lack of change and much of the uncertainty may be because DHS was still organizing to address its mission.

2.2 Staffing IT remains a challenge in most organizations

Survey respondents were asked if they felt that their organizations' IT network management and telecommunications departments were adequately and appropriately staffed. While 41 percent felt they have been adequately and appropriately staffed, 53 percent felt that they have not achieved an adequate level of staffing or an appropriate mix of staff to meet current needs. The remaining respondents did not know if they were adequately and appropriately staffed.

Survey respondents were asked how their organizations determine how many staff are need for IT network management and telecommunications. Table 2.2 shows how staffing levels are determined, and Table 2.3 shows how salary levels are determined in the surveyed organizations.

Table 2.2 *How IT Staffing Levels Are Determined*

Method	Percent
Benchmark against other organizations	24
Input from a staffing consultant	6
Staffing studies conducted by outside firm	12
In-house systems for determining staffing needs	59
I do not know the answer to this question	19
Other	15

Note: Multiple answers accepted.

Table 2.3 *How IT Salary Levels Are Determined*

Method	Percent
Benchmark against other organizations	49
Input from a staffing consultant	8
Salary studies conducted by outside firm	35
In-house systems for determining salary levels	46
I do not know the answer to this question	11

Table 2.3 *How IT Salary Levels Are Determined (continued)*

Method	Percent
Other	10

Note: Multiple answers accepted.

2.3 DRPs are in place, but training lags

Survey respondents were asked if their organizations had a DRP in place. While 65 percent reported that there was DRP in place, 8 percent reported that there was not a DRP in place, and 24 percent reported that the DRP was in the development stages. Respondents were also asked if employees had been trained in how to activate the DRP and respond to a disaster. Table 2.4 shows the reported status of DRP training.

Table 2.4 *DRP Training Status*

Status	Percent
No employees have been trained	12
Very few employees have been trained	29
Most employees have been trained	19
All employees have been trained	8
Training is being developed	11
I do not know the answer to this question	4
Other	7

2.4 IS security plans are in place, but training lags

Survey respondents were asked if their organizations had an IS and network security plan in place. While 73 percent reported that there was an IS and network security plan in place, 7 percent reported that there was not a plan, and 17 percent reported that the plan was in the development stages. Respondents were also asked if employees had been trained on the IS security plan. Table 2.5 shows the reported status of IS security training.

Table 2.5 *IS Security Training Status*

Status	Percent
No employees have been trained	9
Very few employees have been trained	30
Most employees have been trained	28
All employees have been trained	15
Training is being developed	7
I do not know the answer to this question	8
Other	3

In a related question, respondents were asked if their organizations had a computer-incident response plan in place. Only 53 percent reported that there was an incident-response plan in place, 20 percent reported there was not a plan in place, and 16 percent reported that the computer-incident response plan was being developed. The remaining 11 percent were not aware of the status of the plan. Once again, respondents were also asked if employees have been trained on the computer-incident response plan. Table 2.6 shows the reported status of incident-response training. Table 2.7 shows the status of training on antivirus measures and what employees should do if they believe a virus has hit their computer system.

Table 2.6 *Computer-Incident Training Status*

Status	Percent
No employees have been trained	14
Very few employees have been trained	23
Most employees have been trained	32
All employees have been trained	13
Training is being developed	3
I do not know the answer to this question	13
Other	2

Table 2.7 *Antivirus-Measures Training Status*

Status	Percent
No employees have been trained	7
Very few employees have been trained	16
Most employees have been trained	38
All employees have been trained	34
Training is being developed	1
I do not know the answer to this question	2
Other	2

2.5 Privacy plans are in place, and training keeps pace

Respondents were also asked if their organizations had a privacy policy to protect the personal data of customers in place. Remarkably, 81 percent reported that there was a plan in place, while 7 percent reported that a privacy plan was being developed. Another 7 percent reported there was not a privacy plan in place, and 5 percent did not know the status of the plan. Table 2.8 shows the reported status of customer data privacy plan training.

In a related question, respondents were asked if their organizations had a privacy policy to protect the personal data of employees in place. While 72

Table 2.8 *Customer Data Privacy Plan Training Status*

Status	Percent
No employees have been trained	6
Very few employees have been trained	12
Most employees have been trained	37
All employees have been trained	32
Training is being developed	1
I do not know the answer to this question	8
Other	4

Table 2.9 *Employee Data Protection Policy Training Status*

Status	Percent
No employees have been trained	5
Very few employees have been trained	14
Most employees have been trained	35
All employees have been trained	33
Training is being developed	3
I do not know the answer to this question	8
Other	2

percent reported that there was a privacy policy to protect personal data of employees in place, 14 percent reported that there was not a policy in place. Meanwhile, 7 percent reported that a policy was being developed, and 7 percent reported that they were uncertain as to the status of the policy. Table 2.9 shows the reported status of employee personal data protection policy training.

2.6 End-user training remains a weak spot

One of the biggest concerns that many IT managers have is the ability of end users to actually use IT. Survey respondents were asked if they felt that their organizations adequately train end users on how to use computer systems and applications. The lack of end-user skills can result in mishaps and undetected unauthorized activities when end users do not know what to observe or report. As is shown in Table 2.10, respondents were pretty well split on their viewpoints about the adequacy of training for end users in their organization with 47 percent reporting they felt training was adequate, and 45 percent reporting that they did not feel that training was adequate.

Table 2.10 *End Users Adequately Trained*

Response	Percent
Yes	47
No	45
Undecided	8

Table 2.11 *Status of Training on Intellectual Property Management*

Status	Percent
No employees have been trained	16
Very few employees have been trained	28
Most employees have been trained	19
All employees have been trained	25
Training is being developed	4
I do not know the answer to this question	8
Other	0

In a related question, respondents were asked if their organizations trained employees on the ethical management of intellectual property. Neglecting to train employees in this area may lead to such activities as the unauthorized installation of software on their work computers that results in a security problem. It may also result in employees improperly dispensing sensitive information. Table 2.11 shows the status of training on intellectual property management.

In another question related to education, respondents were asked if they felt that public education in the United States is adequately educating children to work in the information age. As is shown in Table 2.12, 56 percent of the survey respondents felt that public education in the United States is not adequately educating children to work in the information age.

Respondents were also asked how their organizations support efforts to reduce the digital divide (Table 2.13). The largest percentage (44%) contribute money or equipment to educational programs; the next largest accepts trainees from educational organizations in cooperative education

Table 2.12 *Adequate Public Education*

Response	Percent
Yes	21
No	56
Undecided	23

Table 2.13 *Organizations' Efforts to Address the Digital Divide*

Method	Percent
Contributes money or equipment to education programs	44
Allows employees to take time off with pay to do volunteer work	29
Accepts trainees from educational organizations in cooperative education programs	35
Does nothing at all	18
I do not know the answer to this question	27
Other	6

Note: Multiple answers accepted.

programs (35%); the third largest allows employees to take time off with pay to do volunteer work (29%).

2.7 Professional concerns about IT and society

Respondents were asked what their greatest concerns about the future impact of IT on society were. Without a doubt the answers to this question demonstrated that the respondents are definitely impassioned individuals. Twenty-nine of the 67 respondents who answered this question commented about the future loss of privacy or freedom as a result of the widespread adaptation of IT. Table 2.14 shows the concerns about IT and society that the survey respondents shared.

Table 2.14 *Concerns about IT and Society*

Responses from Survey Participants	Privacy- or Freedom-Related Response
Advanced IT will reduce the need for people to interact.	
Blurring of the lines between work and personal life beyond what individuals would prefer; decreased control over personal information (i.e., that obtained by telemarketers); "data smog" decreased examination of where our technologies are taking us alienation due to technology that is created without regard to its use or practical effects; extreme corporate intrusion into personal	P

Table 2.14 *Concerns about IT and Society (continued)*

Responses from Survey Participants	Privacy- or Freedom-Related Response
lives in the face of lax governmental controls on how companies use IT to monitor and steer consumers; environmental impact of the continuous cycle of planned obsolescence; and, in the worst case, IT enabling totalitarian states via the currently available technologies of national ID cards, face-recognition technologies, GPS, smart money, RFID tags, and subcutaneous microchips.	
Continuous exploitation by unknown attackers for the benefit of conducting and/or continuing to conduct cyberwarfare.	
Cybercrime and cyberterrorism.	
Dehumanization of society and moral beliefs.	
Digital divide; ethical use of technology; communication exchanges, including rumors, myths, and other nonfactual information.	
Ease of access to private data—either through malicious intent or lax policies.	
General fear that technology leads to job reduction. General fear of "big brother' technology such as GPS and Web browser tracking.	P
Greater depersonalization, less commitment to local talent.	
Greatly reduced face-to-face social interaction.	
Homeland security unfunded mandates.	
I am not an engineer and I feel that the mindset of the technical person feels that everything revolves around technology. These people either forget or do not understand that other issues are more important to the day-to-day business activities of corporate America. I have seen a trend in the last several years to become more dependent on the decisions and recommendations of the IT department. This can lead to many bad corporate decisions and must be tempered.	
I believe that machines are getting faster and smarter, thus allowing users to be less coherent on the general aspects of IT.	
Identity theft and loss of privacy.	P

Table 2.14 *Concerns about IT and Society (continued)*

Responses from Survey Participants	Privacy- or Freedom-Related Response
I'm concerned with the risk of having my life hacked. As technology is used for home automation or personal convenience–type things, the risk of an attacker disrupting your life is much greater. Appropriate investigation into preventing these things needs to occur. I also feel that technology can have a very positive impact on society if used properly. A computer in the home makes life much easier by managing your finances, scheduling contacts, etc. Once all the glitches of using and integrating these types of applications are overcome people could spend less time on these tasks and more time with family, friends, or working on hobbies. Basically quality of life might be improved.	P
I'm most concerned that technology is used by people who understand only a small part of it, but it was developed by people who think it should do everything. If this trend continues, I see problems with people using technology that is doing more than they want it to and are unaware that this is even happening.	
Inappropriate access and use of personal information.	P
Individual privacy rights in the public domain!	P
IT will continue to lead to the displacement of jobs. This will occur as a result of productivity increases (efficiency) and outsourcing to foreign countries.	
Intrusion into business data and personal stored data.	P
Invasion of privacy and too much information being kept, with the inevitable errors.	P
Isolation of people!	
IT provides leverage. Organizations and people who have IT (such as the U.S. government, TIA, or Experian) have leverage over those (especially individuals) who do not. We are not educating new IT workers in ethics or responsibilities or even the relevant laws.	P
It seems to me that most companies continue to develop and enhance IT by taking every expedient to avoid honest thought about solving real problems or satisfying quantifiable needs, while placing marginal consideration on security or personal privacy and the effect of their efforts on society and the economy.	P

Table 2.14 *Concerns about IT and Society (continued)*

Responses from Survey Participants	Privacy- or Freedom-Related Response
It's enabling people to be constantly accessible—not ever able to turn off. We are constantly bombarded with more information than we can process. There is no time off.	
Job loss, privacy loss, security issues.	P
Joblessness.	
Kids accessing porn and getting molested.	
Lack of built-in security and lack of privacy.	
Less personal interaction in business.	
Lessen traditional research and thinking skills. Create less patient society. Also much, much less privacy.	P
Loss of individual privacy.	P
Loss of individual privacy.	P
Loss of privacy.	P
Many people react without thinking of the impact of their answers or actions.	
My greatest concern is educating the employee who is not directly involved in a security project. He or she has an impact on the company's security, our customers' information security, our company's reputation.	P
People will become lazier. Having almost any type of information at your fingertips allows individuals to perform many tasks without understanding the fundamentals of the problem (e.g., mathematics and engineering).	
People will have little privacy.	P
People will lose their skills in interacting with others. They will not think for themselves but will accept anything the computer tells them as the truth.	
Personal privacy concerns (will we get to the point where it is easy to track and retrieve very specific data on individuals), digital divide—people are being left behind.	P
Personal security.	P

Table 2.14 *Concerns about IT and Society (continued)*

Responses from Survey Participants	Privacy- or Freedom-Related Response
Privacy.	P
Privacy.	P
Privacy and identify theft.	P
Privacy and security.	P
Privacy management of personal data is probably the highest concern I have.	P
Protecting personal data.	P
Society will be more informed by various sources rather than just what they were able to get locally from newspaper radio and television.	
Stolen identity.	P
Stress of available "data" and bombardment with it—inadequate security for personal communications of all sorts—lack of understanding of available security and/or scaring people unnecessarily or making them vulnerable to personal attack.	
Technological improvement is faster than social evolution.	
Technology has the tendency to isolate people from one another. Human interaction on a face-to-face level seems to drop off as the technology of IT grows.	
Technology is outpacing the general public's ability to learn about the dangers and risks of using technology—for example, using the Internet to conduct business.	
That proper security measures don't stay current with technology.	P
That society (primarily folks who reach upper-management levels) may become too dependent upon IT and lose the interpersonal skills that are so desperately needed and woefully inadequate to manage a large number of personnel.	
That users do not have time to be adequately trained and retrained as technology is introduced into their job functions. Users don't respond well to change. Even less so if they won't/can't take time for training.	

Table 2.14 *Concerns about IT and Society (continued)*

Responses from Survey Participants	Privacy- or Freedom-Related Response
The ability to infiltrate systems more easily and take personal and other private information for criminal or unethical use.	P
The acceptance and understanding of how technology can remove the divide between being trained in technology to using technology for the better of society.	
The digital divide between the haves and the have-nots of both our society and the world.	
The loss of privacy.	P
The unknowns of security requirements within government combined with a lack of policy enforcement.	
Threats to innovations due to patent litigation.	
Too much trust placed in systems not proven trustworthy. Too much is assumed by the average citizen about these black boxes and their programmers and operators. Too much complexity for anyone to truly manage or control the systems and those who operate them.	P
Uninformed or misinformed politicians will rush to legislate that which should not be legislated and won't legislate what should be legislated.	
We already have trouble communicating with one another in person and as more transactions become automated, human interaction and people skills are likely to deteriorate.	
Widening of the digital divide and the concurrent impacts on society.	
Will IT and the training required to use, improve, and leverage the various technologies it creates be available to all members of society?	

An interesting and perhaps telling note regarding the surveyed population is that 58 percent of them reported that they have read the book *1984* by George Orwell. For those of you who have not read the book and who have concerns about the impact of technology on society, now may be a good time to do so.

Respondents were also asked about what they believe to be the greatest benefits that the Internet provides society. Overwhelmingly, access and speed of access to information was the main theme of responses to this question. Of the 90 responders to the question, 76 referred to access to information as one of the greatest benefits of the Internet. Access to information is considered by many to be essential for the democratic process to be effective and successful. Table 2.15 shows the responses concerning the greatest benefits of the Internet.

Table 2.15 *Views on the Greatest Benefits of the Internet*

Responses from Survey Participants	Relates to Greater Access to Information
1. Easy access to information; consumers can make better decisions with the information. 2. Creates global village.	P
A better background on what is possible if you put your mind and self to a task. There are more than enough examples of how to do things right and how to do things wrong on the Internet. In addition to that—the Internet provides a far greater scope of experience and knowledge than one person could find through traditional means.	P
A forum for debate and a repository for information that is beyond the control of any central authority, a vast online library on virtually every subject imaginable (many subjects about which very little is available anywhere else), the potential for instant communication with nearly any other connected person on the planet, a truly global marketplace, a way to discover events close to home one might not have known about otherwise.	P
A gateway to information on almost any topics right in your own home.	P
Ability to obtain and exchange information.	P
Access.	
Access to all information that was previously inaccessible. Enhanced communication globally.	P
Access to information.	P
Access to information.	P
Access to information.	P

Table 2.15 *Views on the Greatest Benefits of the Internet (continued)*

Responses from Survey Participants	Relates to Greater Access to Information
Access to information—any information at all—we just have to find a better way to let information be free.	P
Access to information, eease of communication.	P
Access to information and free exchange of ideas.	P
Access to information in a timely, qualitative, and quantitative unprecedented level.	P
Access to information, ease of crossing social boundaries.	P
Access to information.	P
Access to news sources and communications unfettered by commercial censorship.	P
Access to research company information.	P
Access to useful information.	P
Access to vast amounts of information.	P
Allows terrific access to information that was previously only available through tedious use of paper documents.	P
Allows users from all over the world to communicate on any number of topics.	
Availability of information.	P
Availability of information cultural exchange of ideas.	P
Availability of information to the masses.	P
Availability of lots of data and information on many topics available relatively easily with search tools. (e.g., medical, home maintenance, vehicle maintenance, recipes, history, art, etc.)—personal connectivity with family, friends, etc, is dramatic.	P
Communication.	
Connectivity, ease of access to information repositories and other resources.	P
Direct access to information. One-stop shopping if you will. Direct communication.	P
Dissemination of information easier	P

Table 2.15 *Views on the Greatest Benefits of the Internet (continued)*

Responses from Survey Participants	Relates to Greater Access to Information
Ease of transferring information.	P
Easy access to information.	P
Easy and rapid access to information, access to information not previously feasible to see. Collaboration on subject matter. Saves time ordering things, doing banking making appointments.	P
E-commerce, communication, telecommuting, etc.	
Entertainment (online gaming), wider range of news sources, connection to others who share similar interests (sewing, crafts, music).	
Exchange of information.	P
Expansion of Internet creates greater expansion of knowledge to greater number of people allowing more informed populace.	P
For one it provides true freedom of speech and enables everyone who has access to gain information on just about any topic.	P
Free speech.	
Freedom and access to information.	P
Freedom for anyone to discover and access any type of information and to freely communicate and exchange information and ideas with anyone and everyone 24 / 7.	P
Freedom of information (not the accuracy), freedom of communication, liberate the knowledge from confines of libraries.	P
Global access to information and products.	P
Global communication and information transfer.	P
Great for information searches. Great for a marketing tool. Great for instant communication between people over long distances.	P
Immediate access to information on almost any subject.	P
Improved communication between diverse cultures, greater access to information.	P
Information.	P

Table 2.15 *Views on the Greatest Benefits of the Internet (continued)*

Responses from Survey Participants	Relates to Greater Access to Information
Information.	P
Information access.	P
Information accessibility, information exchange, information store.	P
Information and education.	P
Information and knowledge.	P
Information is readily available to everyone.	P
Information warehousing.	P
Information.	P
Instant access to information.	P
Instant access to information, access to more people with similar interests in different locations, opportunity for small businesses to sell on large level, location is less important—more opportunities to live away from large cities.	P
Instant access to information and improved communication globally.	P
Instantaneous access to information and ideas.	P
Instantaneous information and a much greater source of information.	P
Intercommunication across all socially/physically dividing boundaries (i.e., religion, race, color, politics, etc.).	
It allows individuals to communicate with each other as well as form virtual communities without regard to race, location, or (usually) socio-economic level. It is a society of the mind, where your ideas are more important than what you look like, sound like, or live.	
Knowledge.	P
Knowledge and information.	P
Making information more readily available to all people regardless of location.	P

Table 2.15 *Views on the Greatest Benefits of the Internet (continued)*

Responses from Survey Participants	Relates to Greater Access to Information
Massive amounts of data and information. Whatever the question the answer can be found on the Internet.	P
More information sharing.	P
Online economic transactions- saving on postage and not limited to the 8 A.M. to 5 P.M. work schedule. More shopping variety. Easy communication—can communicate with anybody anywhere at any time for almost no cost.	
Provides unlimited freedom to information. Provides a platform to research (i.e., family history and genealogy). Connects the world into a global society.	P
Quick and available knowledge of all kinds.	P
Quick and easy access to Information.	P
Rapid access to information.	P
Rapid information and advanced learning.	P
Research tool, learning tool, help people learn about other countries and culture.	P
Saves time.	
Sharing of knowledge and information.	P
Speed and diversity of information available.	P
Speed to information.	P
The greatest benefit is the global audience it provides. The vast number of communities allows people to get many different perspectives in any topic they choose. A large problem with society is with the understanding and acceptance of different people. If people took a second to listen to other perspectives, then it may be possible to begin to understand and maybe even accept.	
The greatest benefits of the Internet today are the availability of information and the ease of communication.	P
The Internet has greatly enhanced learning in our schools and has also allowed family members to keep in closer contact.	P

Table 2.15 *Views on the Greatest Benefits of the Internet (continued)*

Responses from Survey Participants	**Relates to Greater Access to Information**
The Internet shrinks the global divide. Global communications are now commonplace. Ideas, cultures, and information can easily be shared/exchanged. Likewise, solutions can be addressed by a greater audience now.	P
The knowledge that information is out there and instant access to information that previously was extremely difficult to locate.	P
To be able to be friends with people across the world.	
Turning a local community retail-wise to global. I know can shop among worldwide retailers, where a decade ago I was for the most part limited geographically.	
Unlimited access to information. Exposure to previously unimaginable places and possibilities.	P
Variety of means for information, education, and business.	P
Vast amount of all kinds of information and data that we can all use in our everyday lives.	P

Homeland security and the threat of terrorism has created a juxtaposition between this key element of democracy and the need to keep information away from potential terrorists. Even the National Archives of the United States has reevaluated its dissemination of information to assure that no information will be dispensed that could aid terrorism. Governments, organizations, and private business have been rapidly moving to evaluate what information is available on their Web sites and through other normal public challenges that could aid terrorists in planning or executing an attack.

Survey participants were also asked what they felt were the worse things that the Internet enables in society. Table 2.16 shows the response about the worst things that the Internet enables. Interestingly, 32 of the 91 respondents commented that the access to information was the worst thing that the Internet enables. This shows that just as people value the access to information, they can also fear the access to information.

Although there is a high level of personal dilemma about the good and the bad of the Internet, only 8 percent of the survey respondents felt that content and activity on the Internet should be regulated by the govern-

Table 2.16 *Views on the Worse Things That the Internet Enables*

Responses from Survey Participants	Relates to Greater Access to Information
1. Disinformation. 2. People sit in front of their computer/TV and are not as active as they should be. 3. Ease of computer crime.	P
Access.	P
Access to harmful information.	P
Access to hate site, porn site for people who are underage.	P
Access to information. Ease of communication including too much junk mail.	P
Access to information regardless of moral or ethical boundaries.	P
Access to porn and crazy information is too easy. Too many people do not know how to protect themselves from the dangers lurking on the Internet.	P
Access to unlimited information. Never leave home tendency.	P
Addiction to being online. Dissemination of false information. Too easy to obtain personal information about other people.	P
All things can be misused or abused.	
Allows criminals to have easy access to information about our children and private information.	
Allows people to participate in activities they normally would be ashamed to do in person. Allows the bad part of society to be as readily available as the good information.	P
Another avenue for information hackers to steal personal data.	P
As with all technologies it is abused by the dark side of criminals, pornographers, scammers, and thieves. Kind of like the old western movies.	
Availability of socially unacceptable material information available on destructive nature of creating dangerous objects.	P
Boosts technocracy. Provides possibility to be anonymous (hackers' violence). Personality redouble possibility (virtual me).	
Chat rooms.	

Table 2.16 *Views on the Worse Things That the Internet Enables (continued)*

Responses from Survey Participants	Relates to Greater Access to Information
Child porn.	
Child predators!	
Crime.	
Crime.	
Crime.	
Deception.	
Diminishes personal contact.	
Dissemination of pornography and hate-based material.	P
Exploitation of children.	
For the most part the Internet has no boundaries. The Internet may provide too much information.	P
Freedom for anyone to discover and access any type of information and to freely communicate and exchange information and ideas with anyone and everyone 24 / 7.	P
Greed and fraud are more easily perpetuated.	
Hard question to answer. Ease of obtaining bad stuff. Ease of conducting illicit activities.	P
Hate crimes.	
ID fraud.	
Illicit info.	P
Inactivity, sloth, porn available to children, predators, spam.	
Inappropriate and/or offensive spam.	
Inappropriate material available to everyone.	P
Information is unreliable, no check & balance to Internet usage, moral depravity/pornography.	P

Table 2.16 *Views on the Worse Things That the Internet Enables (continued)*

Responses from Survey Participants	Relates to Greater Access to Information
Information that, while not warranting suppression, poses problems when readily available to anyone—bomb-making information. Information on business scams and tax havens, fringe pornography (i.e., bestiality), etc.	P
Instantaneous access to (bad) information and ideas.	P
Intrusive attacks by hackers or cyberterrorists.	
Isolation.	
It allows the same old crimes and abuses to occur only at a distance and in new aspects.	
It brings out the good and bad of all of us. The good to assist others in time of need. The bad that exploits the weak in chat rooms, the gullible with faceless threats of need, the ability to peddle or sell nearly anything, the continuance of fraud schemes much like the ones received via snail mail, and the challenges by some savvy and/or those not so savvy but highly interested in distressing our lives through the implementation of viruses, worms, and Trojan horses.	
It is still allow a person who is going to do bad thing, in the general public to do them on the Internet.	
Junk mail spam, noncertified information, etc.	P
Made it easy for hackers to get into other people's systems. People glued to computers more, leaving them with little time for social interactions.	
Moral degradation the Internet is just as bad as it is good.	
More misinformation blurring of concept of reliable source, pornography, intellectual property theft, less emphasis on critical thinking, less ability to determine who information originated with.	P
Negativity of the human image to the masses.	
No monitoring of what is allowed to be published. Information can be dangerous in the wrong hands—like children, for example. The benefits can be turned around and used in a harmful way in the hands of the wrong person.	P

Table 2.16 *Views on the Worse Things That the Internet Enables (continued)*

Responses from Survey Participants	Relates to Greater Access to Information
Pedophilia and cyberterrorism try to abuse this medium.	
People feel that they are entitled to everything—nobody wants to work for anything.	
People rely on information on the Internet as "the truth." Very easy for people to be taken advantage of if they are not educated on using it defensively.	
People taking advantage of others, more ways to be fraudulent.	
Porn.	
Porn, spam, loss of control over information.	P
Porn.	
Pornography. Gambling. Addictive behaviors.	
Pornography and e-commerce. Here is a tool (the Internet) that the entire world can communicate through. We can have a free exchange of information and ideas to better society and solve problems, yet pornography and e-commerce are two of the most prevalent uses of the Internet technology.	P
Pornography and perverts preying on the young. Another way that crooks can prey on all of us.	
Pornography and spam.	
Pornography has grown at an alarming rate due to the Internet.	
Potential fraud.	
Predators, unethical profiteering.	
Privacy invasion.	
Proliferation of pornography.	
Promotes some bad things like porn, spamming, and gambling.	
Quick and easy access to information.	P
Rapid and anomalous access to people (where trust can be easily made and broken).	

Table 2.16 *Views on the Worse Things That the Internet Enables (continued)*

Responses from Survey Participants	Relates to Greater Access to Information
Rumors, half-facts, no real interaction between people (but calling it total interactive experience).	P
Social and personal isolation in the way of human contact and communications. Also, personal freedom demands a personal responsibility—the Internet allows otherwise anonymous irresponsible behaviors that have not been confronted until now.	
Society feels the need to reinvent the ethical structure that existed in radio, TV, etc.	
Spam, ability to easily misrepresent, access to more people.	
Spam and porn are constantly pushed in your face.	
Spam, sleazy people preying on children.	
Spawned a new breed of cyberperversion and increased the ability to seduce and take advantage of the gullible.	
Spreads misinformation too easily. Easier to be hurtful to others. Time waster. Much easier access to things the general public should not have access to—like how to make chemical weapons. Pornography.	P
Technological predators. False information. Loss of social skills, talking, reasoning, critical thinking skills.	P
That it is more important than it really is.	
The ability to anonymously harass or terrorize anyone else on the Internet no matter where he or she is.	
The ability to find personal information on others and use it unethically and criminally.	P
The anonymity that the Internet provides allows people to act in a way they would not in other situations.	
The efficiency with which less than honorable people can harm others—and be very difficult to trace.	

Table 2.16 *Views on the Worse Things That the Internet Enables (continued)*

Responses from Survey Participants	Relates to Greater Access to Information
The Internet provides a great service in providing access to any kind of information desired. This service is very dangerous as well, since this information may be malicious in nature. For example, this could give some ten-year-old boy access to information on how to make drugs or a bomb or something along those lines.	P
The lack of physical contact. Having said that though—it does tend to break the traditional barriers of language distance and racial concerns that may be experienced with physical contacts which at time can be a concern.	
This is a philosophical question about a technology. Not sure how to answer. It is only another pathway or vehicle or tool that will be used. As such it doesn't enable anything that is not already going on in some form within the fabric of society. All it truly does is make such enablement faster.	
Too often caters to lowest common denominator.	
Undesirable products. Often illegal products.	
Unfortunately it allows dishonest and bad people to do dishonest and bad things to the large number of good and innocent individuals.	
Unfortunately with freedom of speech there is always the abuse. I am not referring to being able to voice my opinion but rather some of the information that may be inappropriately available to kids. Also the technology allows for a push of information whereas I for one do not appreciate spam being pushed to my e-mail or Internet screen.	

ment. Overwhelmingly, 59 percent responded that content and activity on the Internet should not be regulated by the government. Meanwhile, 15 percent were undecided. Table 2.17 shows the views of respondents on government regulation of the Internet, and Table 2.18 shows the comments of those who responded to the question with the answer of "other."

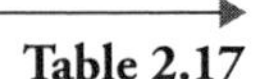

Table 2.17 *Views on Government Regulation of the Internet*

Response	Percent
Yes	8
No	59
Undecided	15
Other	17

Table 2.18 *Views on Government Regulation of the Internet: Responses to "Other"*

Government should provide resources to investigate fraud and national opt out functionality for spam. These services should be optional for people who choose to use them. They should not be mandatory or regulated.
I do feel that certain things should not be viewed by or even made available to certain individuals. Porn, for example, should not be as accessible as it is for young to teenage children. If these sites were not shoved down our throats, I've got to believe that if adults wanted to get to porn sites they'd figure it out with all the forceful advertising. I do believe, however, that since this is not being controlled by the government that it is squarely in the parents' court to prevent this or any questionable entertainment source from being readily available to minors. I mean, come on, with all the available resources today to allow you to monitor every stroke of the keyboard (if you wish), certainly falls upon a parent's realm of responsibility.
I don't think the government should be regulating everything on the Internet. If something is illegal based on that government's laws, then it should be able to act on it within the jurisdiction of its laws.
I feel that fees for e-mails will be necessary. This would cut down the number of e-mails that just spam the Internet. Then stiff fines for violations could be added for major violations.
I think that it needs to be regulated from a criminal perspective. We should not overlook criminal behavior and Web sites promoting such just because they are on the Internet and not on the street.
Not by the government but possibly the private sector.
Only as it relates to criminal or unethical behavior that is destructive in nature (hacking, worms, viruses).
Only if there is a compelling reason that trumps the argument that it not.

Table 2.18 *Views on Government Regulation of the Internet: Responses to "Other" (continued)*

Our children need to be protected in public areas (i.e., schools and libraries). There is no reason that deviant behavior should be allowed. If an institution really feels that strongly that freedom of speech is more important than protecting our children, the organization should be required to establish an over-21 area, just like establishments that serve alcoholic beverages.
Some things should be regulated, such as spam, malicious code, and protection of child exploitation. Most everything else should not be regulated.
Sometimes porn, etc.
Somewhat.
The Internet is a global medium. Any government regulation would only be useful for each specific country.
The United States is only one part of the Internet. If government is to be included, then it should be a UN-led/backed regulation.
There is no government with this much authority. The PRC has tried to manage this and failed.
Unfortunately, yes. If the technology were not abused for children, I would feel otherwise because adults can adjust, but unsuspecting children may not know how to cope with it.
While some material should be subject to regulation, I don't think it will ever happen. How do you overcome the constitution and the freedom of speech?

An interesting note on which to wrap up the presentation of the survey results concerns two questions about how these professionals deal with their children's use of the Internet. Of all of the respondents, 46 percent reported that they counsel their children on the use of the Internet, 17 percent reported that their children are old enough to handle the Internet, and 36 percent reported that they do not have children. (Note that one respondent skipped this question.)

Respondents were also asked, "If you have children, do you monitor their use of the Internet?" The majority, 33 percent reported that they monitor their children's use of the Internet, 6 percent reported that they do not monitor their children's use of the Internet, and 24 percent reported that their children are old enough to handle the Internet.

2.8 Background of survey respondents

The majority of respondents held an IT-related position, with 15 percent holding IT management positions, 27 percent holding IT staff positions, and 28 percent holding IT security positions. Industry sectors were well represented in the group of 100 respondents, with 17 percent working in government, 15 percent in manufacturing, 10 percent in banking and finance, 10 percent in education, 10 percent in healthcare, and 10 percent in professional services. Table 2.19 shows the job function/title of respondents, and Table 2.20 shows the industry sector of respondents.

Table 2.19 *Job Function/Title of Respondents*

Job Function/Title	Percent
CIO/MIS director	15
IT security manager/staff	28
IT staff	27
Department manager	15
Department staff	5
Other	10

Table 2.20 *Industry Sector of Respondents*

Sector	Percent
Banking/finance	10
Education	10
Government	17
Healthcare	10
Insurance	3
Manufacturing	15
Military	2
Professional services	10
Retail/wholesale distribution	2
Telecommunications	4

Table 2.20 *Industry Sector of Respondents (continued)*

Sector	Percent
Transportation	2
Utilities	2
Other	13

2.9 Blending government change with reality

In Chapter 1, we reviewed many of the changes that the federal government has initiated to address homeland security. In this chapter we examined results of a survey that shows the status of homeland security–related IS management practices and that clearly shows that not all organizations have achieved high levels of security planning and training.

Based on the information presented in this chapter, IT managers should follow the steps in Action Checklist Number 2 (see Table 2.21), including evaluating the condition of IS security policies, plans, and procedures in their organizations. The next chapter examines the implementation of the security of critical infrastructures.

Table 2.21 *Action Checklist Number 2*

Action Item	Status (e.g., Completed, Pending, or N/A)
Evaluate changes in IT management practices that were made as a result of terrorist attacks of September 11, 2001, to determine if new procedures are still adequate to address current security conditions or needs.	
Evaluate changes in IT management practices that were made as a result of the establishment of DHS to determine if new procedures are still adequate to address current security conditions or needs.	
Assess the level of training within the IT department to determine if the skill base necessary to evaluate, test, maintain, and improve policies, plans, and procedures exists.	
Evaluate IT staffing to determine if the staffing level and staffing mix are adequate to address current needs.	

Table 2.21 *Action Checklist Number 2 (continued)*

Action Item	**Status (e.g., Completed, Pending, or N/A)**
Determine the status of implementation of DRPs and what related training has been achieved.	
Determine the status of implementation of IS security plans and what related training has been achieved.	
Determine the status of implementation of computer-incident response plans and what related training has been achieved.	
Determine the status of implementation of plans for the management of data privacy and what related training has been achieved.	
Assess the level of training of IT users to determine what security-related training should be implemented.	

3

Security and Critical Infrastructures

In February 2003, DHS published *The National Strategy for the Physical Protection of Critical Infrastructures and Key Assets,* which outlines national goals, objectives, and principles to help physically secure critical infrastructures. The success of the strategy is dependent on steps that public and private entities across the country will take to improve security. This chapter examines the implications of this strategy for IT managers responsible for securing and maintaining IT assets and facilities as well as providing IT support to departments that are responsible for providing physical security, disaster-recovery planning, and business-continuity planning. Areas covered include the following:

- Identifying critical national-infrastructure components
- Treating security improvement as a process
- Leveraging technology for security at a national level
- Applying the national strategy at the organizational level
- The security-improvement process in the organization
- Leveraging technology for security at an organizational level
- Integrating the organizational and national strategies

3.1 Identifying critical national-infrastructure components

It is essential to identify and assure the protection of critical infrastructures. It is also necessary to provide a timely warning system that can help assure the protection of those infrastructures and assets that face a specific or imminent threat. *The National Strategy for the Physical Protection of Critical*

Infrastructures and Key Assets calls for cooperation between government, industry, and private citizens and is designed to protect the following:

- Agriculture and food
- Water
- Public health
- Emergency services
- Defense industrial base
- Telecommunications
- Energy
- Transportation
- Banking and finance
- Chemical industry and hazardous materials
- Postal and shipping
- National monuments and icons
- Nuclear power plants
- Dams
- Government facilities
- Commercial key assets

Key assets and high-profile events are individual targets whose attack could result in massive human casualties and property destruction, but also in profound damage to national prestige, morale, and confidence. Terrorists are expected to target critical infrastructures to achieve three general types of effects:

1. Direct infrastructure effects with cascading disruption or arrest of the functions of critical infrastructures or key assets through direct attacks on a critical node, system, or function
2. Indirect infrastructure effects with cascading disruption and financial consequences for government, society, and economy through public- and private-sector reactions to an attack

3. Exploitation of infrastructure of elements of a particular infrastructure to disrupt or destroy another target

3.2 Treating security improvement as a process

The most important principle of security is that it is a process that requires continuous risk assessments, the evaluation of existing mitigation, and the discovery and eradication of newly found vulnerabilities. In other words, what may be secure one day may not be secure a day, a week, or a month later because of new vulnerabilities or improved terrorist abilities.

To initiate and maintain the process of continuous security improvement, the federal government intends to encourage market solutions wherever possible and to compensate for market failure with focused government intervention. In addition, the government will serve as a facilitator of meaningful information sharing and work to foster international cooperation. The federal government has the capacity to organize, convene, and coordinate broadly across governmental levels to:

- Take inventory of the most critical facilities, systems, and functions and monitor their preparedness across economic sectors and governmental jurisdictions.
- Assure that federal, state, local, and private entities work together to protect critical facilities, systems, and functions that face an imminent threat or whose loss could have significant national consequences.
- Provide and coordinate national-level threat information, assessments, and warnings that are timely, actionable, and relevant to state, local, and private-sector partners.
- Create and implement comprehensive, multitiered protection policies and programs.
- Explore potential options for enablers and incentives to encourage stakeholders to devise solutions to their unique protection impediments.
- Develop cross-sector and cross-jurisdictional protection standards, guidelines, criteria, and protocols.

- Facilitate the sharing of critical-infrastructure and key asset-protection best practices and processes and vulnerability-assessment methodologies.
- Conduct demonstration projects and pilot programs.
- Seed the development and transfer of advanced technologies, while taking advantage of private-sector expertise and competencies.
- Promote national-level critical-infrastructure and key asset-protection education and awareness.
- Improve the federal government's ability to work with state and local responders and service providers.

The high-priority cross-sector security initiatives are designed to address planning and resource allocation; information sharing and indications and warnings; personnel surety; building human capital and awareness; technology and research and development; and modeling, simulation, and analysis. *The National Strategy for the Physical Protection of Critical Infrastructures and Key Assets* clearly states that in the planning and resource allocation process it is incumbent on federal, state, and local governments and private-sector stakeholders to work together to:

- Define clearly their critical-infrastructure and key asset-protection objectives.
- Develop a business case for action to justify increased security investments.
- Establish security baselines, standards, and guidelines.
- Identify potential incentives for security-related activities where they do not naturally exist in the marketplace.

DHS has been charged with creating collaborative mechanisms for public- and private-sector critical-infrastructure and key asset-protection planning. One of the first steps in this process is to identify key protection priorities and develop mechanisms to support these priorities. This will be accomplished in part by a supposed sharing of risk-management expertise between the public and private sectors and the coordination and consolidation of federal and state protection plans. Other activities that DHS will supposedly accomplish to facilitate the process of improving homeland security include the following:

- Identifying options for incentives for private organizations that proactively implement enhanced security measures
- Developing an integrated critical-infrastructure and key asset-geospatial database
- Establishing a task force to review legal impediments to reconstitution and recovery following an attack against a critical infrastructure or key asset
- Conducting critical-infrastructure protection planning with international partners
- Identifying requirements and developing appropriate programs to protect critical personnel
- Coordinating the development of national standards for personnel surety
- Developing a certification program for background-screening companies
- Exploring the establishment of a model security training program for private security officers

3.3 Leveraging technology for security at the national level

The National Strategy for the Physical Protection of Critical Infrastructures and Key Assets government planners concluded that at the national level there was a general lack of focus on long-term research, development, testing, and engineering for critical-infrastructure and key asset protection. The goal was to establish a process to coordinate, with broad sector input, the creation and adoption of national research priorities and support to cross-sector research and development activities. DHS was then charged with the efforts to:

- Coordinate public- and private-sector security research and development activities.

- Coordinate interoperability standards to ensure compatibility of communications systems.
- Explore methods to authenticate and verify personnel identity.
- Improve technical surveillance, monitoring, and detection capabilities.

Government planners also concluded that modeling, simulation, and analysis can also facilitate protection planning and decision support by enabling the mapping of complex interrelationships among the elements that make up the risk environment. The information derived from these exercises and experiments could be helpful in drawing attention to likely cascading consequences that otherwise might have gone unconsidered. It was also recognized that enhancing national modeling, simulation, and analysis capabilities will require a unified effort across the public and private sectors. Thus, DHS has been charged with:

- Integrating modeling, simulation, and analysis into national infrastructure and asset-protection planning and decision-support activities
- Developing economic models of near- and long-term effects of terrorist attacks
- Conducting integrated risk modeling of cyber- and physical threats, vulnerabilities, and consequences
- Developing models to improve information integration

The Technology Administration's National Institute of Standards and Technology (NIST) has provided measurements, standards, and technical advice for many years to help federal, state, and local agencies and the private sector improve security against terrorist, military, natural-disaster, and other types of threats. Since the September 11, 2001, terrorist attacks, NIST has had approximately 120 ongoing and newly initiated research and standards development projects to address homeland security issues, including the following.

3.3.1 Investigation of the World Trade Center collapse

NIST launched a $16 million, 24-month federal building and fire safety investigation to study the structural failure and subsequent progressive collapse of the WTC. The study of the WTC Twin Towers and Building 7 of the complex focuses on the building construction, the materials used, and all of the technical conditions that contributed to the outcome of the WTC disaster. The objectives of the NIST investigation are to determine technically the following:

- Why and how WTC Buildings 1, 2, and 7 collapsed following the initial impact of the aircraft
- Why the injuries and fatalities were so low or high depending on location (by studying all technical aspects of fire protection, occupant behavior, evacuation, and emergency response)
- What procedures and practices were used in the design, construction, operation, and maintenance of the WTC buildings
- Which building and fire codes, standards, and practices warrant revision and are still in use

Scientists and engineers used a NIST-developed computational model to recreate aspects of the fires that occurred following the terrorist attack on the WTC. The model, Fire Dynamic Simulator, and a software package called SmokeView have been used previously to aid in the recreation of building fires that resulted in firefighter fatalities. Preliminary calculations have demonstrated the model's ability to shed light on the impact of building geometry, fuel distribution, and wind conditions on the smoke and fire flows within and outside the Twin Trade towers. Such information may be helpful to firefighters in predicting the likely behavior of future large-scale fires in high-rise buildings.

3.3.2 Anthrax airflow study

Following the release of anthrax spores in the Hart Senate Office Building in Washington, DC, in October 2001, NIST engineers provided help in understanding how spores may have spread through the buildings. NIST experts in ventilation systems and air quality used a sophisticated NIST-developed computer model to understand different ways in which airflow may have transported spores. The results of the modeling were used in developing decontamination strategies.

3.3.3 Cybersecurity standards and technologies

NIST develops cryptographic standards and methods for protecting the integrity, confidentiality, and authenticity of information resources. NIST's first encryption standard has been used widely in the public and private sectors since 1977. In December 2001, NIST and the Department of Commerce announced the newest and strongest-yet encryption standard for the protection of sensitive nonclassified electronic information. Although the Advanced Encryption Standard (AES) was developed for the government, the private sector is using it to safeguard financial transactions and ensure the privacy of digital information—from medical records and tax information to PIN numbers—for millions of Americans. Individual consumers, financial brokers, and large corporations rely on NIST encryption standards for safe and secure electronic transactions, whether they are worth just a few cents or several billion dollars.

NIST also works with government and industry to establish more secure systems and networks by developing, managing, and promoting security-assessment tools, techniques, and services and supporting programs for testing, evaluation, and validation. For example, NIST helps companies incorporate NIST encryption algorithms into commercial products by testing and validating their correct implementation.

NIST, in cosponsorship with the Small Business Administration (SBA) and the National Infrastructure Protection Center, and using NIST publications as core materials, holds regional workshops to advise small businesses and not-for-profit organizations on practical tools and techniques that can help them assess, enhance, and maintain the security of their systems.

3.3.4 Cybersecurity of electric power and industrial control systems

NIST is working with companies and industry organizations to identify the types of vulnerabilities that exist and develop security requirements for the real-time systems that control the power grid and critical industrial production processes. A Process Control Security Requirements Forum has been established to identify and assess threats and risks to process control information and functions, make and promote the adoption of security requirements recommendations, and promote security awareness and integration of security considerations in the life cycle of electric power and industrial process control systems.

NIST also is working with the Institute of Electrical and Electronics Engineers (IEEE), the International Electrotechnical Commission, and the Instrumentation, Systems, and Automation Society to incorporate security requirements into the standards relevant to electric power and industrial control systems.

3.3.5 Ensuring proper doses for irradiation of mail

NIST is a member of a White House task force led by the Office of Science and Technology Policy to ensure that mail intended for Congress and other federal government offices is properly irradiated to kill anthrax bacteria. Very shortly after the first discovery of anthrax in mail to Senator Tom Daschle, the U.S. Postal Service identified commercial facilities in Lima, Ohio, and Bridgeport, New Jersey, that could successfully irradiate mail to help ensure its safety.

These facilities use high-energy electron sources to sterilize a wide range of items, more typically medical instruments and supplies. Such radiation destroys biological agents without affecting most other materials, so the mail is made safe without damage. NIST physicists certified for the task force that these facilities could sterilize mail against anthrax effectively.

NIST collaborated with the U.S. Postal Service and the Armed Forces Radiobiology Research Institute (AFRRI) to determine what dose of radiation produced at the two facilities would be adequate to kill anthrax and yet not damage most mail items. NIST has a long history of involvement in providing calibrations, standards, and measurement methods to ensure accurate radiation doses for x-ray machines, mammography, radiopharmaceuticals, and other products.

The high radiation doses required to kill the anthrax caused some deterioration of the paper in the mail, with the subsequent release of volatile organic compounds (VOCs) that can be irritating to mail-room personnel. NIST is working with AFRRI, the U.S. Postal Service, the National Archives, and the Library of Congress to minimize the release of the VOCs and to understand quantitatively the VOC chemistry and the damage to the paper in the mail.

The electron irradiation process has limited penetrating power and, thus, cannot be used to sanitize parcels that have larger volumes and contain dense objects. For parcel package decontamination, the team from NIST, AFRRI, and the U.S. Postal Service turned to high-energy x-ray irradiation, which is much more penetrating but requires a longer irradiation time to deliver the needed dose. Using procedures analogous to those used in the certification of electron beam irradiation, the White House task force validated the decontamination of parcel packages using high-energy x-rays.

3.3.6 Weapons-detection technologies and standards

With funding from the National Institute of Justice (NIJ), NIST researchers have completed work on new performance standards and operational requirements for both walk-through and hand-held metal detectors. Several additional federal agencies—including the Transportation Security Administration and the Federal Bureau of Prisons—and dozens of state and local law-enforcement and corrections agencies contributed ideas to the project.

The researchers created a sophisticated measurement system that uses specialized computer software to evaluate detector effectiveness. Test objects also were developed to duplicate the response of various threat items, such as razor blades, handguns, and handcuff keys.

Another NIST research group has received funding from the NIJ and the Federal Aviation Administration (FAA) to investigate a new technology for weapons detection based on low-energy, millimeter-size electromagnetic waves. The technology, which currently is under development, involves a radar-like apparatus that could illuminate a group of people or individuals. Clothing is transparent to the waves, but objects concealed beneath the clothing are not. Waves striking guns, knives, and plastic explosives would be reflected back and directed through a set of optics, which focuses the radiation onto an array of tiny antennas mounted on a silicon wafer. The antennas are so small that 120 can fit onto a single wafer. An electronics package would convert the concentrated electromagnetic radiation into images, and these would be projected onto a laptop computer screen.

Millimeter-size waves are expected to locate concealed weapons consistently, without simultaneously creating detailed images of the body. NIST is working to understand fully the performance issues for such detectors to be able to assist the FAA and the NIJ in judging the sensitivity and reliability of commercial products.

3.3.7 Detection of chemical, biological, radiological, and other threats

As the primary reference laboratory for the United States, NIST develops standards, protocols, and new test methods to ensure that chemical and biological compounds can be measured accurately. This includes extensive, ongoing programs for the detection of chemical, biological, radiological, nuclear, and explosive threats.

NIST researchers work continually to improve methods and data for ultrasensitive detection of chemicals, including chemical warfare agents. This research involves both widely used techniques, such as mass spectrometry and chromatography, as well as smaller, portable devices designed to detect more specific biological or chemical agents.

For example, a NIST database developed with the Environmental Protection Agency and the National Institutes of Health is included with most mass spectrometers sold by major manufacturers today.

This database provides the mass spectral information—a kind of chemical fingerprint—needed to identify definitively more than 140,000 different compounds. This database is essential for rapidly identifying specific chemical threats in real time—at airport security checkpoints, for example. NIST also is developing mass spectral libraries for use in the identification of bacteria and other complex protein mixtures that may be used in a biological attack.

Military personnel wear gas masks for protection against chemical and biological assault. With funding from the U.S. Army, NIST is verifying the accuracy of test equipment used to determine if a soldier's gas mask is protecting properly. A gas mask that does not fit well may leak around the edges, there may be small holes in the mask, or the filter may be malfunctioning.

To test for such problems, the army uses a commercial calibration system that compares the concentration of airborne particulate matter inside the soldier's mask while it is being worn with the ambient concentration of particulates outside the mask. Ordinary small particulates in the air serve as a stand-in for chemical or biological agents such as mustard gas or anthrax because their flow behavior is very similar. NIST scientists are working to ensure accurate calibration of test equipment by developing a mechanism to deliver a well-characterized aerosol source, as well as accurate and reproducible measurement capabilities.

Two complementary analytical approaches have been developed by NIST; the first uses electron microscopy and imaging processing to count particles, whereas the second is much faster and uses the measurement of electrical current flow of deliberately charged particles to calculate the particle concentration. Both methods are in the final stages of intercomparison and validation and will result in improved and more reliable calibration of military gas masks.

Other NIST projects are aimed at creating new, portable measurement devices that can detect agents such as sulfur-mustard gas compounds, sarin and other nerve agents, and explosive compounds. For example, gas microsensors based on NIST-patented research show exceptional promise as a low-cost, widely deployable technology for detecting a range of chemical agents that could be used in terrorist attacks. Therefore, NIST is working with the Defense Threat Reduction Agency on the creation of microsensor arrays that use selective thin films and miniheaters embedded in integrated circuits to identify chemical agents at trace levels. The NIST-developed microsensor arrays have been used successfully to detect simulated mustard and nerve agents and, more recently, the chemical agents themselves.

NIST also has initiated work with the Food and Drug Administration on the development of fluorescent standards for microarray-based clinical diagnostics to detect pathogenic microorganisms in the environment. A NIST collaboration with Virginia Polytechnic Institute and State University has been developing a cell-based microfluidic sensor for the detection of environmental toxins in water streams. And a NIST collaboration with the FAA is aimed at checking the performance of systems that sense whether an airline passenger is carrying explosives by identifying minute quantities of particles and vapors as the person walks through a portal device. NIST is using its expertise in a specialized form of mass spectrometry to identify, count, and size explosive particles collected by such detection systems.

NIST is working with other federal agencies to improve the quality and comparability of measurements for both chemical and biological agents. For example, NIST is working with the Department of Defense (DOD) on the use of specialized mass spectrometric techniques for the identification of bacteria and other microorganisms. NIST is focusing on the standardization of methods for sample preparation and data interpretation of results. NIST also has initiated a collaboration to assist the Centers for Disease Control and Prevention in support of their Counter-Terrorism Laboratory Network, which includes laboratories in five states, with plans to expand the number of states participating in the coming years. Additional NIST projects involve improving methods to:

- Use laser-based techniques to enhance detection of chemical agents.
- Use proteins to detect low levels of specific biological pathogens.
- Rapidly sequence DNA for quick identification and for tracing the sources of pathogens.

- Monitor medical markers in routine urine tests as an early warning. system that a population has been exposed to biological pathogens.

3.3.8 Tools for law enforcement

For most of its 100-year history, NIST has worked closely with law-enforcement, corrections, and criminal justice agencies to help improve the technologies available for solving and detecting crimes and for protecting law-enforcement officers. Starting in 1913, a NIST scientist named Wilmer Souder pioneered the use of scientific techniques for forensic investigations and helped the Federal Bureau of Investigation (FBI) establish its crime laboratory in 1932. Since the early 1970s, NIST has issued more than a dozen law-enforcement standards that help law-enforcement agencies ensure that the equipment they purchase and the technologies they use are safe, dependable, and effective.

3.3.9 Standards for biometrics

NIST has provided biometric test data and standard measurement methods for fingerprints and, more recently, face recognition. This work is being extended to include the specific biometric systems and scenarios required for visa systems under the USA Patriot Act, as amended by the Enhanced Border Security and Visa Reform Act. NIST has statutory responsibilities to develop and certify a technology standard that can be used to verify the identity of persons applying for a U.S. visa or using a visa to enter the country. The DOJ and DOS also expect NIST to certify the accuracy of specific government and commercial systems being considered for use in this visa system.

This program will produce standard measurements of accuracy for biometric systems, standard XML-based scoring software, and accuracy measurements for specific biometrics required for the system scenarios mandated under the Border Security Act. This work will have wide impact beyond the mandated systems; standard test methods are likely to be accepted as international standards, and discussions are under way concerning the use of these same standards for airport security.

In conjunction with the FBI, NIST has developed several databases, including one consisting of 258 latent fingerprints and their matching rolled file prints. This database can be used by researchers and commercial developers to create and test new fingerprint identification algorithms, test commercial and research systems that conform to the NIST/American National Standards Institute (ANSI) standard, and assist in training latent fingerprint examiners. The increasing use of specialized “live” fingerprint scanners will help ensure that a high-quality fingerprint can be captured quickly and added to the FBI's current files. Use of these scanners also should speed up the matching of fingerprints against the FBI database of more than 40 million prints.

The Biometric Consortium serves as the federal government's focal point for research, development, test, evaluation, and application of biometric-based personal identification and verification technology. The consortium now has more than 800 members, including 60 government agencies. NIST and the National Security Agency (NSA) cochair the consortium. NIST has collaborated with the consortium, the biometric industry, and other biometric organizations to create a common biometric exchange file format. The format already is part of government requirements for data interchange and is being adopted by the biometric industry. The specification is a candidate for fast-track approval as an ANSI standard and as an international standard for exchange of many types of biometric data files, including data on fingerprints, faces, palm prints, retinas, and iris and voice patterns.

3.3.10 Standards for forensic DNA typing

NIST has developed a series of standard reference materials (SRMs) that can be used by forensic and commercial laboratories to check the accuracy of their analyses. The NIST SRMs include samples of human DNA that have been carefully analyzed according to a standard FBI matching method. By extracting the DNA provided in the NIST SRM and analyzing it with their own laboratory equipment and test methods, forensic and commercial laboratories can verify that their methods are accurate.

NIST experts in DNA analysis met with scientists from the Armed Forces Institute of Pathology (AFIP) in October 2001 to discuss details of a specialized DNA analysis technique that AFIP is using to identify remains of victims at the Pentagon and Pennsylvania crash sites. NIJ officials also contacted NIST scientists for consultation on DNA analysis of human remains from the WTC. A NIST forensic scientist also serves on the NIJ-convened World Trade Center Kinship and Data Analysis Panel, which is composed of 25 experts from the forensic DNA community.

It was clear from the outset that the large number of victims and degraded condition of tissue samples from the attack pose particular problems for forensic DNA typing, so NIST developed a new technique using smaller portions of DNA at specific chromosome sites. The new technique improves DNA typing assays for degraded DNA and is now being compared with the methods currently used by a commercial DNA testing laboratory for the analysis of 13,000 bone fragments from the WTC site. NIST also is verifying two new commercial methods that have been developed to analyze degraded DNA samples.

The massive effort to identify victims from the WTC—the world's largest human identification case ever—includes a program devoted to analyzing mitochondrial DNA (mtDNA), a small circular strand of genetic material located within the cell's mitochondria that converts nutrients into energy. Each human cell can have hundreds to several thousand molecules of mtDNA, compared with only one copy (two intertwined strands) of genomic DNA in the cell nucleus. A NIST SRM is being used for quality control in the mtDNA studies.

3.3.11 Enhanced surveillance cameras

The proper rendering of shadow and dark detail by cameras is important in many security applications, such as surveillance within airplane cabins or terminals. Cameras, however, do not work nearly as well as the human eye, which is much better at distinguishing subtle differences between varying shadows and dark details. This is particularly true when bright areas dominate the scene under view. In this situation, conventional cameras suffer from substantial amounts of glare that make it difficult to see details in shadowed areas. By mimicking the eye and surrounding the camera with liquid instead of air, NIST researchers (with interagency Technology Support Working Group funding) hope to improve the performance of surveillance cameras substantially. This, in turn, may improve the reliability of other technologies, such as face recognition within airports.

3.3.12 Forensic tools for investigating computer or magnetic data evidence

While computer forensics experts know these tricks, they frequently face the daunting task of searching up to 100,000 files on a single desktop computer for evidence. NIST computer scientists are helping to speed up this process dramatically with a new tool, the National Software Reference Library. Working with software manufacturers and others who provided copies of their programs, NIST collected signature formats for more than 6 million different computer files. These signatures are checked against the actual contents of the file rather than other identifiers such as the file name or header. The library allows law-enforcement agencies to eliminate 25 percent to 95 percent of the total files in a computer, concentrating only on those that really might contain evidence.

There is also a critical need in the law-enforcement community to ensure the reliability of computer forensic tools, so that they consistently produce accurate and objective test results. NIST's Computer Forensic Tool Testing (CFTT) project aims to establish a methodology for testing these software tools through the development of tool requirements specifications, test procedures, test criteria, test sets, and test hardware. The results provide the information necessary for toolmakers to improve tools, for users to make informed choices about acquiring and using computer forensics tools, and for interested parties to understand the tools' capabilities. The approach is based on well-recognized international methodologies for conformance testing and quality testing.

Several federal agencies support the effort, including the NIJ, the U.S. Secret Service, the FBI, the U.S. Customs Service, and the Defense Computer Forensics Laboratory.

In another project, NIST researchers collaborated with the National Telecommunications and Information Administration on a new technique for retrieving data from damaged or altered magnetic tapes and computer disks. The method uses high-resolution magnetic sensors to map microscopic magnetic fields on a sample. The map then is used to rebuild the original magnetic signal. The researchers demonstrated the technique by recovering audio data from a tape fragment provided by the National Transportation Safety Board that was too damaged to be played in a conventional tape deck. For the FBI, they used the technique to reveal magnetic marks produced by the erase and record heads during the recording process. Such evidence could be critical for proving that an original tape or disk had been altered.

3.3.13 Crimes involving pipe bombs or handguns

NIST chemists, in conjunction with the NIJ, have come up with a reliable way to associate the composition of unfired gunpowder or ammunition with residues collected at handgun or pipe bomb crime scenes. To develop the method, the NIST researchers collected gunpowder residues from handguns fired at a test range and analyzed them for nitroglycerin and stabilizer additive content. This enabled the determination of a numerical identification ratio, which often can link the residues to unfired powders. In another project, NIST asked 15 forensic laboratories to analyze test samples of two commercial gunpowders. This voluntary interlaboratory comparison demonstrated the labs' proficiency in gunpowder measurements, thereby making forensic gunpowder analysis more defensible in criminal prosecutions. As a follow-up to this work, NIST now is preparing a smokeless powder reference material, which forensic laboratories will be able to use in checking the accuracy of their bomb and gunpowder residue analyses.

3.3.14 Standardization of communications for first responders

Federal, state, and local police, fire, and rescue personnel are assigned to use widely separated radio frequencies. They also use different types of computer hardware and software systems with access to different law-enforcement databases. At a large disaster site, such as the WTC, responders from different agencies may not be able to use their radios to talk to each other. At other times, a police officer may let a traffic offender go with a ticket, unaware that the offender was wanted on serious charges in another jurisdiction.

NIST, again with funding from the NIJ, is working with the public safety community to standardize techniques for wireless telecommunications and IT applications. NIST also is working with standards development organizations to have first responder requirements included within the scope of standardization efforts. For example, NIST is coordinating first responders' standards needs with the IEEE committee that is developing standard message sets for transferring information among public-safety, transportation, and hazardous material–incident command centers. In addition to standardization, NIST is helping other agencies select promising interim solutions and is analyzing long-term solutions, such as a software-defined radio, for research and development investment.

NIST also is working on the development, deployment, and standardization of Web-based technologies for integrating sensors, real-time video, smart tags, and embedded microprocessor devices to provide next-generation personnel support for remote monitoring, control, and communications in the field. This technology can enable rapid access to real-time sensor and video information and allow sharing and collaborative use of IT applications. Wearable computers and small, embedded devices integrated with the latest technology for remote sensing, real-time conferencing, and other data-intensive applications could provide an immediate feedback channel for law-enforcement agents and emergency responders. NIST is working to demonstrate how these technologies can be extended and rapidly deployed to create easily configurable networks.

3.3.15 Simulation tools

When properly used, simulation tools can enhance planning and training and help personnel evaluate different response options during and after catastrophic events. Complex scenarios cannot be modeled very accurately, however, because no single simulation tool can represent all aspects of an emergency situation. Individual simulation packages and databases can address individual phenomena and behaviors, but they cannot be integrated together easily to provide an overall picture of events.

To address this need, NIST is helping to establish a framework to allow a broad range of simulation systems to share information, including models and results. NIST is working with the response community, industry, and academia to identify information sources, simulation systems, and data requirements; develop an emergency response simulation framework and standard interfaces; and develop and demonstrate distributed simulations using commercial software and the new framework. The ability to integrate information from different simulations will be a valuable tool for responders and allow agencies to develop and coordinate emergency response simulations and scenarios independently.

3.3.16 Search-and-rescue robots

A NIST project aimed initially at protecting emergency personnel by minimizing the amount of time rescuers spend searching earthquake-damaged buildings has helped provide a new tool for rescue workers at the WTC. Search-and-rescue robots had never before been used at a disaster site, and they demonstrated promise in being able to penetrate areas too small and too hazardous for people to access. Teams of robots—led by the independent Center for Robot-Assisted Search and Rescue—were able to locate full and partial remains of several victims at the WTC site. Just a month before, several of the robots had run through a NIST-designed test course at the International Joint Conference on Artificial Intelligence.

To provide an objective evaluation of the performance of autonomous, intelligent, mobile robots for search-and-rescue operations, NIST engineers designed and built a standard test arena for robots, complete with overturned furniture, collapsed floors, broken pipes, and mannequin victims. The arena has different levels of difficulty to help assess different types of robotic ability. Because the robots, built by universities and industry, compete quite literally on the same playing field, their performance can be measured objectively. Since one of NIST's goals is to foster cooperation among robotics researchers around the world, NIST supplies its test arenas to two international robotics conferences, which include competitions to see how well search-and-rescue robots perform on the NIST arena. Winners of the annual RoboCupRescue and the American Association for Artificial Intelligence Rescue Robot competitions share their techniques so all participants can build better robots.

3.4 Applying the national strategy at the organizational level

There are several key questions that managers need to address when considering how to address homeland security issues. First, is any part of their organizations a component of the critical national infrastructure? Second, which parts of the critical national infrastructure are their organizations most dependent on? Third, are the organizations' facilities located near facilities or structures that are components of the critical national infrastructure?

These questions can be answered through a structured threat-assessment process. The updated risk assessments can help organizations to develop a business case for action to justify increased security investments. Risk assessments need to cover all operational aspects of an organization, including IT support.

If managers do conclude that their organizations or parts of them are components of the critical national infrastructure, then, depending on the sector that the unit is a component of, there are several steps that should be taken to apply the national strategy. These are covered on a sector-by-sector basis in Chapter 5.

Most organizations will likely find that they are dependent on components of the critical national infrastructure. It is difficult not to be dependent on telecommunications, banking, and public utilities. Thus, if there were to be a major disruption in any those sectors because of a terrorist attack, the organization would be impacted in some way. These disruptions can, in part, be mitigated or minimized through the implementation of a DRP and a business-continuity plan.

If managers conclude that their organizations' facilities are located near facilities or structures that are components of the critical national infrastructure, then it is likely that a major terrorist attack on those components would impact operations. The best illustration of this is that when the WTC was attacked on September 11, 2001, over 20 buildings in the area sustained damage, and many organizations were forced to relocate temporarily or permanently. These disruptions can also, in part, be mitigated or minimized through the implementation of a DRP and a business-continuity plan.

3.5 The security-improvement process in the organization

Once threat assessments are conducted, DRPs and business-continuity plans need to be developed or revised to address newly determined threats. These plans can help to mitigate or minimize disruptions that can result from a terrorist attack on a component of the critical national infrastructure.

It is important to maintain the perspective that security improvement is an ongoing process. In addition to developing the DRPs and business-continuity plans, organizations need to establish a process that stays in step with the national initiatives that will do the following:

- Maintain an updated inventory of an organization's critical facilities, systems, and functions and monitor its security methods and preparedness to deal with disputations.
- Coordinate with federal, state, local, and private entities in planning and response activities.
- Monitor and respond to national-level threat information, assessments, and warnings.
- Examine incentives provided by federal, state, or local government to devise solutions to unique protection impediments.
- Monitor and respond to cross-sector and crossjurisdictional protection standards, guidelines, criteria, and protocols.
- Monitor the development of and utilize emerging protection best practices and processes and vulnerability-assessment methodologies.
- Monitor the results of demonstration projects and pilot programs and assess outcomes for potential application in the organization.
- Implement appropriate asset-protection education and awareness campaigns.
- Monitor and respond to efforts made by the federal, state, and local governments to improve incident response.
- Establish a personnel surety program for all key personnel.

The federal government plans to coordinate public- and private-sector security research and development activities and interoperability standards of communications systems to utilize technology better to improve homeland security. As new technologies evolve, organizations need to establish a process that stays in step with the national initiatives. An internal organizational process should be established to monitor technology development, standards for technology use, and technologies that have been tested and proven effective.

3.6 Integrating organizational and national strategies

IT managers will play a key role in determining the level and type of security needed for their organizations. Action Checklist Number 3 (see Table 3.1) shows the steps that IT managers, in conjunction with other departmental managers, should take to help integrate their organizations' security strategies with *The National Strategy for the Physical Protection of Critical Infrastructures and Key Assets.*

The next chapter focuses on information sharing that can occur between federal, state, local, and private entities to improve homeland security.

Table 3.1 *Action Checklist Number 3*

Action Item	Status (e.g., Completed, Pending, or N/A)
Conduct a structured threat assessment to determine if the organization is a component of the critical national infrastructure.	
Conduct a structured threat assessment to determine the level of dependency on components of the critical national infrastructure.	
Conduct a structured threat assessment to determine the proximity of the organization's facilities to facilities or structures that are components of the critical national infrastructure.	
Initiate a security-improvement process.	
Establish an internal organization process to monitor technology development, standards for technology use, and technologies that have been tested and proven effective.	

4

Information Sharing for Protecting National Assets

The National Strategy for the Physical Protection of Critical Infrastructures and Key Assets states that in order to meet the challenges associated with the terrorist threat, public and private stakeholders must have the ability to work together seamlessly. The federal government, particularly the intelligence and law-enforcement communities, plays a significant role in providing, coordinating, and ensuring that threat information is understood across all levels of government.

In addition, it is recognized that state and local law enforcement, as well as private-sector security entities, are valuable sources of localized threat information. These organizations possess a better understanding of the vulnerabilities impacting their facilities, systems, and functions than the federal government. Development of accepted and efficient processes and systems for communication and exchange of crucial security-related information is critical to improving homeland security.

This chapter provides an overview of the information-sharing efforts implemented to improve homeland security. Areas covered include the following:

- The information-sharing mission
- Information-sharing mechanisms
- Deciding how to participate in information sharing

4.1 The information-sharing mission

State and local governments and private-sector officials have indicated that the threat information they receive from the federal government is often vague, duplicative, and in some cases conflicting. They argue that in the past they have seldom received indications and warnings that are specific, accurate, and timely enough to support resource-allocation decisions. Conversely, when relevant timely information is shared, they point out that it often fails to reach the appropriate parties because of security-clearance requirements. *The National Strategy for the Physical Protection of Critical Infrastructures and Key Assets* states that adequate protection of critical infrastructures and key assets requires the following:

- Improved collection of threat information
- Comprehensive and relevant threat assessment and analysis
- Robust indications and warning processes and systems
- Improved coordination of information-sharing activities

The Homeland Security Act of 2002 provides that critical-infrastructure information voluntarily submitted to DHS, when accompanied by an express statement of the expectation that it will be protected, will be exempt from disclosure under the Freedom of Information Act and state Sunshine laws. Further, if such information is submitted in good faith, it may not be directly used in civil litigation without the consent of the person submitting it.

The act also provides for the establishment of government procedures for receiving, handling, and storing voluntarily submitted critical-infrastructure information and for protecting the confidentiality of such information. It also provides for the development of mechanisms that, while preserving confidentiality, also permit the sharing of such information within the federal government and with state and local governments.

The act authorizes the federal government to provide advisories, alerts, and warnings to relevant businesses, targeted sectors, other government actors, and the general public regarding potential threats to critical infrastructure. The act also stipulates that the federal government must protect the source of any voluntarily submitted information forming the basis of a warning, as well as any proprietary or other information that is not properly in the public domain.

The act enables private-sector individuals to enter into voluntary agreements to promote critical-infrastructure security, including appropriate forms of information sharing, without incurring the risk of antitrust liability. Under this new legal regime, DHS will be able to give proper assurances to private-sector owners and operators of critical infrastructure that the sensitive or proprietary information that they furnish will be protected. These assurances are designed to encourage the private sector to share that vital information with the government. Specific initiatives include efforts to:

- Define protection-related information-sharing requirements and establish effective, efficient information-sharing processes.
- Implement the statutory authorities and powers of the Homeland Security Act of 2002 to protect security and proprietary information regarded as sensitive by the private sector.
- Promote the development and operation of critical sector Information-Sharing Analysis Centers.
- Improve processes for domestic-threat data collection, analysis, and dissemination to state and local government and private industry.
- Support the development of interoperable secure communications systems for state and local governments and designated private-sector entities.
- Complete implementation of the Homeland Security Advisory System (covered in Chapter 1).
- Establish the Cyber Warning and Information Network (CWIN).

4.2 Information-Sharing Mechanisms

In Chapter 1 we discussed various tip systems that the government has established to help facilitate the flow of information about potential terrorist activities. These include providing the FBI and other organizations with tips about the activities of individuals, organizations, or groups.

In addition there is the CWIN, which is a group of organizations, including the NIPC, the Critical Infrastructure Assurance Office (CIAO), and others, that have some responsibility for the security of federal systems. The private-sector Information-Sharing and Analysis Centers are also included in the network. (Specific cyberthreat analysis is presented in later chapters.)

The NIPC, with help from representatives of private industry, the academic community, and government agencies, developed the InfraGard initiative to share information about cyberintrusions, exploited vulnerabilities, and infrastructure threats. The field offices of the FBI have established InfraGard chapters, and there are now 72 chapters with over 1,500 organizations across the United States as members. The National InfraGard Program provides four basic services to members:

1. An alert network using encrypted e-mail
2. A secure Web site for communication about suspicious activity or intrusions
3. Local chapter activities and a help desk for questions
4. The ability of industry to provide information on intrusions to the local FBI field office using secure communications

General membership in InfraGard is open to all parties interested in supporting the purposes and objectives of InfraGard. On the local level InfraGard is organized into 72 chapters, each of which is associated with a field office of the FBI. InfraGard members are responsible for promoting the protection and advancement of the critical infrastructure, cooperating with others in the interchange of knowledge and ideas, supporting the education of members and the general public, and maintaining the confidentiality of information obtained through involvement. Table 4.1 shows the InfraGard chapter locations.

Table 4.1 *InfraGard Chapters*

Albany	El Paso	Northwest Florida
Albuquerque	Fort Wayne	Norfolk
Anchorage	Harrisburg	Oklahoma City
Atlanta	Honolulu	Omaha
Austin	Houston	Orlando
Baltimore	Indianapolis	Philadelphia
Baton Rouge	Iowa	Phoenix
Birmingham	Jackson	Pittsburgh
Boston	Jacksonville	Portland
Buffalo	Kansas City	Richmond
Charlotte	Knoxville	Rochester
Chattahoochee Valley	Las Vegas	Sacramento

Table 4.1 *InfraGard Chapters*

Chicago	Little Rock	Salt Lake City
Cincinnati	Los Angeles	San Antonio
Cleveland	Louisville	San Diego
Columbia	Madison	San Francisco
Columbus	Memphis	San Juan
Connecticut	Miami	Seattle
Dallas	Milwaukee	Springfield
Dayton	Minneapolis	Southern Arizona
Delaware	Mobile	St. Louis
Denver	Nashville	Tampa
Detroit	New Jersey	Vermont
Eastern Carolina	New Orleans	Washington
	New York	West Virginia

InfraGard Secure Access members can report incidents through the secure Web site using the online report in the incident reports area. Members may also report by:

- Contacting the Watch and Warning Unit at (202) 323-3205
- Contacting your InfraGard coordinator
- Faxing your incident report via unsecured fax to the Watch and Warning Unit (202) 323-2079 or (202) 323-2082
- E-mailing it using your secure e-mail to the Watch and Warning Unit at infragard-hq@fbi.gov

As discussed in Chapter 1, the FBI public Web site has an online incident-reporting form. This form may be used by anyone who wishes to report an incident to the FBI. The information is then verified and sanitized so it can be passed to InfraGard secure members in the form of analytical products or threat assessments.

4.2.1 National bylaws of InfraGard

Preamble

InfraGard is dedicated to increasing the security of the critical infrastructures of the United States of America. All InfraGard participants are committed to the proposition that a robust exchange of information about threats to and actual attacks on these infrastructures is an essential element to successful infrastructures protection efforts. The goal of InfraGard is to enable that information flow so that the owners and operators of infrastructures can better protect themselves and so that the U.S. government can better discharge its law-enforcement and national security responsibilities.

Article I

Nature of InfraGard: InfraGard is a cooperative undertaking between the Federal Bureau of Investigation (hereinafter, the "FBI") and other non-FBI members (hereinafter, the "Membership"). The Membership includes an association of businesses, academic institutions, state and local law-enforcement agencies, and other participants. All decisions made on behalf of InfraGard shall be by consensus between the FBI and the Membership. The FBI will be represented at the national level by the Director of the National Infrastructure Protection Center (or an FBI official designated by the NIPC Director) and at the local level by the Assistant Director in Charge (ADIC) or Special Agent in Charge (SAC) of the local FBI field office (or an FBI official designated by the ADIC or SAC). The Membership will be represented at the national level by the National Executive Committee, and at the local level by the Executive Committee of the local InfraGard chapter. These bylaws are intended to cover actions and decisions made on behalf of InfraGard, or identified in some way with InfraGard (such as through the use of the InfraGard name). Nothing in them is intended to limit the ability of the FBI or any member of InfraGard to act outside of InfraGard. As used in this document, "InfraGard" is understood to mean the FBI and the Membership acting in consensus at the national or local level.

Article II

Purpose and Objectives: The purpose and primary objective of InfraGard is to increase the security of the U.S. national infrastructures through ongoing exchanges of information relevant to infrastructure protection and through education, outreach, and similar efforts to increase awareness of infrastructure protection issues.

Article III

Membership: General membership shall be open to all parties interested in supporting the purposes and objectives of InfraGard as stated in this document and who meet such other qualifications, as the InfraGard Membership shall establish. Membership will be considered without regard to race, religion, color, national origin, age, sex, sexual orientation, or disability. All members shall execute the "National Membership Application/Agreement" prior to admission. The InfraGard Membership may expel any member based on that member's violation of these bylaws, the National Membership Application/Agreement, or any other duly enacted requirements of InfraGard. Additionally, the InfraGard Membership may exclude or expel from membership any organization, individual, or other entity whose past behavior or public statements create substantial doubt that the organization, individual, or entity in question would actually abide by the requirements of InfraGard membership if admitted. Membership does not entitle an InfraGard participant to obtain information from the FBI.

Article IV

Local Chapters: On the local level, InfraGard initially will be organized into 56 chapters (hereinafter "Local Chapters"), each associated with a field office of the FBI. The Membership of each Local Chapter will elect an Executive Committee, consisting of at least three members, with each member having one vote. The Executive Committee will be responsible for administration of the Local Chapter and for liaison with the FBI representative (who will attend all Executive Committee meetings). The Executive Committee may organize itself in whatever manner seems appropriate to the local circumstances, and may establish officers and subordinate committees as appropriate. In addition to electing the Executive Committee, the Local Chapter may choose to enact its own Bylaws addressing matters of membership, administration, organization, or other matters, so long as such Bylaws are enacted by a two-thirds vote of the Local Chapter and are fully consistent with the National ByLaws, National Membership Agreement, and other duly enacted national requirements of InfraGard.

Article V

National Organization: InfraGard will hold an annual National Convention at which each Local Chapter will be represented. A majority of the total number of Local Chapters, each having one vote, shall constitute a quorum for the transaction of business of InfraGard at the national level. At the first National Convention, the Local Chapters will elect by simple majority a National Executive Committee consisting of seven members. The membership term on the National Executive Committee shall be two years and shall be staggered. To implement a staggered election cycle, three of the initial members of the National Executive Committee shall be elected to one-year terms. The National Executive Committee will be responsible for administration of the Local Chapters and for liaison with the FBI national representative (who will attend all National Executive Committee meetings). The National Executive Committee shall, as needed, develop proposed national policy for InfraGard in response to proposals by Local Chapters or the FBI. The National Executive Committee will circulate any such proposed policy to the Local Chapters and shall enact such policy with the concurrence of the FBI and a majority of the Local Chapters. A majority of the National Executive Committee members shall constitute its quorum, and each member shall have one vote. Prior to the first National Convention, a Provisional National Executive Committee will serve, elected by the Indiana, Northern Ohio and Southern Ohio Local Chapters, acting pursuant to such Bylaws as these Local Chapters adopt. At least two months prior to the annual National Convention, the [Provisional] National Executive Committee shall make nominations for election to it, with the slate of nominees being equal in number to the number of seats vacant or to be vacated at the end of the year. Members of the [Provisional] National Executive Committee may be nominated for reelection. The list of nominees shall be sent to each Local Chapter, together with at least one month's notice of the annual National Convention. Further nominations in writing, signed by at least 20 InfraGard members or selected by any Local Chapter, shall be presented for election if received by the [Provisional] National Executive Committee ten days prior to the National Convention.

Article VI

New Local Chapters: Any grouping of the InfraGard Membership may request provisional recognition as a new Local Chapter through the National Executive Committee, which may approve such request with the concurrence of the FBI. A grouping of the InfraGard Membership obtaining provisional recognition as a Local Chapter shall be known as a "Provisional Chapter." At the National Convention, as its first order of business, the Membership will recognize and approve Provisional Chapters through a simple majority vote, with each existing Local Chapter casting one vote. Provisional Chapters that are approved will be recognized as Local Chapters following the approval or denial of all Provisional Chapters existing at the time of the National Convention.

Article VII

Funding: Absent other arrangements, all participants in InfraGard will bear their own expenses. Local Chapters may, if they choose, enact membership dues or otherwise collect funds from the local Membership. Any funds so collected will be administered by the local Executive Committee in compliance with rules enacted by the Local Chapter for the proper handling of InfraGard funds. The National Executive Committee may also collect and administer funds if so authorized by a two-thirds vote of Local Chapters. All funds collected from the Membership will remain in the possession of the Membership and shall not be held, administered, or distributed by the FBI. No funds collected from the Membership shall be used to fund official FBI activities or otherwise augment the authorized budget of the FBI.

Article VIII

Statement of Ethics: All InfraGard participants will conduct themselves in compliance with all applicable federal, state, and local laws. InfraGard is committed to establishing an atmosphere of trust among its members. InfraGard participants will not betray that trust by engaging in illegal activity, by knowingly submitting false or misleading information to InfraGard, or by seeking some commercial or other advantage at the expense of other members through actions taken within InfraGard.

Article IX

Amendments: The National Executive Committee, the FBI, or any Local Chapter, can propose amendments to these National ByLaws. Such amendments will be considered at the National Convention and will be adopted with the concurrence of the FBI and a simple majority of the Local Chapters. The FBI will give the strongest consideration in favor of adopting any amendment proposed by the majority of Local Chapters.

4.2.2 Code of ethics of InfraGard

As an InfraGard member it is my responsibility to:

- Promote the protection and advancement of the critical infrastructure of the United States of America.
- Cooperate with others in the interchange of knowledge and ideas for mutual protection.
- Support the education of members and the general public in a diligent, loyal, honest manner, and not knowingly be a part of any illegal or improper activities.
- Serve in the interests of InfraGard and the general public in a diligent, loyal, and honest manner, and will not knowingly be a party to any illegal or improper activities.
- Maintain confidentiality, and prevent the use for competitive advantage at the expense of other members, of information obtained in the course of my involvement with InfraGard, which includes but is not limited to the following:
    - Information concerning the business of a fellow member or company
    - Information identified as proprietary, confidential, or sensitive
- Abide by the National and Local Chapter InfraGard Bylaws.
- Protect and respect the privacy rights, civil rights, and physical and intellectual property rights of others.

4.3 What information to share and how to report incidents

If your systems are hacked or intruded upon by an unauthorized party, you should call your local FBI office or contact the NIPC. In the event that you experience a crime against your computer systems, the FBI and the NIPC recommend that you respond quickly. Contact law enforcement. Traces are often impossible if too much time is wasted before alerting law enforcement or your own incident-response team.

If you are unsure of what actions to take, do not stop system processes or tamper with files. This may destroy traces of intrusion. Follow organizational policies and procedures. (Your organization should have a computer incident–response capability and plan in place.) Do not contact the suspected perpetrator.

Also remember to use the telephone to communicate. (Attackers may be capable of monitoring e-mail traffic.) Contact the incident–response team for your organization. (Quick use of technical expertise is crucial in preventing further damage and protecting potential evidence.) You should also establish points of contact with general counsel, emergency response staff, and law enforcement. (Preestablished contacts will help in a quick-response effort.)

It is advisable to make copies of files an intruder may have altered or left. If you have the technical expertise to copy files, this action will assist investigators as to when and how the intrusion may have occurred.

You should also identify a primary point of contact to handle potential evidence. This will help to facilitate the establishment of a chain of custody for evidence. (Potential hardware and software evidence that is not properly controlled may lose its value.)

Compile as much information and data as possible about the incident. Information that law-enforcement investigators will find helpful includes the following:

- Date, time, and duration of incident
- The name, title, telephone number, fax number, and e-mail of the point of contact for law enforcement, as well as the name of your organization, address, city, state, zip code, and country
- The physical locations of computer systems and/or networks that have been compromised
- Whether the systems are managed in-house or by a contractor
- Whether the affected systems or networks are critical to the organization's mission
- If your organization is a part of the critical infrastructure, which sector was affected:
  - Agriculture and food
  - Water
  - Public health
  - Emergency services
  - Defense industrial base
  - Telecommunications
  - Energy
  - Transportation
  - Banking and finance
  - Chemical industry and hazardous materials

  - Postal and shipping
  - National monuments and icons
  - Nuclear power plants
  - Dams
  - Government facilities
  - Commercial key assets

- The nature of the problem, which could include intrusion, system impairment, denial of resources, unauthorized root access, Web site defacement, compromise of system integrity, theft, or damage
- Whether the problem has been experienced before
- The suspected method of intrusion or attack, which could include a virus, an exploited vulnerability, a denial of service, a distributed denial of service, a trapdoor, or a Trojan horse
- The suspected perpetrators and the possible motivations of the attack, which could include an insider or disgruntled employee, a former employee, or a competitor. (If the suspect is an employee or former employee, you should determine and report the type of system access that the employee has or had.)
- An apparent source (IP address) of the intrusion or attack if known and whether there is any evidence of spoofing
- What computer system (hardware, operating system, or applications software) was affected
- What security infrastructure was in place, which could include an incident-response team, encryption, a firewall, secure remote access or authorization tools, an intrusion detection system (IDS), security auditing tools, access control lists, or packet filtering
- Whether the intrusion or attack resulted in a loss or compromise of sensitive, classified, or proprietary information
- Whether the intrusion or attack resulted in damage to systems or data
- What actions to mitigate the intrusion or attack have been taken, which could include the system being disconnected from the network, system binaries checked, backup of affected systems, or log files examined
- What agencies have been contacted, which could include state or local police, CERT, or FedCIRC

- When your system was last modified or updated and the name of the company or organization that did the work (address, phone number, point of contact information)

It is also necessary to determine a dollar value for damage, business loss, and cost to restore systems to normal operating conditions. The following information is helpful in determining dollar amounts:

- In the event that repairs or recovery were performed by a contractor, you should determine the charges incurred for services.
- If in-house staff were involved in determining the extent of the damage, repairing systems or data, or restoring systems to normal operating conditions, you should determine the number of hours staff expended to accomplish these tasks and the hourly wages, benefits, and overhead associated with each employee involved in the recovery.
- If business was disrupted in some way, you should determine the number of transactions or sales that were actually disrupted and their dollar value.
- If systems were impaired to the point that actual disrupted transactions or sales cannot be determined, then you should determine the dollar value of transactions or sales that would occur on a comparable day, for the duration of the system outage.
- If systems are used to produce goods, deliver services, or manage operations, then determine the value of the loss due to that disruption. (You may have had similar experiences if operations were disrupted because of inclement weather, fires, earthquakes, or other disruptive incidents.)
- If systems were physically damaged, you need to know what you paid to acquire and install the systems.
- If systems were stolen, you need to know what you paid to acquire and install the systems and the cost of actions taken to ensure that information on the stolen systems cannot be used to access systems.
- If intellectual property or trade secrets were stolen, then you need to determine the value of that property.
- If intellectual property or trade secrets were used by a competitor or other party, then you need to determine the impact on your business.

A good source of information about dealing with intrusions is available from the High Tech Crime Investigation Association Web site www.htcia.org, and specific information is available at the San Diego Chapter's Web site, www.htcia-sd.org. The San Diego Chapter has also published a guide for working with law-enforcement agencies when you have had a computer incident; this is available at www.htcia-sd.org/htciaguide.pdf.

4.4 Deciding how to participate in information sharing

Many organizations have been very hesitant to participate in the activities of the IS security community, including becoming a member of InfraGard as well as professional organizations that support security efforts. There are several reasons for a lack of participation, including the following:

- Organizations have policies or practices that prohibit sharing information.
- Management, legal counsel, and public-relations staff are concerned that revealing information about failures in computer security will negatively reflect on the reputation of the organization.
- In publicly traded companies, managers are concerned that negative press could negatively impact stock price or erode investor confidence.
- If an organization reports an incident and the case goes to trial, the litigation process will consume resources and expose the organization to public scrutiny.

Every organization needs to make a rational decision about how to participate in the reporting and information-sharing process. I have a bias toward participation and information sharing and have attended many meetings of InfraGard chapters and organizations such as the High Tech Crime Investigation Association. Having attended the meetings I have concluded that there are several immediate benefits for reporting and information sharing:

- Liaisons with the FBI and other law-enforcement organizations can be established.

- Internal security staff becomes more familiar with the IS security community and sources of support and assistance.
- Internal security staff members are exposed to ongoing training activities.
- Internal security staff has access to additional warning and alert systems.

It is important to bear in mind that in the war against terrorism, any organization that experiences an attack or an intrusion into its IS that may be related to terrorism is likely to suffer negative consequences if the events are not reported to law enforcement.

Action Checklist Number 4 (see Table 4.2) shows what steps an organization needs to take in order to start participating in the information-sharing process. The next chapter focuses on corporate actions required for homeland security by sector.

Table 4.2 *Action Checklist Number 4*

Action Item	Status (e.g., Completed, Pending, or N/A)
Establish policies for reporting computer-related incidents.	
Develop procedures for reporting computer-related incidents.	
Assign staff responsibilities for reporting computer-related incidents.	
Assign staff responsibilities for participating InfraGard or professional organizations.	

5

Homeland Security Initiatives by Sector

The *National Strategy for Homeland Security* has identified 13 critical sectors. The critical-infrastructure sectors identified are agriculture and food, water, public health, emergency services, government, the defense industrial base, information and telecommunications, energy, transportation, banking and finance, chemicals and hazardous materials, and postal and shipping. Each of the sectors faces a unique set of challenges to improve homeland security. This chapter covers major security-related initiatives that IT managers can help address within each sector.

5.1 Agriculture and Food

The agriculture and food sectors include the supply chains for feed, animals, and animal products; crop production and the supply chains of seed, fertilizer, and related materials; and the postharvesting components of the food supply chain, which include processing, production, packaging, storage, and distribution. The retail sales that support institutional food services and restaurant and home consumers are also considered part of the sector. Table 5.1 shows security initiatives in the agriculture and food sector.

Table 5.1 *Security Initiatives in Agriculture and Food*

Initiatives
Evaluate sector security and identify vulnerabilities.
Devise methods to address vulnerabilities.
Enhance detection and testing capabilities.
Assess transportation-related security risks.
Monitor potential infrastructure protection incentives.

5.2 Water

The water sector consists of two basic components: fresh water supply and wastewater collection and treatment. Infrastructures are diverse, complex, and distributed, ranging from systems that serve a few customers to those that serve millions. On the supply side there over 170,000 public water systems that depend on reservoirs, dams, wells, and aquifers, as well as treatment facilities, pumping stations, aqueducts, and transmission pipelines. The wastewater sector has over 19,500 municipal sanitary sewer systems, including an estimated 800,000 miles of sewer lines that collect and treat sewage and process water from domestic, commercial, and industrial sources. The wastewater sector also includes storm, water systems, which collect and sometimes treat storm-water runoff. Table 5.2 shows DHS security initiatives in the water sector.

Table 5.2 *Security Initiatives in Water*

Initiatives
Identify high-priority vulnerabilities and improve site security.
Improve sector monitoring and analytic capabilities.
Improve sectorwide information exchange and coordinate contingency planning.
Work with other sectors to manage unique risks resulting from interdependencies.

5.3 Public health

The public health sector consists of state and local health departments, hospitals, health clinics, mental health facilities, nursing homes, blood-supply facilities, laboratories, mortuaries, and pharmaceutical stockpiles. Table 5.3 shows security initiatives in the public health sector.

Table 5.3 *Security Initiatives in Public Health*

Initiatives
Designate trusted communicators.
Review mission-critical operations, establish protection priorities, and ensure adequate security and redundancy for critical laboratory facilities and services.
Develop criteria to isolate infectious individuals and establish triage protocols.

Table 5.3 *Security Initiatives in Public Health (continued)*

Initiatives
Enhance protection of emergency stockpiles of medical supplies and domestic and international pharmaceutical manufacturing facilities.
Explore options for incentives to increase security spending.

5.4 Emergency services

The emergency services infrastructure consists of fire, rescue, emergency medical service (EMS), and law-enforcement organizations that save lives and property in the event of an accident, natural disaster, or terrorist incident. Table 5.4 shows security initiatives in emergency services.

Table 5.4 *Security Initiatives in Emergency Services*

Initiatives
Adopt interoperable communications systems.
Develop redundant communications networks.
Coordinate national preparedness exercises.
Implement measures to protect our national emergency response infrastructure.
Enhance and strengthen mutual-aid agreements among local jurisdictions.

5.5 Defense industrial base

The defense industrial base includes those manufacturer, research organizations, and service providers with the primary purpose of supporting the DOD and military allies of the United Sates. Table 5.5 shows security initiatives in the defense industrial base.

Table 5.5 *Security Initiatives in the Defense Industrial Base*

Initiatives
Build critical-infrastructure protection requirements into contract processes and procedures.
Incorporate security concerns into production and distribution processes and procedures.

5.6 Telecommunications

The telecommunications sector provides voice and data service to public and private users through a public-network infrastructure encompassing the Public Switched Telecommunications Network (PSTN), the Internet, and private enterprise networks. The PSTN provides switched circuits for telephone, data, and leased point-to-point services. It consists of physical facilities, including over 20,000 switches, access tandems, and other equipment. These components are connected by nearly 2 billion miles of fiber and copper cable. The physical PSTN remains the backbone of the infrastructure, with cellular, microwave, and satellite technologies providing extended gateways to the wireline network for mobile users.

The Internet consists of a global network of packet-switched networks that use a common suite of protocols. Internet Service Providers (ISPs) provide end users with access to the Internet. Larger ISPs use Network Operation Centers (NOCs) to manage their high-capacity networks, linking them through Internet peering points or network access points. Smaller ISPs usually lease their long-haul transmission capacity from the larger ISPs and provide regional and local Internet access to end users via the PSTN. Internet access providers interconnect with the PSTN through points.

Supporting the underlying PSTN and ISPs are operations, administration, maintenance, and provisioning systems, which provide the vital management and administrative functions, such as billing, accounting, configuration, and security management. Table 5.6 shows security initiatives in telecommunications.

Table 5.6 *Security Initiatives in Telecommunications*

Initiatives
Define an appropriate threshold for security.
Expand infrastructure diverse routing capability.
Understand the risks associated with vulnerabilities of the telecommunications infrastructure.
Coordinate with key allies and trading partners.

5.7 Energy

The energy sector is divided into two segments in the context of critical-infrastructure protection: electricity and oil and natural gas. The electric industry services almost 130 million households and institutions. The United States consumed nearly 3.6 trillion kilowatt hours in 2001. Oil and natural gas facilities and assets are widely distributed, consisting of more than 300,000 producing sites; 4,000 off-shore platforms; more than 600 natural gas processing plants; 153 refineries; and more than 1,400 product terminals and 7,500 bulk stations, backup processes, systems, and facilities. Table 5.7 shows security initiatives in electrical energy, and Table 5.8 shows security initiatives in the oil and natural gas sector.

Table 5.7 *Security Initiatives in Electrical Energy*

Initiatives
Identify equipment stockpile requirements.
Reevaluate and adjust nationwide protection planning, system restoration, and recovery in response to attacks.
Develop strategies to reduce vulnerabilities.
Develop standardized guidelines for physical security programs.

Table 5.8 *Security Initiatives in Oil and Natural Gas*

Initiatives
Plan and invest in research and development for the oil and gas industry to enhance robustness and reliability.
Develop strategies to reduce vulnerabilities.
Develop standardized guidelines for physical security programs.
Develop guidelines for measures to reconstitute capabilities of individual facilities and systems.
Develop a national system for locating and distributing critical components in support of response and recovery activities.

5.8 Transportation

The transportation sector consists of several modes: aviation, maritime traffic, rail, pipelines, highways, trucking and busing, and public mass transit.

The aviation system consists of two main parts: (1) airports and the associated assets needed to support their operations, including the aircraft that they serve, and (2) aviation command, control, communications, and IS needed to support and maintain safe use of our national airspace. Table 5.9 shows security initiatives in the aviation sector.

Table 5.9 *Security Initiatives in Aviation*

Initiatives
Identify vulnerabilities, interdependencies, and remediation requirements.
Identify potential threats to passengers.
Improve security at key points of access.
Increase cargo-screening capabilities.
Identify and improve detection technologies.

The rail mode provides transportation for mining, manufacturing, and agriculture products; liquid chemicals and fuels; and consumer goods. In addition, more than 20 million intercity travelers use the rail system annually, and 45 million passengers ride trains and subways operated by local transit authorities. Table 5.10 shows security initiatives in rail transportation.

Table 5.10 *Security Initiatives in Rail Transportation*

Initiatives
Develop improved decision-making criteria regarding the shipment of hazardous materials.
Develop technologies and procedures to screen intermodal containers and passenger baggage.
Improve security of intermodal transportation.
Clearly delineate roles and responsibilities regarding surge requirements.

The highways, trucking, and busing mode is heterogeneous in nature. There is a multitude of owners and operators nationwide, and the trucking and busing infrastructure is highly resilient, flexible, and responsive to market demand. For the same reason, the sector is fractionated and regulated by multiple jurisdictions at the federal, state, and local levels. Table 5.11 shows security initiatives in highways, trucking, and busing.

Table 5.11 *Security Initiatives in Highways, Trucking, and Busing*

Initiatives
Develop improved decision-making criteria regarding the shipment of hazardous materials.
Develop technologies and procedures to screen intermodal containers and passenger baggage.
Improve security of intermodal transportation.
Clearly delineate roles and responsibilities regarding surge requirements.

The United States also has a vast pipeline industry, consisting of many hundreds of thousands of miles of pipelines, many of which are buried underground. These lines move a variety of substances, such as crude oil, refined petroleum products, and natural gas. Table 5.12 shows security initiatives in pipeline management.

Table 5.12 *Security Initiatives in Pipelines*

Initiatives
Develop standard reconstitution protocols.
Develop standard security assessment and threat deterrent guidelines.
Work with other sectors to manage risks resulting from interdependencies.

The maritime shipping infrastructure includes ports and their associated assets, ships and passenger transportation systems, costal and inland waterways, locks, dams and canals, and the network of railroads and pipelines that connect these waterborne systems to other transportation networks. There are 361 seaports in the United States, and their operations range widely in size and characteristics. Table 5.13 shows security initiatives in the maritime shipping sector.

Mass-transit systems are mostly owned and operated by state and local agencies. A city relies on its mass-transit system to serve a significant portion of its workforce in addition to being a means of evacuation in case of

Table 5.13 *Security Initiatives in Maritime Shipping*

Initiatives
Identify vulnerabilities, interdependencies, best practices, and remediation requirements.
Develop a plan for implementing security measures corresponding to varying threat levels.
Develop processes to enhance maritime domain awareness and gain international cooperation .
Develop a template for improving physical and operational port security.
Develop security and protection guidelines and technologies for cargo and passenger ships.
Improve waterway security.

emergency. Table 5.14 shows security initiatives in mass-transit system management.

Table 5.14 *Security Initiatives in Mass Transit System Management*

Initiatives
Identify critical planning areas and develop appropriate guidelines and standards.
Identify protective impediments and implement security enhancements.
Work with other sectors to manage unique risks resulting from interdependencies.

5.9 Banking and finance

The banking and financial services sector infrastructure consists of a wide variety of physical structures, financial utilities, and human capital. Most of the industry's activities and operations take place in large commercial office buildings. Physical structures to be protected house retail or wholesale banking operations, financial markets, regulatory institutions, and physical repositories for documents and financial assets. The financial utilities infrastructure includes such electronic devices as computers, storage devices, and telecommunication networks. In addition to the sector's key physical components, many financial services employees have highly specialized skills and are, therefore, considered essential elements of the industry's critical infrastructure. Table 5.15 shows security initiatives in the banking and finance sector.

Table 5.15 *Security Initiatives in Banking and Finance*

Initiatives
Identify and address the risks of sector dependencies on electronic networks and telecommunications services.
Enhance the exchange of security-related information.

5.10 Chemical industry and hazardous materials

The chemical sector is highly diverse in terms of company sizes and geographic dispersion. Its product and service delivery system depends on raw materials, manufacturing plants and processes, and distribution systems, as well as research facilities and supporting infrastructure services, such as transportation and electricity products. Table 5.16 shows security initiatives in the chemical industry and hazardous materials arena.

Table 5.16 *Security Initiatives in the Chemical Industry and Hazardous Materials*

Initiatives
Promote enhanced site security.
Review current laws and regulations that pertain to the sale and distribution of pesticides and other highly toxic substances.
Continue to develop the chemical ISAC and recruit sector constituents to participate

5.11 Postal and shipping

Each day the postal service deals with more than 600 million pieces of mail, and each day more than 300,000 city and rural postal carriers deliver that mail to more than 137 million delivery addresses nationwide. USPS employs more than 749,000 full-time personnel in rural and urban locations across the country and generates more than $60 billion in revenues each year. USPS and private-industry mailing and shipping revenues exceed $200 billion annually. The size and pervasiveness of the system as a whole have important implications in terms of the potential secondary effects of a malicious attack. Table 5.17 shows security initiatives in postal and shipping.

Table 5.17 *Security Initiatives in Postal and Shipping*

Initiatives
Improve protection and response capabilities.
Assure security of international mail.
Promote and support ISAC participation.
Conduct enhanced risk analyses of key facilities.
Improve customer identification and correlation with their mail.
Identify conflicts with respect to coordinated multijurisdictional responses.

5.12 Protection of key assets

Key assets include an array of facilities, sites, and structures whose disruption or destruction could have significant consequences. One category of key assets consists of national monuments, symbols, and icons that represent heritage, traditions, values, and political power. Table 5.18 shows security initiatives in the protection of monuments, symbols, and icons. Table 5.19 shows security initiatives in the protection of government facilities.

A second category of key assets includes facilities and structures that represent economic power and technological advancement and that may house significant amounts of hazardous materials, fuels, and chemical catalysts that enable production and processing functions. Table 5.20 shows security

Table 5.18 *Security Initiatives in the Protection of Monuments*

Initiatives
Define criticality criteria for national monuments, icons, and symbols.
Conduct threat and vulnerability assessments.
Retain a quality security force.
Conduct security-focused public outreach and awareness programs.
Collaborate with state and local governments and private foundations to assure the protection of symbols and icons outside the federal domain.
Evaluate innovative technologies.
Make provisions for extra security during high-profile events.

Table 5.19 *Security Initiatives in the Protection of Government Facilities*

Initiatives
Develop a process to screen nonfederal tenants and visitors entering private-sector facilities that house federal organizations.
Determine the criticality and vulnerability of government facilities.
Develop long-term construction standards for facilities requiring specialized security measures.
Implement new technological security measures at federally occupied facilities.

initiatives in the protection of nuclear facilities. Table 5.21 shows security initiatives in the protection of dams.

Table 5.20 *Security Initiatives in the Protection of Nuclear Facilities*

Initiatives
Coordinate efforts to perform standardized vulnerability and risk assessments.
Establish common processes and identify resources needed to augment security at nuclear power plants.
Criminalize the carrying of unauthorized weapons or explosives into nuclear facilities.
Enhance the capabilities of nuclear power plant security forces.
Seek legislation to apply sabotage laws to nuclear facilities.
Enhance public outreach and awareness.

Table 5.21 *Security Initiatives in the Protection of Dams*

Initiatives
Develop risk-assessment methodologies for dams.
Develop protective action plans.
Establish a sector ISAC.
Institute a national dam security program.
Develop emergency action plans.
Develop technology to provide protective solutions

A third category of key assets includes such structures as prominent commercial centers, office buildings, and sports stadiums, where large numbers of people regularly congregate to conduct business or personal transactions, shop, or enjoy a recreational pastime. Table 5.22 shows security initiatives in the protection of commercial centers.

Table 5.22 *Security Initiatives in the Protection of Commercial Centers*

Initiatives
Share federal building security standards and practices with the private sector.
Facilitate efficient dissemination of threat information.
Implement the Homeland Security Advisory System.
Explore options for incentives for the implementation of enhanced design features or security measures.
Improve building codes for privately owned facilities.

5.13 Leveraging IT in security initiatives

There are numerous ways that IT can be leveraged to improve security. Possible methods range from support for advanced physical security systems to applying artificial intelligence to process and environmental control. IT managers can find or develop applications to contribute to improved security in each sector. IT managers first need to know what the major security initiatives are and which were presented in this chapter.

Action Checklist Number 5 (see Table 5.23) shows the steps necessary to evaluate, select, deploy, and monitor IT solutions to improve security. The next chapter focuses on why a national strategy to secure cyberspace is important.

Table 5.23 *Action Checklist Number 5*

Action Item	Status (e.g., Completed, Pending, or N/A)
Evaluate security initiatives for sectors in which the organization has operations.	
Assess organizational plans to meet security needs.	

Table 5.23 *Action Checklist Number 5 (continued)*

Action Item	Status (e.g., Completed, Pending, or N/A)
Evaluate IT solutions that address security needs or support new security requirements.	
Compare IT solutions that address security needs or support new security requirements for effectiveness, usability, and return on investment.	
Select and acquire IT products or services.	
Deploy and test applicable IT solutions.	
Monitor performance of IT solutions and tune, enhance, or migrate product sets.	

6

Why a National Strategy to Secure Cyberspace Is Important

IT managers have many concerns about cybersecurity, with 84 percent of those surveyed for this book stating that they believe that at some time in the future, terrorists will launch cyberattacks against the United States. Another 11 percent remained undecided about the potential threat of cyberattacks, while only 3 percent stated that they did not consider cyberattacks to be inevitable. (More details on the survey are shown in Chapter 2.)

The annual Computer Crime and Security Survey conducted by the Computer Security Institute (CSI) with the participation of the Computer Intrusion Squad of the San Francisco office of the FBI provides an annual look at the impact of computer crime in the United States. Respondents in those studies reported, among other things, that average annual total losses over the three years prior to 2000 were $120,240,180, while average annual losses during 2001 reached $377,828,700.

A CIO KnowPulse Poll of 170 CIOs conducted in fall 2001 revealed that the majority (67%) of CIOs is not very confident or not at all confident that law enforcement will provide their companies with sufficient advance warning of a threat to computer systems. Another 27 percent is somewhat confident, with only 2 percent feeling very confident, and 2 percent feeling extremely confident. While nearly one-half (49%) of CIOs have been given additional responsibility or accountability for security infrastructure since September 11, 2001, more than one-third (39%) still do not have cybersecurity experts on staff or contracted. Just under half (47%) will increase the company's budget for information security following the September 11, 2001, terrorist attacks on the United States.

This chapter explores why a national strategy to secure cyberspace is important to the United States. Areas covered include the following:

- The DHS cybersecurity organization

- The nature of information warfare
- The emergence of the blended threat
- Redefining cyberattacks in the age of terrorism
- Measuring the impact of cyberattacks

6.1 The DHS cybersecurity organization

Dale L. Watson, executive assistant director of counterterrorism and counterintelligence of the FBI, testified before the Senate Select Committee on Intelligence on February 6, 2002. Watson pointed out that during the past several years, the FBI had identified a wide array of cyberthreats, ranging from defacement of Web sites by juveniles to sophisticated intrusions sponsored by foreign powers.

Some of these incidents pose more significant threats than others. The theft of national security information from a government agency or the interruption of electrical power to a major metropolitan area obviously would have greater consequences for national security, public safety, and economy than the defacement of a Web site. But even the less serious categories have real consequences and, ultimately, can undermine public confidence in Web-based commerce and violate privacy or property rights. An attack on a Web site that closes down an e-commerce site can have disastrous consequences for a Web-based business. An intrusion that results in the theft of millions of credit card numbers from an online vendor can result in significant financial loss and, more broadly, reduce consumers' willingness to engage in e-commerce.

Watson contended that beyond criminal threats, cyberspace also faces a variety of significant national security threats, including increasing threats from terrorists. Terrorist groups are increasingly using new IT and the Internet to formulate plans, raise funds, spread propaganda, and engage in secure communications. Cyberterrorism—meaning the use of cybertools to shut down critical national infrastructures (e.g., energy, transportation, or government operations) for the purpose of coercing or intimidating a government or civilian population—is clearly an emerging threat.

In pursuit of stronger cybersecurity, DHS created the National Cyber Security Division (NCSD) under the department's Information Analysis and Infrastructure Protection Directorate. The NCSD was established to provide for 24/7 functions, including conducting cyberspace analysis, issuing alerts and warnings, improving information sharing, responding to major incidents, and aiding in national-level recovery efforts.

The foundation of NCSD was transferred to DHS from the former CIAO, the NIPC, the Federal Computer Incident Response Center, and the National Communications System. With 60 employees, the Division is organized around three units designed to:

1. Identify risks and help reduce the vulnerabilities to the government's cyberassets and coordinate with the private sector to identify and help protect critical cyberassets.
2. Oversee a consolidated cybersecurity tracking, analysis, and response center (CSTARC), which will detect and respond to Internet events; track potential threats and vulnerabilities to cyberspace; and coordinate cybersecurity and incident response with federal, state, local, private-sector, and international organizations.
3. Create, in coordination with other appropriate agencies, cybersecurity awareness and education programs and partnerships with consumers, businesses, governments, academia, and international communities.

The NCSD will work closely with the DHS S&T Directorate to implement all required programs for research and development in cybersecurity. While S&T will provide the actual research and development functions and execution, the NCSD will provide detailed requirements for the direction of the research and development in response to needs of public- and private-sector organizations.

6.2 The nature of information warfare

In *Information Warfare: How to Survive Cyber Attacks*, I conclude that a wide range of information warfare strategies exists and that countries need to be prepared to defend against them. The ten types of information warfare and their potential impacts on private companies are listed in Table 6.1. However, each of the ten categories of information warfare has a price tag, a required organizational structure, and a timeline for preparation and implementation.

Given these cost structures, the types of information warfare that will most likely be waged against large industrial computer-dependent countries are sustained terrorist information warfare, random terrorist information warfare, sustained rogue information warfare, random rogue information warfare, and amateur rogue information warfare.

Table 6.1 *Information Warfare Strategies*

Type of Information Warfare	Potential Direct Impact on Private Companies in Full-Scale Information Wars	Potential Indirect Impact on Private Companies in Less Than Full-Scale Wars
Offensive ruinous information warfare	Destructive attacks on corporate systems by aggressors	Residual viruses or other destructive code launched during attacks or loss of communications systems
Offensive containment information warfare	Destructive attacks on corporate systems by aggressors	Residual viruses or other destructive code launched during attacks or loss of communications systems
Sustained terrorist information warfare	Repeated or sustained destructive targeted attacks on corporate systems by terrorist groups	Hits by viruses and other destructive code launched to attack general populations or loss of communications systems
Random terrorist information warfare	Random destructive targeted attacks on corporate systems by terrorist groups	Hits by viruses and other destructive code launched to attack general populations or loss of communications systems
Defensive preventive information warfare	Accidental disruption of communications during the initiation of preventive measures	Accidental disruption of communications during the initiation of preventive measures
Defensive ruinous information warfare	Destructive attacks on corporate systems by attacked countries to destroy an aggressor	Hits by viruses and other destructive code launched during defensive responses or loss of communications systems
Defensive responsive containment information warfare	Destructive attacks on corporate systems from countries attempting to contain an aggressor	Hits by viruses and other destructive code launched during defensive responses or loss of communications systems
Sustained rogue information warfare	Repeated or sustained targeted attacks on corporate systems by criminal groups	Hits by viruses and other destructive code launched to attack general populations or loss of communications systems
Random rogue information warfare	Random targeted attacks on corporate systems by criminal groups	Hits by viruses and other destructive code launched to attack general populations or loss of communications systems

Table 6.1 *Information Warfare Strategies (continued)*

Type of Information Warfare	Potential Direct Impact on Private Companies in Full-Scale Information Wars	Potential Indirect Impact on Private Companies in Less Than Full-Scale Wars
Amateur rogue information warfare	Random targeted attacks on corporate systems by amateur groups	Hits by viruses and other destructive code launched to attack general populations or loss of communications systems

Source: Information Warfare: How to Survive Cyber Attacks, McGraw-Hill, 2001.

To finance, organize, and mount offensive ruinous information warfare and offensive containment information warfare is so expensive that the publicly political enemies of the large industrial countries cannot afford to use such strategies. But that does not mean that the lesser tactics would not be extremely damaging to infrastructures and economies.

The strategies that would be most effective against smaller, somewhat computer-dependent countries are offensive ruinous information warfare and offensive containment information warfare. In the case of aggressor countries or groups, defensive responsive containment information warfare is the most likely tactic. The strategies that will be the most effective against countries that have done little in terms of developing a computer dependency are those of offensive containment information warfare.

The smaller, less developed countries in no way can afford to mount and sustain defensive ruinous information warfare or defensive responsive containment information warfare strategies. At best, they could mount random terrorist information warfare or random rogue information warfare strategies and most likely would depend on amateur rogue information warfare carried out by a few patriots or geographically dispersed allies.

The private sector in industrial computer-dependent countries does need to be concerned about large-scale offensive ruinous information warfare in widespread conflicts that get out of hand. However, the most likely immediate threats to corporate operations outside of organized conflicts are random terrorist information warfare, sustained rogue information warfare, random rogue information warfare, and amateur rogue information warfare.

The most vulnerable corporations are those that are heavily involved in and derive the majority of their revenues from electronic commerce, or what we so lovingly call dot-coms. It will cost corporations much more to defend themselves against these information warfare strategies than it will cost terrorist or rogues to mount such attacks.

In addition, the only organizations in the industrialized countries that can afford to counter effectively or ultimately eliminate the attackers, especially if they are outside the country of the corporation that is being attacked, are maintained and controlled by the military. Because civilian law enforcement is in a weak position to deal with information warfare attacks on private corporations, those companies without strong ties to the military will become easy targets with little recourse.

6.3 The emergence of the blended threat

Terrorists are expected to launch attacks that have direct infrastructure effects with cascading disruption or arrest of the functions of critical infrastructures or key assets through direct attacks on a critical node, system, or function. In addition, attacks can also exploit various elements of a particular infrastructure to disrupt or destroy another target. Taking this proposition to a higher level, simultaneous physical attacks combined with cyberattacks that can disrupt communications or the operations of responders can have devastating effects. The combined attacks can result in indirect infrastructure effects with cascading disruption and financial consequences for government, society, and economy through public- and private-sector reactions to an attack.

In a fictional work, *ExopaTerra*, created by Baley Montag, the United States is confronted with a fierce multifront blended attack in which terrorists launch a series of both physical and cyberattacks focused on the West Coast. The scenario unfolds as follows:

5:30 A.M. PST

A hostage situation occurs in Singapore. Groups of people take over a 22-story building with offices of several international companies, including six global computer companies that are headquartered in the United States.

A plane crashes; it was heading from Hong Kong to LAX.

A new computer virus is spotted in Europe, a mass mailer, moving moderately fast, but it has a payload. Within minutes a report of the virus is received from Japan.

6:00 A.M. PST

There is another hostage situation, in Rome, in another office building with international companies. It is an 18-story building with plenty of connectivity, including satellite dishes on the roof.

A plane returned to the Tokyo airport; it was bound for LAX.

6:30 A.M. PST

Computer virus reports come in from Washington, DC, Boston, New York, Hong Kong, Tokyo, Bangkok, and Sydney.

A refinery explosion occurs in Oakland. Weeks earlier there had been a report that software had been pirated that helped to control the process in the refinery.

A second refinery explosion is reported in the Bay Area. The refinery fires have about half of the East Bay Emergency Service teams tied up at this point.

7:00 A.M. PST

About a dozen U.S. government Web sites have been hacked and defaced. The hackers leave their calling card; it says *ExopaTerra*.

There is a problem with mass transit in New York City; the computers have crashed. An electrical failure is being blamed.

FAA computers are out at San Francisco International; traffic is being diverted, and all outgoing flights have been delayed.

Word from Tokyo is that the flight was turned around because a guy refused to quit playing with his cell phone. The flight was headed to LAX, the same destination as the Hong Kong flight that crashed earlier.

Another computer virus is on; it is a Trojan horse, and it leaves a backdoor open for entry into any system it hits.

A young man comes running into the director's office at BART: "We have lost control. It is as if somebody has taken over the system. We can't do a thing."

8:00 A.M. PST

The clock strikes 8:00. A BART train crashes into another one sitting at an underground station in downtown San Francisco.

More computer virus reports; e-mail systems are clogged everywhere on the East Coast, and it is spreading fast.

The San Francisco, San Jose, and Oakland airports remain closed.

One of the major banks in San Francisco is suffering from a never-ending chain of intrusion attempts.

The police in Rome are planning to go in, but it will be two or three hours until they are ready. Several computer companies are working to take the Rome building out of their network, but there are other networks that go into that building as well.

The Singapore police are still holding; it will probably be three or four more hours before they move in. In that building are the regional office for IQ Computers and BizX, a large database and financial management software company.

There is more detail on the virus from Japan; it is spreading quickly and variants have already been identified.

The *San Francisco Chronicle*'s Web site is running a front-page story on a possible anthrax attack in the city today.

There is a mass mailing of an e-mail saying that there is going to be an anthrax attack in San Francisco today. It goes to thousands of e-mail addresses in the Bay Area.

9:00 A.M. PST

Hackers from a military base in Japan are hitting a brokerage in San Francisco.

Another plane is down off the Pacific Coast; it was coming from South Korea; it was an hour away and about an hour late for its scheduled arrival at LAX.

The virus attacks are being logged as the biggest ever; replications are in the billions, and there are dozens of variants.

San Francisco is starting to panic; there are traffic jams everywhere, smoke from the refinery fires is drifting around the bay. Clouds reach more than two miles into the air.

The governor of the state of California is convinced that the city is being attacked by terrorists and has closed the bridges in and out of San Francisco. The traffic jams are horrendous.

10:00 A.M. PST

One of the ATM networks in the Bay Area has been hit and taken down.

The cell phone system in San Francisco is grid locked; it will likely be that way for the rest of the day.

Another refinery is hit, this time in Houston. There was no damage because the security team locked the attackers out. They did trace the attack back to the building in Rome.

Riot-geared police in Rome are bringing out about ten people from the building and putting them in vans. The police had raided the building and used tear gas to force out the intruders. They are putting the terrorists in vans when suddenly the police vans are attacked with rockets. Panic ensues and dozens are killed.

11:00 A.M. PST

There is a train wreck in the East Bay. Somebody from a South Korean contractor's office logged on, walked right in, knew what he was doing, and flipped a few switches. Two trains collided. Both trains were moving corrosive industrial materials and a variety of liquid and solid chemicals. As the trains collided, dozens of rail cars were derailed, with some cars bursting into flames, resulting in a chemical spill that released toxic gases. The black poisonous clouds have started to spread over East Bay communities. Emergency crews are responding.

The credit card clearance system serving the Bay Area is not functioning, just in time for lunch.

12:00 P.M. PST

The ATMs and the credit card clearance system serving San Francisco are going up and down every few minutes.

Computer viruses are still spreading, and e-mail is clogged up.

San Francisco transportation systems are virtually shut down. The airports remain closed, even though the computers seem to be back up. BART will be out of service for at least 24 more hours. There are no trains running. The bridges are still closed.

There is action starting at the Singapore building; the terrorists are using the connections in the offices of IQ Computers and BizX to hit those corporate computers.

The 911 system in the Bay Area is clogged and dysfunctional.

Reports of rolling power outages throughout Northern California start emerging.

It is confirmed that a pipeline is hit in the Bay Area.

1:00 P.M. PST

Another plane is down over the Pacific Ocean, a 747 coming into LAX from South Korea. It was one of those whose landing was delayed; it was 30 minutes late and 30 minutes out of LAX when it went down.

The sabotaged pipeline in the bay has been shut off; in less than 60 minutes it dumped 295,000 gallons of oil into the San Francisco Bay.

The police in Singapore made their move; they captured about a dozen people. They shot a dozen more.

Communications in the Bay Area are either clogged or completely out, including the cell phone system, the landline phones, and the 911 system. Rolling blackouts are still occurring.

The credit card clearance system in the Bay Area keeps going in and out, as does the ATM system.

The hotels are all full in San Francisco and have been since the morning. Many businesses are locking their doors and throwing their employees out into the streets, even though there are no hotel rooms and there is no way to get out of the city.

There is no sign of the computer viruses slowing down.

It looks like the night will shape up this way: continuous disruption of systems, random power outages, marshal law, and hundreds of thousands of people trapped in the city of San Francisco.

2:00 P.M. PST

The federal government decided to mobilize Regular Army troops that could use helicopters to move into the city to help mitigate the chaos.

The Coast Guard has been put on high alert and begun routine patrols of the San Francisco Bay. Naval vessels have been ordered to move into defense positions in the bay.

Most people in the Bay Area are not receiving television signals.

The police are busy dealing with traffic situations at the bridges and along the freeways that lead to the bridges that go in and out of San Francisco. There have been numerous traffic accidents, many of which have required emergency medical service teams. Abandoned vehicles are everywhere.

Amtrak is not running trains into, out of, or through the Bay Area. The airports will not open until tomorrow morning at the earliest and maybe not until the next day.

3:00 P.M. PST

There are riots in San Francisco; street gangs are running wild, looting, shooting, and burning.

The credit card clearance system has been resolved; somebody had made one of the internal servers into a drone that would corrupt the other servers every few minutes.

4:00 P.M. PST

The FBI is searching every ship in every port on the West Coast to look for explosive devices.

Electricity is going on and off all over the Bay Area.

The death toll on planes that have crashed is now over 900.

Emergency services are not functioning in most of the Bay Area. In addition to 911 being out, local numbers for ambulance, fire, and police services are clogged. The Department of Health estimates that more than 200 people have died because they could not get emergency services.

5:00 P.M. PST

There are fires popping up all across the Bay Area. There are normally about 30 fires per day in the entire area. The fire department estimates that there have been over 400 fires in buildings. There is no idea of the potential death toll because the fire department has responded to very few of the incidents.

The Marian nuclear power plant is reporting a problem. They swear they have not been hacked, but things are looking bad.

6:00 P.M. PST

There is an explosion on the ship filled with used tires in San Francisco; the fire is burning out of control, and black toxic smoke is filling the air.

The port authority police in Los Angeles, along with U.S. customs agents are doing a check on the freighter filled with fertilizer. There is small explosion, but it fails to set off the fuel tanks. The fire is put out quickly.

6.4 Redefining cyberattacks in the age of terrorism

One of the more unique twists that Baley Montag puts on cyberattacks in *ExopaTerra* is the method by which attacks occurred. There is certainly a large amount of hacking and illegal system access. However, the damage done with the BART system, railroad switching devices, pipeline control systems, and financial services systems is perpetrated by individuals who are trained in IT and understand exactly how to use the software on control system computers.

In the past it was generally a disgruntled insider who had enough knowledge about a system to sabotage operations. Random and even deliberate hackers may know how to access systems and damage files and impede operations. However, such damage may be relatively easy to deal with and recover from.

As terrorists become more sophisticated, and there is little doubt that they will, defenders need to prepare for the possibility that the attackers may know just as much about the system they are attacking as the defenders. The attack on the railroad system in *ExopaTerra* is perpetrated by a engineer in Korea who is being threatened by the loss of his family if he did not cooperate with the terrorist organization.

When financial incentives have failed, terrorists and criminals have forced many people to cooperate with them through threats of violence, blackmail, or holding family members hostage. This is not likely to change in the future. It also has rather serious implications for IT managers when products are being selected and deployed across the enterprise.

It is very important to measure, as a part of the total cost of ownership, the security that comes with a product. This translates into examining what type of security the creator of the product has for source code and client or customer records. It applies equally to service organizations that provide coding, network design or management, and security planning and implementation. It is seriously time to add trust and security to the price tag of all IT products.

6.5 Measuring the impact of cyberattacks

The potential impact on organizations as a result of cyberattacks is shown in Table 6.2. At the simplest level, measuring the economic cost of direct damage to a target organization's computer systems and the cost to repair damage or restore systems and functionality can be measured by tracking the time that it requires technicians to perform the tasks necessary to restore systems.

Table 6.2 *Impact of Cyberattacks on an Organization*

Type of Impact
Direct damage to target organization's computer systems
Cost to repair damage or restore target organization's systems and functionality
Decrease in productivity of employees in target organization
Delays in order processing or customer service in target organization
Decrease in productivity in customer's organization because of delays in target organization
Delays in customer's business because of delays in target organization
Negative impact on local economies where target organization is located
Negative impact on local economies where target organization's customers are located
Negative impact on value for individual investors in target organization
Negative impact on value of investment funds holding target organization securities

Table 6.2 *Impact of Cyberattacks on an Organization (continued)*

Type of Impact
Negative impact on regional economies where target organization, customer, or investor organizations are located
Negative impact on national economies where target organization, customer, or investor organizations are located

When a cyberattack affects tens of thousands of organizations, the challenge of collecting data on the cost to restore systems is almost insurmountable for most investigators. Although the methodology required to track time expenditures and corresponding cost for a single organization is straightforward, the resources required to collect data from thousands of organizations and compile it into a form that is usable for litigation purposes is not readily available to the criminal justice system.

Many organizations are unsure how to measure a decline in productivity that results from a cyberattack. In addition, the focus on restoring operations as quickly as possible usually overrides the desire to collect data on the loss of productivity or the many other types of impact that a malicious code attack can have on an organization. Regardless of the difficulty or the lack of interest in collecting data that can be used to quantify the types of impacts shown in Table 6.2, the potential oscillatory effect that downtime of computer systems has on an organization will be related to the duration of system outages. The impact on an organization can also be viewed in terms of when the impact may occur:

- Immediate economic impact can include damage to systems that requires human intervention to repair or replace, disruption of business operations, and delays in transactions and cash flow.
- Short-term economic impact can include loss of contracts with other organizations in supply chains or the loss of retail sales, have a negative impact on an organization's reputation, and be a hindrance to developing new business.
- Long-term economic impact can include a decline in market valuation, erosion of investor confidence, decline in stock price, and reduced goodwill value.

Cyberattacks can also impact individual citizens. The potential impact on individuals is shown in Table 6.3. Individual citizens can suffer the same basic damages that a large organization suffers when cyberattackers and

Table 6.3 *Impact of Cyberattacks on Individuals*

Type of Impact
Direct damage to target individual's computer systems
Cost to repair damage or restore target individual's computer systems and functionality
Decrease in productivity of target individual
Loss of contribution to employer of target individual
Loss of contribution to family of target individual
Loss of contribution to social groups of target individual
Loss of contribution to community of target individual
Decline in economic participation in target individual's local community
Decline in economic participation in target individual's region
Decline in economic participation in e-commerce sector
Potential long-term decline in economic participation in e-commerce sector

malicious code run amuck on the Internet. Individual citizens must also pay the price to repair damage or restore their computer systems and, thus, the functionality those systems provide. As with the impacts on organizations, it is more complicated to measure other types of damage and impact. In the case of the individual citizen, the potential oscillatory effect of system outages can have far reaching consequences on the family, social groups, and communities of which the individual is a member.

It is important to consider the impact of computer crimes on individuals and the social groups of which individuals are members. The home computer has become a far more significant tool and platform for participation in society and the workforce. Large numbers of people telecommute on at least a part-time basis. This can range from work-at-home days to the ability to check e-mail prior to departing for the airport when people are not going to stop at the office that morning.

In addition, the use of home computer systems for participation in educational activities and programs has become commonplace. Home computer systems are also used to aid household management, check recreational schedules, and conduct e-commerce. The ability to use home computer systems in these manners allows individuals and families to maximize the use of their time and potentially save on transportation costs.

The impact of cyberattacks can also be examined from a societal perspective. Table 6.4 shows how the effects of malicious code attacks on organizations and individuals are reflected in a society. Attacks that cripple computer systems consume resources that may otherwise be expended for other purposes.

Table 6.4 *Impact of Cyberattacks on Societies*

Type of Impact
Disruption of individual activities
Disruption of family activities
Disruption in participation in education
Disruption in social-group activities
Disruption in community activities
Disruption of local commerce and e-commerce
Disruption of government operations/functions
Disruption of business activities
Disruption of seasonal social calendars

The process of collecting data on the impact of cyberattacks is certainly possible, but it is very cumbersome and expensive. When cyberattacks impact only one organization, the complexity of the data-collection process will depend on the extent of damage and the duration of system outages. In the case of cyberattacks, several key data points are needed to determine the immediate economic impact caused by the attack.

Actual loss means the reasonably foreseeable pecuniary harm that results from the offense. In most computer-crime cases, actual loss includes the following pecuniary harm, regardless of whether such pecuniary harm was reasonably foreseeable:

- Reasonable costs to the victim of conducting a damage assessment

- The cost of restoring the system and data to their condition prior to the offense
- Any lost revenue due to interruption of service

Table 6.5 *Data Required to Determine Impact of Cybercode Attacks in an Organization*

Types of Data
Time required to inspect systems to detect malicious code or deliberately placed code resulting from the attack.
Time required to eradicate the malicious code or deliberately placed code resulting from the attack.
Time required to apply patches to systems.
Time required to certify systems and return to service.
Time required to determine which, if any, files were damaged, altered, or stolen.
Time required to restore files that were damaged or altered.
Salaries, benefits, and overhead that comprise the per-hour costs of technicians working on computer system restoration and file recovery.
The value of stolen data or information.
Salaries, benefits, and overhead that comprise the per-hour costs associated with activities required as a result of data being stolen, such as canceling credit card numbers and issuing new cards.
Hours of lost productivity because of system outages.
Salaries, benefits, and overhead that comprise the per-hour costs of employees with reduced productivity.
Lost revenue because of system outages.

Table 6.5 shows the data required to determine the economic impact of a malicious code attack on an organization.

Calculating the cost of restoring systems is the easiest step in determining the damage caused by a computer system attack. The hours spent on the applicable activities are multiplied by the per-hour costs, as shown in Table 6.6. The time required for the various activities will depend on the nature of the attack, the type of systems attacked, and the extent of damage that occurred. The per-hour costs will depend on the skill level required to perform the work, local salary levels, and local benefits and overhead costs.

Table 6.6 *Calculating the Cost of Restoring Systems after Cyberattacks*

Activity	Measure (hours)
Time required to inspect systems to detect malicious code or deliberately placed code resulting from the attack	
Time required to eradicate the malicious code or deliberately placed code resulting from the attack	
Time required to apply patches to systems	
Time required to certify systems and return to service	
Time required to determine which, if any, files were damaged, altered, or stolen	
Time required to restore files that were damaged or altered	
	Total Hours
Salaries, benefits, and overhead that comprise the per-hour costs of technicians working on computer system restoration and file recovery	$ cost per hour
Multiply the number of hours by the hourly costs	$ total costs

The complexity of calculating the cost of lost productivity will vary by organization. Some organizations have a good grasp on the productivity levels of individual employees or workgroups. This is especially true in organizations that have quota systems covering activities such as the number of sales calls per hour that must be made. Other organizations may have determined the value of an employee hour because there was a risk analysis or cost-benefit analysis performed to determine the return on investment for computer security expenditures or performance-enhancing software that is deployed in the organization. However, in the absence of such data, an organization will need to build the data-collection process from the ground up, which can be a time-consuming and expensive activity.

Measures of lost revenue because of system outages can be as complex as calculating lost productivity. A shortcut to determining lost revenue is to use the revenue of comparable days as a benchmark. If systems were out for the entire day on a Thursday and Friday during the summer, the revenue levels of previous similar days can be used as a benchmark. It is important to factor in trends in revenue decline or growth.

If revenue on an average day has increased by 10 percent for the last several months compared with one year prior, then the summer days of the previous year can be used with 10 percent added. Conversely, if revenue on an average day has declined by 10 percent, then the revenue level of comparable days one year prior can be reduced by 10 percent. In this example it is also important to examine revenue during the following week to determine if any sales during those days would have occurred during the days of the system outages.

The value of stolen data or information can be extremely difficult to establish unless there are actions required as a direct result of the data being stolen. Salaries, benefits, and overhead that comprise the per-hour costs associated with activities required as a result of data being stolen, such as canceling credit card numbers and issuing new cards, can be determined in a manner similar to that used to calculate the restoration of computer systems. In cases where data is stolen, and there is a regulatory consequence for the data being compromised, such as fines or required audits because of the compromise, then those resulting costs can be used to determine partially the impact of the data being stolen.

In addition to not wanting to participate, many organizations do not have the resources to collect such data. There is also very little motivation to spend time and money when it is likely that the organization will not be compensated for the cost of collecting data or for any damages incurred because of the attack. Collecting data from organizations in one country poses many challenges, but collecting data from organizations in dozens of countries around the world is extremely difficult.

6.6 Evaluating the cybervulnerability of an organization

Cybervulnerability means far more than just the level of security that an organization has on its own systems. Those details can be addressed through developing an IS security plan and a computer-incident response plan, covered in Action Checklist Number 2 presented at the end of Chapter 2.

A comprehensive look at cybervulnerability includes an examination of what will happen in an organization if its business partners and service providers suffer a debilitating attack. Action Checklist Number 6 (see Table

6.7) shows steps that IT managers can take to evaluate the overall cybervulnerability of their organizations.

The next chapter focuses on participating in a national cyberspace security response system.

Table 6.7 *Action Checklist Number 6*

Action Item	**Status (e.g., Completed, Pending, or N/A)**
Evaluate the methods by which the organization communicates and conducts business transactions with suppliers.	
Determine the vulnerabilities in the systems used to work with suppliers and develop an action plan to improve security in those systems.	
Evaluate the methods by which the organization communicates and conducts business transactions with customers.	
Determine the vulnerabilities in the systems used to work with customers and develop an action plan to improve security in those systems.	
Evaluate the methods by which the organization communicates and conducts business transactions with service providers.	
Determine the vulnerabilities in the systems used to work with service providers, and develop an action plan to improve security in those systems.	

7

Participating in a National Cyberspace Security Response System

The *National Strategy to Secure Cyberspace* provides a framework for organizing and prioritizing cybersecurity efforts by setting the direction for federal government departments and agencies that have roles in cybersecurity. In addition, it identifies steps that state and local governments, private companies and organizations, and individual citizens can take to participate in national efforts. The strategic objectives of the *National Strategy to Secure Cyberspace* are the following:

- Preventing cyberattacks against national critical infrastructures.
- Reducing national vulnerability to cyberattacks.
- Minimizing damage and recovery time from cyberattacks that do occur.

This chapter discuses the goals of priority I of the *National Strategy to Secure Cyberspace,* which calls for participation in a national cyberspace security response system and establishes the steps that an organization should take, including the following:

- Prepare to participate in a public-private architecture for responding to national-level cyberincidents, which may mean that under certain alert conditions, organizations will need to reports various types of activities and intrusion attempts.
- Prepare to contribute to the development of tactical and strategic analysis of cyberattacks and vulnerability assessments, which will require more detailed reporting of activities and intrusion attempts on an ongoing basis.

- Join in a shared synoptic view of the health of cyberspace with government agencies and other organizations.
- Be a recipient of information from an expanded CWIN when DHS is coordinating crisis management activities for cyberspace security and participate in national incident–management efforts.
- Participate in the development of national public-private continuity and contingency planning efforts, as well as mobilization exercises to test plans.

7.1 The architecture for responding to national-level cyberincidents

The development of an architecture and process to respond to national-level cyberincidents is well underway. As discussed in previous chapters, the federal government has reorganized several agencies and created an NCSD under DHS's Information Analysis and Infrastructure Protection Directorate. The NCSD was established to provide for 24/7 functions, including conducting cyberspace analysis, issuing alerts and warnings, improving information sharing, responding to major incidents, and aiding in national-level recovery efforts.

However, for such a system to work, several other processes and mechanisms will need to be established. First and foremost, organizations of all types will need to report suspicious and malicious activities to the NCSD or the FBI. Second, these reports will need to be analyzed quickly to determine if they represent an actual or eminent threat. Third, once a threat is identified, a warning will need to be issued about the nature of the threat.

To a limited extent, these steps have been followed in the past. The main problem with past efforts has been mostly centered on the speed. This includes how quickly reports are provided to authorities, how quickly they have been analyzed, and how quickly warnings have been issued. It is assumed that the new NCSD structure will provide for faster turnaround in all the steps required for issuing a warning.

Even if the reporting, analysis, and warning processes are improved, most organizations will still face a significant challenge in turning the warning into actionable information. There are several obstacles, including the following:

- Of the 100 name-brand organizations surveyed, 53 percent felt that they have not achieved an adequate level of staffing or an appropriate mix of staff to meet current needs.
- While 73 percent of the organizations surveyed reported that there was an IS and network security plan in place, only 41 percent report that all or most employees have been trained on the IS security plan.
- Only 53 percent of the organizations surveyed reported that there was a computer-incident response plan in place, and only 39 percent report that all or most employees have been trained on the computer-incident response plan.
- On the virus protection front, 72 percent of the organizations surveyed report that all or most of their employees have been trained on how to handle or report computer viruses.
- Respondents were pretty well split on their viewpoints about the adequacy of training for end users in their organizations, with 47 percent reporting they felt training was adequate and 45 percent reporting that they did not feel that training was adequate.

The status of developing and implementing computer security and computer-incident response plans, as well as the level of training that has been achieved, as reported by the 100 name-brand organizations, clearly shows that many weaknesses remain. This means that there are still many holes that need to be plugged before an architecture and process to respond to national-level cyberincidents can really be effective in protecting a significant number of organizations.

7.2 Tactical and strategic analysis of cyberattacks and vulnerability assessments

To advance the national ability to analyze cyberattacks and vulnerabilities, several things need to change in how the government and private-sector user organizations interact, as well has in how technology producers report vulnerabilities to the government.

The analysis of cyberattacks will require more detailed reporting of activities and intrusion attempts on an ongoing basis. However, most organizations are still leery of reporting incidents. The 100 name-brand organizations were asked if they ever reported a computer crime or intrusion to law enforcement. As shown in Table 7.1, only 26 percent reported that they had. In Chapter 4

Table 7.1 *Reporting Computer Incidents to Law Enforcement*

Response	Percent
Yes	26
No	36
I do not know the answer to this question	35
Other	3

it was recommended that IT managers analyze how to participate in the reporting process, and guidelines were provided for what to report.

To analyze vulnerabilities successfully, two primary areas need to be examined: (1) how technology is produced and what types of flaws and vulnerabilities exist in products sold on the open market, and (2) how users configure and deploy that technology in their organizations and how well field systems are configured to minimize the vulnerabilities that may be inherent in the technology.

The NIST and the NSA have been actively evaluating the vulnerabilities of information and network technology and issued many standards and recommendations. However, several certified security professionals that were interviewed for this book reported that many organizations are still deploying technology with weak configurations that increases the vulnerability of their systems and networks.

To eliminate vulnerabilities in cyberspace, it is also necessary to identify those vulnerabilities as quickly as possible. This will require more vigorous testing before technology producers release new products or upgrades to existing products. It will also require reporting of vulnerabilities that are discovered in products. Given the competition in the technology marketplace, it is not likely that technology producers will willingly reveal what they know about vulnerabilities until those vulnerabilities are discovered by independent testers.

Regardless of the position technology producers take on reporting vulnerabilities, it should be recognized that the manufacturers of IT and networking products have remained liability free for flaws, defects, or vulnerabilities in their products. The manufacturers of IT and networking products protect themselves through licensing agreements that displace all the liability to the user as part of the agreement for the product to be licensed to the user. This situation is not likely to change in the near future.

7.3 A shared view of the health of cyberspace

Over the last decade there has emerged a relatively widely shared view of the importance of the health of cyberspace. Although there has been considerable agreement that the health of cyberspace is important, there is a lack of consensus about what steps to take to maintain or improve the health of cyberspace.

Responses from the survey of 100 name-brand companies conducted for this book illustrate some of the social and cultural obstacles that exist when actions are considered to regulate the Internet. Respondents were asked about what they felt were the greatest benefits that the Internet provides society. Overwhelmingly, access and speed of access to information was the main theme of responses to this question. Of the 90 responders to the question, 76 referred to access to information as one of the greatest benefits of the Internet.

Survey participants were also asked what they felt were the worst things that the Internet enables in society. Interestingly, 32 of the 91 respondents commented that the access to information was the worst thing that the Internet enables. Basically, one can conclude that the respondents feel that when information is used by good people for good things, then access is good, but if information is used by bad people for bad things, then access is bad.

Although there is a high level of personal dilemma about the good and the bad of the Internet, only 8 percent of the survey respondents felt that content and activity on the Internet should be regulated by the government. Overwhelmingly, 59 percent responded that content and activity on the Internet should not be regulated by the government. Meanwhile 15 percent were undecided.

The global nature of the Internet means that the view of the health of cyberspace must be shared well beyond the borders of the United States and other computer-dependent nations. In the case of the "I Love You" virus in 2000, the common view was that the government of the Philippines did not move quickly enough in the global interest when apprehending the suspect in the case. It took several days for Philippine law enforcement to apprehend the suspect, although it was determined that he could have been responsible for the incident.

It is also important to note that even when there is a shared view among groups of people, action may be difficult to achieve. The Telecommunications Act of 1996, for example, contained section 501, The Communications Decency Act (CDA) of 1996, much of which was overturned by the federal courts shortly after the act was passed. The act would have made it a crime to transmit knowingly any communication accessible to minors that is considered "obscene, lewd, lascivious, filthy, or indecent" and would have also prevented any publicity of abortion services. Punishment was to include a sentence of up to two years in prison and a $100,000 fine.

In June 1996, a three-judge panel in Philadelphia ruled parts of the act unconstitutional. This decision was appealed by the U.S. Justice Department. On June 26, 1997, the U.S. Supreme Court agreed with the district court judges that the CDA was unconstitutional. The judges considered that it lacked the precision that the First Amendment requires when a statute regulates the content of speech. In order to deny minors access to potentially harmful speech, the CDA effectively suppressed a large amount of speech that adults have a constitutional right to receive and to address to one another. That burden on adult speech is unacceptable if less restrictive alternatives would be at least as effective in achieving the legitimate purpose that the statute was enacted to serve.

Basically, the first substantial effort of the U.S. Congress to regulate the Internet, the CDA, was met with outrage. Among other actions taken by opposing groups, the Electronic Frontier Foundation launched the Blue Ribbon Campaign, a call for Internet users to protest against the intended legislation by displaying the anticensorship Blue Ribbon on their pages. It was a heated social and cultural debate about regulating the Internet, and that debate still rages around the world. It is an issue that will not be resolved any time soon. It also shows that the achievement of a universal consensus on the health of cyberspace is far away from realization.

7.4 The CWIN

The CWIN, a group of organizations, including the NIPC, the CIAO, and others that have some responsibility for the security of federal systems, is the core of the cyberwarning network. However, there are many other mechanisms that contribute to the warning system, including the following:

- The cybersecurity organizations of other national governments
- The customer-support mechanisms of technology producers
- The customer-support mechanisms of technology service providers
- Professional IS security organizations

Computer security professionals interviewed for this book recommend that organizations not rely upon a single source for warnings and alerts. As previously mentioned, organizations need to evaluate how they will assimilate and act on warnings of malicious cyberbehavior.

7.5 Continuity and contingency planning efforts

The U.S. government is urging that organizations participate in the development of national public-private continuity and contingency planning efforts, as well as mobilization exercises to test plans. In many organizations disaster-recovery planning is improving. In a survey of 256 managers and planners that I conducted during the fourth quarter of 2002, four out of ten organizations reported that spending for disaster-recovery planning had increased since the terrorist attacks of September 11, 2001. The survey was conducted for a book entitled *Guide to Disaster Recovery* published by Course Technology in June 2003.

However, there are still many obstacles to achieving a high level of participation in such efforts. As noted in Chapter 2, 46 percent of the 100 name-brand organization surveyed for this book reported that the terrorist attacks of September 11, 2001, have not changed their IT management policies or practices at all. In addition, while 65 percent reported that DRPs are in place, 8 percent reported that there was not a DRP in place, and 24 percent reported that a DRP was in the development stages. Only 27 percent of the organizations reported that most or all employees have been trained on disaster-recovery procedures.

It is also important to note that rehearsing and testing disaster-recovery or contingency plans can be a very expensive process. During the survey of 256 managers and planners that I conducted during the fourth quarter of 2002, only two out of ten organizations reported that they rehearsed their entire DRP, while five out ten reported that they rehearsed or tested only parts of their DRP.

Each organization needs to address how it is approaching rehearsing and testing DRPs, if not for the sake of national initiatives, then at least to determine if DRPs have become outdated, personnel have changed, or buildings have been remodeled.

In addition, coordination with local authorities and emergency responders on disaster-recovery planning is advisable. They will be the first responders during any disaster and, in many locations, have been receiving advanced training on responding to incidents, especially those that may be terrorist related.

7.6 Mobilizing organization resources for priority I

Action Checklist Number 7 (see Table 7.2) shows which steps IT managers in all types of organizations can take to synchronize their efforts with those of the government to achieve the goals of participating in a national cyberspace security response system. The next chapter focuses on participating in a national threat and vulnerability reduction program.

Table 7.2 *Action Checklist Number 7*

Action Item	Status (e.g., Completed, Pending, or N/A)
Evaluate the organization's ability to participate in and benefit from a national cyberincident response system.	
Develop processes and procedures to utilize information provided by the national cyberincident response system.	
Determine if the organization is using reports, analyses, standards, and recommendations provided by researching agencies such as the NSA and the NIST to improve IS security.	
Evaluate how computer security standards and procedures are set in the organization.	
Determine if the organization's view of the health of cyberspace is influenced by political, economic, or business issues that could impact IT policies and computer-incident response plans.	
Evaluate the sources of cybersecurity information that the organization has, including vendors, service providers, and other organizations, that can be used to maintain security during threat situations.	
Determine if DRPs are up-to-date and if any changes or updates need to be made to the plans.	

8

Participating in a National Threat and Vulnerability Reduction Program

This chapter discuses the goals of priority II of the *National Strategy to Secure Cyberspace,* which calls for participation in a national threat and vulnerability reduction program. To meet the goals of priority II, an organization should take or be prepared to take the following steps:

- Assist in enhancing law-enforcement's capabilities for preventing and prosecuting cyberspace attacks, which will mean reporting more incidents and filing necessary complaints to support the prosecution of perpetrators.
- Be forthwith in providing information that will contribute to national vulnerability assessments so that all organizations will better understand the potential consequences of threats and vulnerabilities.
- Deploy new and more secure protocols and routing technologies in order to reduce vulnerabilities, which will require upgrading or replacing less secure technology.
- Deploy and use digital control systems and supervisory control and data-acquisition systems that the government has labeled as trusted or that in some other way meets government standards.
- Deploy and upgrade software that can reduce and remediate vulnerabilities, which will mean installing patches more frequently or eliminating less secure software from the product mix used by the organization.
- Help to analyze infrastructure interdependencies and improve the physical security of cybersystems and telecommunications systems to make them meet potential government standards.

- Contribute to a process that helps to prioritize federal cybersecurity research and development agendas and assess and secure emerging systems.

8.1 Law-enforcement capabilities

Assisting in the efforts to enhance law-enforcement's capabilities for preventing and prosecuting cyberspace attacks will mean reporting more incidents and filing necessary complaints to support the prosecution of perpetrators. The importance of reporting incidents to law enforcement and how to report incidents is discussed in depth in Chapter 4.

In addition to increased and improved reporting of computer-related incidents, organizations also need support of training programs for law-enforcement professionals, as well as IT security professionals to work with law enforcement. There has been considerable effort put forth to train more IT security professionals. This effort will better enable the enforcement of laws, because organizations will have more qualified staff to assist law-enforcement actions. Although there have been several national initiatives to improve training, much of the actual training takes place at the local level.

One example of how the gap between national initiatives and local resources has been bridged is the National INFOSEC Education & Training Program supported by the NSA, the National Science Foundation (NSF), and other federal agencies.

The NSF provides financial support for the Federal Cyber Service: Scholarship for Service Program designed to increase the number of qualified students entering the fields of information assurance (IA) and computer security and to increase the capacity of the U.S. higher-education enterprise to continue to produce professionals in these fields. The program has two tracks.

The scholarship track provides funding to colleges and universities to award scholarships in the IA and computer security fields. Scholarship recipients will become part of the Federal Cyber Service of IT specialists, who ensure the protection of the U.S. government information infrastructure. Upon graduation, after their two-year scholarships, the recipients are required to work for a federal agency for two years in fulfillment of their Federal Cyber Service commitment.

The capacity-building track provides funds to colleges and universities to improve the quality and increase the training of IA and computer security professionals through the professional development of IA faculty and the development of academic programs. Partnerships designed to increase participation by underrepresented groups are particularly encouraged.

The NSA certifies academic programs for participation in the Federal Cyber Service: Scholarship for Service Program as Centers of Academic Excellence in Information Assurance Education. NSA grants the designations following a rigorous review of university applications against published criteria based on training standards established by the National Security Telecommunications and Information Systems Security Committee (NSTISSC). The NSTISSC has established standards for IS security professionals that provide the minimum training and education standards for properly executing the duties and responsibilities of:

- Information systems security (INFOSEC) professionals
- Designated approving authority (DAA)
- System administration (SA) in IS security
- IS security officers (IAD)

The Information Assurance Courseware Evaluation Process takes the next step in meeting national education and training requirements in IA. The process systematically assesses the degree to which the various institutional, college, and university curriculums satisfy NSTISSI standards. The NSTISSC Education, Training, and Awareness Issue Group (ETAIG) established the Information Assurance Courseware Evaluation Working Group (IACEWG) to develop and implement this process. The process certifies institutions as meeting all of the elements of a specific standard with a designated set of courseware. The certification does not make a judgment as to the quality of the presentation of the material within the set of courseware, but only that all of the elements of a specific standard are covered.

The process assesses the curriculum of an institution, college, or university against the NSTISSI standards. The data for this evaluation is electronically submitted by the institution in a standardized format through an interactive Web site that will also maintain the privacy of the information. All submissions must be made electronically. Much of the required information was previously developed by institutions requesting designation as a Center of Academic Excellence under the Centers of Academic Excellence in Information Assurance Education (CAEIAE) program.

The IACE submission will identify specific courses of instruction and will provide a mapping of the course content against the elements of an NSTISSI standard. The mapping will be performed for all the applicable courses, and an evaluation will be made by a review board to determine the degree to which the institution meets the standards. After working with the institution to ensure all the elements of the standard are met, the institution will receive formal certification. It is important to note that this process certifies the institution, not the individual attending the institution. Certified institutions will be authorized to issue certificates to their students.

Each year, newly designated CAEIAEs are recognized in a formal presentation at the annual Conference of the Colloquium for Information Systems Security Education. The colloquium conference provides a forum for key officials in government, industry, and academia to focus on current and emerging requirements in IA education and to encourage the development and expansion of curricula at graduate and undergraduate levels. As of summer 2003, the 50 universities designated as CAEIAEs are the following:

- Air Force Institute of Technology
- Auburn University
- Capitol College
- Carnegie Mellon University
- Drexel University
- East Stroudsburg University
- Florida State University
- George Mason University
- George Washington University
- Georgia Institute of Technology
- Idaho State University
- Indiana University of Pennsylvania
- Information Resources Management College of the National Defense University
- Iowa State University
- James Madison University
- Johns Hopkins University

- Mississippi State University
- Naval Postgraduate School
- New Jersey Institute of Technology
- New Mexico Institute of Mining and Technology
- North Carolina State University
- Northeastern University
- Norwich University
- Pennsylvania State University
- Polytechnic
- Portland State University
- Purdue University
- Stanford University
- State University of New York, Buffalo
- State University of New York, Stony Brook
- Stevens Institute of Technology
- Syracuse University
- Texas A&M University
- Towson University
- University of California, Davis
- University of Dallas
- University of Idaho
- University of Illinois, Urbana-Champaign
- University of Maryland, Baltimore County
- University of Maryland, University College
- University of Massachusetts, Amherst
- University of Nebraska, Omaha
- University of North Carolina, Charlotte
- University of Pennsylvania
- University of Texas, San Antonio
- University of Tulsa

- University of Virginia
- U.S. Military Academy, West Point
- Walsh College
- West Virginia University

8.2 National vulnerability assessments

The national effort to identify vulnerabilities is moving ahead at a frantic pace. For this effort to be successful, organizations need to be forthwith in providing information that will contribute to national vulnerability assessments. It is also important that all organizations better understand the potential consequences of threats and vulnerabilities.

To address technology vulnerabilities the Computer Security Division at the NIST has established a computer security resources center (csrc.nist.gov) and a venerability and threat portal (icat.nist.gov/vt_portal.cfm).

The threat portal provides access to the ICAT Metabase. The ICAT Metabase is a searchable index of computer vulnerabilities that links users into a variety of publicly available vulnerability databases and patch sites, enabling them to find and fix the vulnerabilities existing on their systems.

ICAT allows searches at a fine granularity, a feature unavailable with most vulnerability databases, by characterizing each vulnerability according to over 40 attributes (including software name and version number). ICAT does not compete with publicly available vulnerability databases, but instead is a search engine that drives traffic to them. The ICAT developers were supported by numerous agencies and organizations, including the following:

- The Center for Education and Research in Information Assurance and Security (CERIAS) at Purdue University
- FedCIRC
- Internet Security Systems X-Force
- National Information Assurance Partnership (NIAP)
- SysAdmin, Audit, Network, Security (SANS) Institute
- Security Focus

Among the 40 pieces of data and information that ICAT provides on over 5,000 vulnerabilities is a classification of a severity. Vulnerabilities can have one of three severity levels: high, medium, or low.

A vulnerability is high severity if it:

- Allows a remote attacker to violate the security protection of a system (i.e., to gain some sort of user or root account)
- Allows a local attack that gains complete control of a system
- Is important enough to have an associated CERT/CC advisory

A vulnerability is medium severity if it:

- Does not meet the definition of either high or low severity

A vulnerability is low severity if it:

- Does not typically yield valuable information or control over a system, but instead gives the attacker knowledge that may help the attacker find and exploit other vulnerabilities
- Believed by the NIST staff to be inconsequential for most organizations

It is important to note that so far much of the effort to assess vulnerabilities has focused on technology. The ultimate goal of the *National Strategy to Secure Cyberspace* is to go beyond technology and to view vulnerabilities in a more holistic manner. This includes examining how organizations are interconnected and how disruptions or attacks can be prevented or contained. This is discussed in more detail in the following sections.

8.3 Deploying more secure technology and trusted systems

One approach to improving security is to eliminate or reduce the population of older and less reliable equipment. IT environments and networks can then be upgraded or replaced with more secure protocols and routing technology in order to reduce vulnerabilities. It is also important to be very selective about what technology is deployed.

The U.S. government is recommending that organizations use only digital control systems and supervisory control and data-acquisition systems that the government has labeled as trusted or that in some other way meet government standards. The U.S. government has established a program to support the security and trustworthiness of IT products that are part of the national information infrastructure, both in the public and private sectors. The NIST and NSA have worked with government and industry to develop and apply information security technology, assurance metrics, and standards necessary for the protection of information critical to overall economic and national security interests. These efforts have focused primarily on government-sponsored initiatives to produce effective IT security evaluation criteria (e.g., the Trusted Computer System Evaluation Criteria and the Federal Criteria for IT Security) and to evaluate products developed by industry in response to those criteria.

The development of similar IT security evaluation criteria by Canada and several European countries during the last decade has prompted the effort to begin harmonizing existing evaluation criteria into common criteria that are internationally accepted and standards based. The Common Criteria is the result of a multiyear effort by the governments of the United States, Canada, the United Kingdom, France, Germany, and the Netherlands to develop harmonized security criteria for IT products.

At the same time the Common Criteria were being developed, there was a parallel effort to transition trusted product evaluations from the government to the private sector. NSA began the transition of its commercial IT product evaluation capability to the private sector with the establishment of the Trust Technology Assessment Program (TTAP). Under this program, IT security evaluations were conducted by commercial testing laboratories using the Trusted Computer Systems Evaluation Criteria (TCSEC) in accordance with cooperative research and development agreements. The transition continues under the Common Criteria Evaluation and Validation Scheme (CCEVS) with commercial testing laboratories conducting Common Criteria–based evaluations of IT products on a fee-for-service basis using the Common Evaluation Methodology.

The NIAP CCEVS is an activity jointly managed by the NIST and the NSA and staffed by personnel from those agencies. The focus of the CCEVS is to establish a national program for the evaluation of IT products for conformance to the International Common Criteria for IT Security Evaluation. The validation body approves participation of security testing laboratories in the scheme in accordance with its established policies and procedures. During the course of an evaluation, the validation body provides technical guidance to those testing laboratories, validates the results of IT security evaluations for conformance with the Common Criteria, and serves as an interface to other countries for the recognition of such evaluations.

IT security evaluations are conducted by commercial testing laboratories accredited by the NIST's National Voluntary Laboratory Accreditation Program (NVLAP) and approved by the validation body. These approved testing laboratories are called Common Criteria Testing Laboratories (CCTL). NVLAP accreditation is one of the requirements for becoming a CCTL. The purpose of the NVLAP accreditation is to ensure that laboratories meet the requirements of ISO/IEC Guide 25, General Requirement for the Competence of Calibration and Testing Laboratories and the specific scheme requirements for IT security evaluation.

The validation body assesses the results of a security evaluation conducted by a CCTL within the scheme and, when appropriate, issues a Common Criteria certificate. The certificate, together with its associated validation report, confirms that an IT product or protection profile has been evaluated at an accredited laboratory using the Common Evaluation Methodology for conformance with the Common Criteria. The certificate also confirms that the IT security evaluation has been conducted in accordance with the provisions of the scheme and that the conclusions of the testing laboratory are consistent with the evidence presented during the evaluation. The validation body maintains a NIAP Validated Products List (VPL) containing all IT products and protection profiles that have successfully completed evaluation and validation under the scheme.

More information about Common Criteria can be obtained at www.commoncriteria.org, along with an updated list of tested products. Tested products are classified into the following categories:

- Antivirus
- Biometrics
- Certificate management
- Firewalls
- Guards
- IDSs

- Mobile code
- Network management
- Operating systems
- PC access control
- Peripheral switch
- Public-key infrastructure (PKI)/key management infrastructure
- Secure messaging
- Sensitive data protection
- Single-level Web servers
- Smart cards
- Trusted database management systems (DBMS)
- Virtual private networks (VPNs)

8.4 Upgrading software to remediate vulnerabilities

One of the most frequently discussed areas of IT security during the last several years has been how long it takes to eradicate a vulnerability once it is identified. Many vulnerabilities can be reduced or eliminated by installing current patches. In the case of Code Red, for example, the vulnerability had been known for months before it was exploited in the Code Red attack. Other vulnerabilities can be reduced or eliminated by configuring software in a more secure manner.

In addition to the software producer, there are several organizations that can provide information about the configuration of operating system and applications software. The NSA, for example, provides the following publications at its Web site:

- *Guide to the Secure Configuration and Administration of iPlanet Web Server, Enterprise Edition 4.1*
- *Guide to the Secure Configuration and Administration of Microsoft Internet Information Server 4.0*
- *Guide to the Secure Configuration and Administration of Microsoft Internet Information Server 4.0 (Checklist Format)*

- *Secure Configuration of the Apache Web Server, Apache Server Version 1.3.3 on Red Hat Linux 5.1*
- *Microsoft NetMeeting 3.0 Security Assessment and Configuration Guide*
- *The 60 Minute Network Security Guide*
- *Guide to Securing Microsoft Internet Explorer 5.5 Using Group Policy*
- *Guide to the Secure Configuration and Administration of Microsoft SQL Server 2000*
- *Guide to Securing Netscape 7.02*

Software configuration is controlled through a formal and structured configuration management process. This involves identifying the configuration of a system or component, controlling changes to the configuration, and maintaining the integrity and traceability of the configuration throughout the life cycle of the technology. Proper configuration management enables an organization to answer the control and track the following activities:

- The process for making changes to computers, applications, or network equipment
- Who is authorized to make changes
- Who made which changes to the systems or applications
- What changes were made
- When were the changes made
- Why were the changes made

8.5 Physically Securing Technology Facilities

Organizations also need to analyze infrastructure interdependencies and improve the physical security of cybersystems and telecommunications systems to make them meet potential government standards. Those organizations with in-house telecommunications and network facilities can provide a point of entry into regional or national network infrastructures. Thus, the physical security of these facilities can be equally as important as the cybersecurity of the networks.

Implementing physical security to such facilities requires that the access and the activities of employees, service provider staff, and contractors be controlled, managed, and monitored. Efforts to manage the physical security of computer and network facilities should at minimum include those items in the security checklist shown in Table 8.1.

Table 8.1 *Physical Security Checklist for Technology Facilities*

Physical Security Method	Status (e.g., Completed, Pending, or N/A)
Only personnel who require access to perform their official duties will be permitted in the facilities.	
A facilities access roster will be established.	
A log is kept of all personnel who are issued the combination/key to the computer room and each person will be required to sign for that combination/key.	
A cipher lock or suitable substitute will be placed on each door to the facilities.	
The combination of a cipher lock will be changed frequently, especially when a person who was previously given the combination leaves the organization.	
Keys or access card keys will be returned to the organization upon separation, transfer, or termination of an employee.	
Loss of keys or disclosure of cipher key code will be reported to the security director immediately.	
There will be signs posted designating the facilities as a restricted area.	
Contract personnel and others not authorized with unrestricted access, but who are required to be in the controlled area, will be escorted by an authorized person at all times when they are within the controlled area.	
All access to the facilities will be logged, and logs will be regularly reviewed by management.	
There shall be no signs to indicate that information system or network equipment is located in any particular building or area.	
Media used to record and store sensitive software or data will be labeled, protected, controlled, and secured when not in use.	

Table 8.1 *Physical Security Checklist for Technology Facilities (continued)*

Physical Security Method	Status (e.g., Completed, Pending, or N/A)
Physical access controls will also be implemented in locations of wiring used to connect elements of the systems, supporting services (such as electric power), backup media, wiring closets, and any other elements required for the facilities operation	

8.6 Prioritizing cybersecurity research

In general, the government has multiple layers and sources of input when it comes to prioritizing research and development agendas. However, it may be in the best interest of an organization to participate in the process of setting priorities for cybersecurity research. This will most likely depend on the industry sector in which the organization operates and the level of dependency that an organization has on computer systems or networks. It may also be influenced by past experiences such as system attacks.

If IT managers have an interest in making recommendations on cybersecurity research, they should contact DHS, the NIST, or their local congressional representatives for guidance on how to best participate.

8.7 Mobilizing organizational resources for priority II

Action Checklist Number 8 (see Table 8.2) shows which steps IT managers in all types of organizations can take to synchronize their efforts with those of the government to achieve the goals of participating in a national threat and vulnerability reduction program. The next chapter focuses on launching a national cyberspace security awareness and training program.

Table 8.2 *Action Checklist Number 8*

Action Item	Status (e.g., Completed, Pending, or N/A)
Determine how IT security staff are trained and develop a program to improve training.	
Determine if there are opportunities to work with local law-enforcement agencies on joint training exercises.	

Table 8.2 *Action Checklist Number 8 (continued)*

Action Item	Status (e.g., Completed, Pending, or N/A)
Determine how the organization obtains information on vulnerabilities and develop steps to obtain more timely information on vulnerabilities.	
Determine if the organization actually uses information on vulnerabilities to keep security methods updated and make changes in the approach if necessary.	
Determine if the technology used by the organization meets the Common Criteria standards and make plans to migrate away from technologies that do not meet the standards.	
Determine if the technology-acquisition process used by the organization requires that products meet Common Criteria standards and modify procedures as necessary.	
Evaluate the configuration-management processes and procedures of the organizations to determine if they provide sufficient levels of control to improve security and modify procedures as necessary.	
Evaluate the process and procedures for installing patches to eliminate vulnerabilities and modify procedures as necessary.	
Evaluate the physical security of computer and network facilities to determine if they meet minimum standards or customary standards for the industry sector and modify physical security procedures as necessary.	
Determine if the organization wants to make recommendations for priorities in cybersecurity research.	

9

Launching a National Cyberspace Security Awareness and Training Program

Creating a culture of security was the title of a presentation made by Federal Trade Commission (FTC) commissioner Orson Swindle at the Privacy 2002: Information, Security, and New Global Realities conference in Cleveland, Ohio, on September 26, 2002. In this presentation Swindle stated, "Starting with ourselves, we must convince our families, friends, colleagues, and employees why computer security is important. I strongly urge corporate executives, educators, business managers, and community leaders to take the lead. It's simply the right thing to do. Get the word around in your circle of influence."

This chapter covers activities that have occurred, as well as work that needs to be done, to meet the goals of priority III, which is to develop and foster participation in a national cyberspace security awareness and training effort. An organization should take or be prepared to take the following steps:

1. Participate in a comprehensive national awareness program to help enable businesses, the general workforce, and the general population to secure their own parts of cyberspace.
2. Improve in-house training and education programs to support the national cybersecurity needs.
3. Accept and have staff participate in private-sector supported and widely recognized professional cybersecurity certifications.

9.1 Raising national awareness

There has been considerable effort put forth by numerous organizations to raise the awareness of the importance of cybersecurity. The work of the FBI, the NIPC, and InfraGard has helped to raise awareness of cybersecurity issues. There is a great deal of information available from all of their Web sites that could be helpful in creating internal cybersecurity awareness programs in an organization.

The computer-focused media, as well as the media in general, have also done an exceptional job in raising awareness about cybersecurity issues. Major virus attacks, for example, have been covered in news magazines, on national and local television news programs, and newspapers from New York City to Peoria, Illinois, to McAllen, Texas.

One of the leading organizations in the effort to improve awareness of cybersecurity issues is the National Cyber Security Alliance (NCSA) (www.staysafeonline.info). The NCSA was founded by a group of public and private organizations, including AOL, ATT, Apple Computer, Cisco Systems, Computer Associates, the Government Services Agency (GSA), InfraGard, McGraw-Hill, SANS, and TrendMicro. I was a member of the founding task force and made a monetary and time contribution as vice president of research for Computer Economics of Carlsbad, California.

The NCSA has been working to promote cybersecurity to businesses and individual computer users. Resources and guides available from the NCSA that may be helpful in internal awareness campaigns include the following:

- Security Fundamentals: Intro, Dangers/Defenses, Viruses, Passwords, and Wrap-up. This free course will provide you with an introduction to and a general awareness of computer security–related issues. It will allow you to identify what you can do in your role within your organization or at home to protect your networks, systems, and information against cyberattacks.
- *Beginner's Guide to Computer Security.* All computers, from the family home computer to those on desktops in the largest corporations in the country, can be affected by computer security breaches. However, security breaches can often be easily prevented. How? This guide provides you with a general overview of the most common computer security threats and the steps you, your family, or your business can take to protect your computer against these threats.
- *Safe at Any Speed: How to Stay Safe Online if You Use High-Speed Internet Access.* More people everyday are surfing the Internet using a high-speed DSL or cable connection. A high-speed Internet connection has many benefits, but it is also a tempting target for malicious people on the Internet because of those benefits. If you use a high-speed

connection to access the Internet, you need to take some additional steps to protect your computer and the information stored on your computer.

- *Home Network Security.* Do you have a home network to share a printer or an Internet connection? Or do you operate a small business that networks its computers for e-mail or to share a connection to the Internet? Networks, just like stand-alone desktop computers, can be vulnerable to security threats. This guide will help you to understand networks and network security better. The information in this guide is especially important if you have an always-on or broadband Internet connection.
- *A Glossary of Computer Security.* Have you ever wondered what a firewall or smurfing is? Or what the difference is between a virus and a worm? This glossary will provide you with the definitions to these terms, as well as some other common computer security terms.
- *Overview: Security.* The Internet has fundamentally changed the way organizations approach security today. Companies face a myriad of network security risks: Web site vandalism, viruses, Trojan horses, denial-of-service attacks, data destruction and theft, and others. These security breaches can compromise application availability, data confidentiality, and data integrity and, most importantly, can interrupt business and cost resources to respond to attacks and fix any vulnerability. This document provides an overview of security for small businesses.
- *What You Need to Implement a Network Security Solution.* A breach in network security could cost your company a great deal in lost productivity, lost data, repair work, and loss of confidence among customers, partners, and employees. To prevent a breach, you just need a solid security strategy and a well-planned implementation. This document discusses network security tools, benefits of network security, strategic and deployment considerations, timelines, and measures of success.
- "Building In-Depth Security for Small and Midsize Business Networks." Network security is becoming an increasingly important concern for small and medium-size companies. A breach in security can have a significant impact on customers, costs, and operations. This white paper discusses the security requirements that small to medium-size businesses face and how to design secure wired and wireless networks.

The NCSA also provides a list of ten tips that can readily help improve cybersecurity. The tips may be helpful in creating awareness or training materials for use in an organization. These tips can be very helpful if employees access the organization's computer systems or networks from home. A full explanation of the tips is provided at the NCSA Web site. The ten tips can be summarized as follows:

1. Use protection software and antivirus software and keep it up to date.
2. Don't open e-mail from unknown sources.
3. Use hard-to-guess passwords.
4. Protect your computer from Internet intruders—use firewalls.
5. Don't share access to your computers with strangers. Learn about file-sharing risks.
6. Disconnect from the Internet when not using it.
7. Back up your computer data.
8. Regularly download security protection update patches.
9. Check your security on a regular basis. When you change your clocks for daylight-savings time, reevaluate your computer security.
10. Make sure your family members and/or your employees know what to do if your computer becomes infected.

The SBA and NIST have combined efforts to reach businesses of all sizes with the latest cybersecurity advice. The SBA Solutions Newsletter has run numerous articles, including the following, that provide good advice to those businesses that may not have full-time IT staff:

- "Virus Protection" (July 2003)
- "Preparing for Contingencies and Disasters" (June 2003)
- "Choosing a GOOD Password" (May 2003)

9.2 Launching an internal awareness campaign

A strong internal awareness program will inform employees of the importance of computer security and motivate them to learn policies and procedures. Public-relations departments are usually very good at managing such campaigns. However, if the present public relations staff does not have experience on managing internal awareness campaigns, it is advisable either to send them to training or hire an external consultant to assist in the development of the campaign.

There are numerous potential elements to an internal awareness campaign and as many as possible should be used to increase the awareness of cybersecurity efforts. Methods that can be used in the awareness campaign include the following:

- Attention-getting logos and headlines on the enterprise intranet
- Articles in employee newsletters explaining the importance of computer security
- Banners and posters in break rooms and employee cafeterias
- Posters in vending areas
- Posters in restroom and lounge areas
- Banners in parking areas
- Brown-bag lunches to discuss the plan
- Pamphlets included in paycheck envelopes
- Direct mailings of pamphlets or letters to employees' homes
- Brief discussions of the plan in staff meetings
- Mini training sessions at workshops or retreats
- Motivational speakers at large enterprise events
- Celebrity endorsement of campaign goals

The U.S. FTC has launched a cybersecurity awareness campaign and provides helpful information about educating computer users on the importance of cybersecurity at its Web site (www.ftc.gov/bcp/conline/edcams/infosecurity/index.html). The article shown in Figure 9.1 has been created by the FTC and is available for use in corporate newsletters.

Are You a Safe Cyber Surfer?

(NAPSI)-Are you a safe cyber surfer? The stakes are high if you're not.

Every time you buy stuff online, do your banking, or pay bills over the Internet, check in with your office by e-mail or just surf the Web for fun, you open a gateway to the personal information on your computer—including credit-card numbers, bank balances, and more. You may also be in for costly computer repairs and lost data due to damaging computer viruses that can invade your computer through e-mail connections.

Fortunately, there are steps you can take to protect your computer, your information, and your peace of mind from computer creeps who try to slow down a network operation, or worse yet, steal personal information to commit a crime. Here are some tips to help you from the security experts at the FTC:

Make sure your passwords have both letters and numbers and are at least eight characters long. Avoid common words: some hackers use programs that can try every word in the dictionary. Don't use your personal information, your login name, or adjacent keys on the keyboard as passwords—and don't share your passwords online or over the phone.

Protect yourself from viruses by installing antivirus software and updating it regularly. You can download antivirus software from the Web sites of software companies, or buy it in retail stores; the best recognize old and new viruses and update automatically.

Prevent unauthorized access to your computer through firewall software or hardware, especially if you are a high-speed user. A properly configured firewall makes it tougher for hackers to locate your computer. Firewalls are also designed to prevent hackers from getting into your programs and files. Some recently released operating system software and some hardware devices come with a built-in firewall. Some firewalls block outgoing information as well as incoming files. That stops hackers from planting programs called spyware that cause your computer to send out your personal information without your approval.

Don't open a file attached to an e-mail unless you are expecting it or know what it contains. If you send an attachment, type a message explaining what it is. Never forward any e-mail warning about a new virus. It may be a hoax and could be used to spread a virus.

```
   When something bad happens—you think you've been hacked
or infected by a virus—e-mail a report of the incident to
your Internet provider and the hacker's Internet provider,
if you can tell what it is, as well as your software ven-
dor.
   To learn more, visit the Web site at www.ftc.gov/infose-
curity or call toll free, 1-877-FTC-HELP (1-877-382-4357).
```

Source: U.S. FTC.

Figure 9.1 *FTC Article about Cybersecurity.*

9.3 Launching an in-house training program on cybersecurity

One of the most important steps in implementing homeland security initiatives is the training of all employees on computer security policies and procedures. Simply stated: What good are great policies and procedures when no one knows what they are? Training of new employees should be done as appropriate for their level and area of responsibility.

There should be a generalized training session that addresses computer security policies and procedures in general, as well as how they apply to the specific technology architecture in the organization. This training should address at least the following areas:

- Password administration, protection, and usage
- Antivirus measures and how to report suspicious e-mail
- How to report a suspected intrusion
- How to work with IT security staff during a computer incident
- Physical security of workstations and computer and telecommunications facilities

In addition to technology-related training, the training of current employees should start at the executive level, and all executive staff should be required to attend the training. The computer security issues on which executive level staff should be trained include the following:

- The work of IT staff to develop the policies and procedures

- An explanation of the major laws impacting the security requirements of the organization
- How policies and procedures are being implemented to protect the organization

Recognize that executive-level staff often have short attention spans because they are so busy with such a wide variety of tasks and responsibilities; they will always feel like they should be doing something other than going to a briefing session on the computer security policies and procedures. This briefing should be limited to no more than two hours.

A second training effort should be directed at middle-level managers and supervisors, who need to understand the computer security policies and procedures thoroughly to assure that the decisions they make during the course of business negotiation and operations management are consistent with the computer security policies and procedures. The range of recommended computer security policies and procedures issues in which management- and supervisory-level staff should be trained is broader than that for the executive-level staff. Middle managers and supervisor have more hands-on responsibility for the day-to-day operation of the enterprise and need a far more detailed understanding of the computer security policies and procedures than executive-level staff. This training will require eight hours to accomplish, allowing time for discussion and questions and answers. Training topics include the following:

- The work that the IT staff has done to develop the policies and procedures
- An explanation of the major laws impacting the security requirements of the organization
- How policies and procedures are being implemented to protect the organization
- Specific data for which the organization must maintain security
- The roles each department plays in maintaining enterprise information and protecting that information
- What policies will be communicated to all employees in the organization
- Any consequence employees will face for violating computer security policies and procedures

- How to contact the IT department if there is a computer security incident
- How to work with the IT department if there is a computer security incident

A third type of training should be directed toward employees who manage workgroups or projects that specifically involve data for which information security must be maintained. It is important that they have a good understanding of the computer security policies and procedures, as well as a detailed understanding of the specific data, applications, or business processes in which they are involved. This training will take as many as four hours to accomplish, with time allowed for discussion and questions and answers.

Training topics include the following:

- The work that the IT staff has done to develop the policies and procedures
- An explanation of the major laws impacting the security requirements of the organization
- How policies and procedures are being implemented to protect the organization
- Specific data for which the organization must maintain security
- The roles each department plays in protecting security
- Project-specific computer security policy and procedure requirements for the areas in which they are involved

In addition, employees who do not fit into these categories should be given at least some level of training so that they understand the overall enterprise policies and philosophy toward computer security. A generalized privacy training program should be developed that covers the importance of security, the laws covering security of information in the organization, and what they should do to help maintain security. This training should be brief and can be accomplished in about one hour.

Each employee who attends training should be required to sign a statement that he or she has received the training, and that signed statement should be kept on file. As employees move into different task-specific jobs or are promoted to a supervisory or management position, they should go through the training that has been designated as appropriate for that position. The signed statement should be dated and include a description of the training and the course outline for the training session the employee attended.

9.4 Professional cybersecurity certifications

Chapter 8 discusses many aspects of the educational programs that have been funded by the U.S. government that will help to train both law-enforcement professionals and IT security staff. In addition, there is a growing movement for certification of IT security professionals. Many technology producers, including Microsoft and Cisco, set standards for certifying IT professionals on their products and the security aspects of their products. These programs, combined with independent offerings, have created a plethora of computer security certification opportunities.

International Information Systems Security Certifications Consortium (ISC2) is a not-for-profit organization dedicated to maintaining a common body of knowledge for information security, certifying industry professionals and practitioners in an international IS standard, administering training and certification examinations, and ensuring credentials are maintained, primarily through continuing education. ISC2 is based in Framingham, Massachusetts. More information is available at the organization's Web site at www.isc2.org.

The organization is run by an elected board of directors. IS professionals in over 60 countries worldwide have attained certification in one of the two designations administered by ISC2:

- Certified Information Systems Security Professional (CISSP)
- System Security Certified Practitioner (SSCP)

The CISSP certification is the mostly widely recognized professional certification in the IT security area. The CISSP examination consists of 250 multiple-choice questions. Candidates have up to six hours to complete the examination. The following ten CISSP IS security test domains are covered in the examination pertaining to the common body of knowledge:

1. Access control systems and methodology
2. Applications and systems development
3. Business-continuity planning
4. Cryptography
5. Law, investigation, and ethics
6. Operations security
7. Physical security
8. Security architecture and models
9. Security management practices
10. Telecommunications, network, and Internet security

The SSCP certification examination consists of 125 multiple-choice questions. Candidates have up to three hours to complete the examination. Seven SSCP IS security test domains are covered in the examination pertaining to the common body of knowledge:

1. Access controls
2. Administration
3. Audit and monitoring
4. Risk, response, and recovery
5. Cryptography
6. Data communications
7. Malicious code/malware

When it comes to vendor-neutral organizations, SANS is probably the leading private organization in the computer security training business. Many SANS resources, such as news digests, research summaries, security alerts, and award-winning papers are free to all who ask. Income from printed publications funds university-based research programs. Income from SANS educational programs funds special research projects and SANS training programs. More information is available at their Web site at sans.org.

In 1999, SANS founded the Global Information Assurance Certification (GIAC). GIAC offers certifications that address a range of skill sets, including security essentials, intrusion detection, incident handling, firewalls and perimeter protection, operating system security, and more. GIAC is unique in the field of information-security certifications by not only testing a candidate's knowledge, but also testing a candidate's ability to put that knowledge into practice in the real world.

GIAC certifications address a range of skill sets, including entry-level information-security officer skills and broad-based security essentials, as well as advanced subject areas such as audit, intrusion detection, incident handling, firewalls and perimeter protection, forensics, hacker techniques, and Windows, and UNIX operating system security. GIAC certifications available for open registration are the following:

- GIAC Security Essentials Certification (GSEC)
- GIAC Certified Firewall Analyst (GCFW)
- GIAC Certified Intrusion Analyst (GCIA)
- GIAC Certified Incident Handler (GCIH)
- GIAC Certified Windows Security Administrator (GCWN)
- GIAC Certified UNIX Security Administrator (GCUX)
- GIAC Information Security Officer (GISO)
- GIAC Systems and Network Auditor (GSNA)
- GIAC Certified Forensic Analyst (GCFA)
- GIAC IT Security Audit Essentials (GSAE)

Additional SANS courses include the following:

- Advanced Network Penetration Testing Methodology—Hands-on
- National Information Leadership Conference IV
- Securing Windows 2000—The Gold Standard
- Reverse Engineering Malware
- CCNA +S
- Wireless Networks

- Building a Syslog Infrastructure
- Securing IIS 5.0
- E-Money

In January 2003, the Information Systems Security Association (ISSA) announced that it will be conducting a review of professional computer security certifications to provide guidance for both security practitioners and the companies looking to hire them. The study will provide a road map that explains the relevance of particular certifications to job functions, as well as identifying the strengths and weaknesses of each. More information about the study will be available at www.issa.org when the study is completed.

9.5 Mobilizing organizational resources for priority III

Action Checklist Number 9 (see Table 9.1) shows which steps IT managers in all types of organizations can take to synchronize their efforts with those of the government to achieve the goals of participating in a national cyberspace security awareness and training program. The next chapter focuses on working to secure governments' cyberspace.

Table 9.1 *Action Checklist Number 9*

Action Item	Status (e.g., Completed, Pending, or N/A)
Develop and launch a technology-focused cybersecurity training program for various types of employees, including executives, managers, supervisors, project leaders, and end users in all capacities.	
Develop and launch an information security–focused training program for different types of employees based on their levels and areas of responsibilities.	
Evaluate the need for certified computer security professionals in the organization and determine a course of action to increase the level of certification of in-house staff.	

10

Working to Secure Governments' Cyberspace

The U.S. government has increased IT security spending and has been hiring more IT security professionals. As mentioned in previous chapters, the government is also building a cybercorps by funding scholarships for individuals going to certified IA programs at schools that have been designated as centers of excellence in IA education. Private-sector organizations will derive several benefits from the efforts of the government to make its computers and networks more secure, including the following:

- Potential technology transfer in the form of practices, standards, and research and development efforts
- A larger and better-trained computer security workforce
- Fewer computers that can become the source of viruses and worms
- Fewer computers that can be used as slaves or drones during large-scale information warfare attacks

To meet the goals of priority IV and participate in securing governments' cyberspace, an organization should take or be prepared to take the following steps:

- Provide information to the government that helps to assess threats and vulnerabilities to federal cybersystems continuously.
- Assure that all users in an organization who may need to use federal cybersystems are trustworthy individuals trained on security issues.
- Provide information to the government that may help to secure federal wireless local area networks and keep those networks secure.

- Assist in improving security in government outsourcing and procurement by providing information as requested about contractors, equipment, software, and services.
- Assist state and local governments in establishing IT security programs and encourage such entities to participate in information-sharing and analysis centers with similar governments.

10.1 Continuously assessing threats and vulnerabilities

EO 13231, Critical Infrastructure Protection in the Information Age, which was signed by the president of the United States on October 16, 2001, was designed to protect the operation of IS essential to the critical infrastructure. The EO also established the President's Critical Infrastructure Protection Board, which is charged with recommending policies and coordinating programs for protecting IS for critical infrastructure, including emergency preparedness communications and the physical assets that support such systems.

Any organization that electronically interacts with any government entity should be prepared to provide information to those entities about computer usage and security practices. This will help to provide ongoing assessments of threats and vulnerabilities. The organizations that are most likely to be able to provide helpful information to government entities are the following:

- Technology producers that sell equipment or software to government entities
- Government contractors that participate in electronic data interchange, online acquisition, e-commerce, or other forms of electronic interaction with government entities
- Other government entities that participate in electronic data interchange or other forms of electronic interaction with government entities
- Organizations in any of the critical industries (agriculture and food, water, public health, emergency services, defense industrial base, telecommunications, energy, transportation, banking and finance, chemical industry and hazardous materials, postal and shipping) that

electronically interact with government entities or that have information regarding specific threats or vulnerabilities

Risk assessments, whether they pertain to information security or other types of risk, are a means of providing decision makers with information needed to understand factors that can negatively influence operations and outcomes and to make informed judgments concerning the extent of actions needed to reduce risk. As reliance on computer systems and electronic data has grown, information security risk has joined the array of risks that governments and businesses must manage. The U.S. General Accounting Office (GAO) has identified the basic elements of a risk-assessment process. Regardless of the types of risks being considered, all risk assessments generally include the following elements:

- Identifying threats, including such things as intruders, criminals, disgruntled employees, terrorists, and natural disasters, that could harm and, thus, adversely affect critical operations and assets
- Estimating the likelihood that such threats will materialize, based on historical information and the judgment of knowledgeable individuals
- Identifying and ranking the value, sensitivity, and criticality of the operations and assets that could be affected should a threat materialize in order to determine which operations and assets are the most important
- Estimating, for the most critical and sensitive assets and operations, the potential losses or damage that could occur if a threat materializes, including recovery costs
- Identifying cost-effective actions, including implementing new organizational policies and procedures as well as technical or physical controls, to mitigate or reduce the risk
- Documenting the results and developing an action plan

The GAO has further determined that reliably assessing information security risks can be more difficult than assessing other types of risks, because the data on the likelihood and costs associated with information security risk factors is often more limited and because risk factors are constantly changing. For example:

- Data is limited on risk factors, such as the likelihood of a sophisticated hacker attack and the costs of damage, loss, or disruption caused by events that exploit security weaknesses.
- Some costs, such as loss of customer confidence or disclosure of sensitive information, are inherently difficult to quantify.
- Although the cost of the hardware and software needed to strengthen controls may be known, it is often not possible to estimate precisely the related indirect costs, such as the possible loss of productivity that may result when new controls are implemented.
- Even if precise information were available, it would soon be out of date due to fast-paced changes in technology and factors such as improvements in tools available to would-be intruders.

10.2 Trusted individuals

It is likely that organizations that may need to use federal cybersystems will be held responsible for the trustworthiness of individuals who are assigned to interact electronically with the government. In addition, organizations will be required to provide training on security issues for individuals who are assigned to use government computers. The organizations most likely to be effected by such requirements are the following:

- Government contractors that participate in electronic data interchange, online acquisition, e-commerce, or other forms of electronic interaction with government entities
- Other government entities that participate in electronic data interchange or other forms of electronic interaction with government entities

This will require that electronic interaction with government entities have an audit trail. A record of user activity will need to be maintained and users will need to be identified and authenticated so that they can be held accountable for their actions. An audit trail in computer usage often results in the recording of the following functions:

- Type of event
- When the event occurred

- User ID associated with the event
- Program or command used to initiate the event
- Log-in attempts
- Password changes
- File creations, changes, or deletions

Audit trails are generally reviewed on a periodic basis. When anomalies are identified, they are reported to an appropriate supervisor for follow-up action. In addition, federal government policies generally require that audit files be stored in a locked room and kept for a period of three years.

It is advisable that employees in organizations that have some sort of formalized electronic interaction with the governments be asked to sign an agreement to safeguard sensitive data and to use computer systems properly. A typical agreement is shown in Figure 10.1.

In addition to a signed agreement from the employee, it is also advisable for there to be a warning banner on the systems being used by the employee that states the appropriate-use policy of the organization. A typical warning banner is shown in Figure 10.2.

It may also be advisable to seek, if it is not already required, an interconnection security agreement (ISA), which documents and formalizes the interconnection of two systems owned by two different organizations. An ISA establishes the requirements for data exchange between two organizations. It specifies the requirement, and, more specifically, the security safeguards for the systems being interconnected. It is then adjudicated and signed by the respective designated individuals from those two organizations. Areas covered by a typical ISA include the following:

- General information and a description of data
- Services offered or used
- Data sensitivity levels
- User community characteristics and locations
- Information-exchange security requirements
- Trusted-behavior expectations
- Formal security policies

Figure 10.1 *Sample agreement to safeguard information.*

AGREEMENT TO SAFEGUARD SENSITIVE INFORMATION

I, ______________________________, acknowledge that I have access to sensitive data maintained by (name of organization).

I agree that I will obtain, use, or disclose such data only in connection with the performance of my official duties solely for authorized purposes.

I agree to maintain the confidentiality of information in accordance with the federal regulations. (List regulations)

I understand that failure to safeguard sensitive data may result in the imposition of penalties, including fines, costs of prosecution, dismissal from office, discharge from employment, and imprisonment. (42 U.S.C. s.653 (1); 26 U.S.C. ss.7213, 7213A, 7431, 5 U.S.C. s.552a (i)).

If I observe any conditions that could cause said information to be compromised in any way, I understand that it is my responsibility to take action to safeguard (name of agency) data and report the incident to my manager.

I agree that my obligation to safeguard the confidentiality of data shall survive the termination of my employment with (name or organization).

ACKNOWLEDGES AND WITNESSED:

____

(Employee)(Date)

____

(Supervisor/Witness)(Date)

- Incident-reporting process
- Audit-trail responsibilities and process

10.3 Wireless security

NIST held a workshop on 802.11 Wireless LAN Security in Falls Church, Virginia, in December, 2002. The workshop comprised approximately 30 individuals from the U.S. federal government, the WiFi industry, and the security and academic communities. Participants included individuals from NIST, the NSA, the National Communication System (NCS), U.S. Secret Service (USSS), Boeing Corporation, Cisco Systems, Microsoft Corpora-

Figure 10.2 *Sample appropriate-use warning banner.*

```
********************************************************
WARNING
********************************************************
This system is for official use by authorized users. Accessing
and using this system constitutes consent to monitoring,
interception, retrieval, recording, reading, copying,
searching, or capturing and disclosure of any information as
to any information processed, stored, or manipulated within
the system, including but not limited to information stored
locally on the hard drive or other media in use with this unit
internally or externally (e.g., floppy disks, tapes, CD-ROMs,
PDAs, etc.) by law enforcement and other personnel in
conjunction with a report of improper or unauthorized use.
Unauthorized or improper use of this system is a violation of
federal law and may be prosecuted, resulting in criminal or
administrative penalties including fines and/or imprisonment.
If criminal activity is discovered, the information will be
provided to the appropriate law-enforcement officials.
Suspected access violations or rule infractions should be
reported to the division head, regional director, or the IT
security manager. The IT security manager can be reached at
(XXX) XXX-XXXX.
********************************************************
WARNING
********************************************************
```

tion, Intel Corporation, TruSecure, Agere Systems, Booz-Allen-Hamilton, Vigil Security, Virginia Polytechnic Institute, the University of Maryland, and the Burton Group. At the conclusion of the second day, the broad-based group of crossindustry and government attendees developed a high-level strategy for the industry that included the following:

- Analyze thoroughly and holistically the short-term solution, WiFi Protected Access (WPA), and develop implementation guidance to help consumers properly use it securely (NIST SP800-48).
- Launch an education campaign to encourage consumers to transition from the use of equipment based on the current Wired Equivalent Privacy (WEP) protocol and to inform them that the vision for the industry is the ubiquitous deployment of the more secure solution—Robust Security Networks (RSN).

- Develop better communications and interactions (perhaps through the use of a formal liaison relationship) between groups within the IEEE and the Internet Engineering Task Force (IETF) that are involved in developing security mechanisms for WiFi.
- Analyze the RSN solution to ensure that nothing in the architecture and codified in the IEEE specifications will preclude equipment embodying the technology from ultimately gaining Federal Information Processing Standard (FIPS)140-2 validation.
- Perform several activities related to the RSN solution, including (1) comprehensively analyzing all aspects of the security protocol, algorithms, and features, (2) identifying extant vulnerabilities based on the WiFi threat model, and (3) developing the necessary security improvements and driving these through the established IEEE standardization process.
- Locate financial resources to fund work, such as security review and security mechanism development, within several working groups involved in the standardization of back-end security protocols, equipment provisioning, and securely roaming.

The process developed by the Defense Information Systems Agency (DISA) for securing wireless devices will apply in some form to all private-sector organizations in which employees use government systems. Table 10.1 summarizes the DISA general standards for securing wireless devices.

Table 10.1 *General Standards for Securing Wireless Devices*

Standard
Ensure that all wireless systems are approved before the system is installed or used to transfer, receive, store, or process information. This applies to wireless local area network (WLAN) devices (access points, routers, bridges, switches, IDSs, firewalls, and laptops), wireless cellular and satellite telephones, PDAs, SMS devices, two-way pagers, and two-way e-mail devices.
Ensure that multifunctional wireless devices meet the security requirements for all functions. For example, both the cellular phone and PDA sections apply to devices combining the cellular phone and PDA functions. If there are conflicts between security requirements for each function, the most stringent requirement will be used. Multifunctional devices combined with cameras are also evaluated using the PDA section guidance.

Table 10.1 *General Standards for Securing Wireless Devices (continued)*

Standard
Ensure that wireless devices that connect directly or indirectly (hotsync) to the network are added to site system security authorization agreements (SSAAs).
Ensure that all wireless devices, particularly laptops, comply with applicable operating system STIGs. (As of spring 2003 there were no STIGs available for either the Palm or the Windows Pocket PC operating systems.)
Ensure that vendor-supported, approved, antivirus software is installed and configured in accordance with the Desktop Application STIG on all wireless devices, particularly laptops and PDAs, and kept up-to-date with the most recent virus definition tables. This applies to all wireless, handheld, or mobile devices.
Ensure that WLAN systems are compliant with overall network security architecture and appropriate enclave security requirements before they are installed.
Ensure that wireless devices that do not meet all wireless security requirements are not used to transfer, receive, store, or process information.
Ensure that password-protection mechanisms such as encryption will be placed on folders and files on all 802.11-enabled devices, if available.
Ensure that approved personal firewalls and IDSs will be implemented on each wireless client.
Ensure that infrared WLAN receivers and transmitters are turned off when not in use.
Ensure that WLAN network interface cards (NICs) that do not have the capability to disable peer-to-peer WLAN communications are not used.
Ensure that the SSID broadcast mode is disabled. WLAN access points that do not allow the SSID broadcast mode to be disabled will not be used.
Ensure that MAC address filtering is enabled at each access point.
Ensure that WLAN devices are not used to transfer, receive, store, or process classified information categorized as sensitive compartmented information (SCI) and top secret (TS).
Ensure that WLAN devices are not permitted in any sensitive compartmented information facility (SCIF), regardless of the classification or sensitivity level of the device.
Ensure that computers with embedded WLAN systems that cannot be removed by the user will not be used to transfer, receive, store, or process classified information.
For WLANs approved for processing secret or confidential information, ensure that the SecNet 11 or other NSA approved Type I network interface card is used.

Table 10.1 *General Standards for Securing Wireless Devices (continued)*

Standard
For WLANs approved for processing secret or confidential information, ensure that high-assurance PKI certificates will be used for authentication in compliance with policy. (SecNet 11 does not provide user identification and authentication.)
For WLANs approved for processing secret or confidential information, ensure that file-system encryption is used on all WLAN client devices with an NSA-approved Type 1 encryption software or technique.
Ensure that if the WLAN provides seamless roaming between access points (session persistence), the WLAN provides a session time-out capability. The session time-out will be set for 15 minutes or less, depending on local security policy.
Ensure that the WLAN access point is set to the lowest possible transmit power setting that will meet the required signal strength of the area serviced by the access point.
Ensure that a FIPS 140-1/2 compliant VPN (with 3DES or AES) will be used to secure the WLAN system.
Ensure that PKI certificates are used for identification and authentication of the user on unclassified WLAN systems.
Ensure that if a WLAN device is used to access to a network via the Internet through a public WLAN/Internet gateway (e.g., airport or hotel "hotspot"), the device must comply with requirements for PDA remote Internet access listed in the wireless checklist.
For internal enclave WLANs, the information assurance officer (IAO) will ensure that access points are logically placed in a screened subnetwork (DMZ) or virtual LAN (VLAN) and separated from the wired internal network.
Ensure that an IDS will be used to monitor the wireless network. An optional firewall may be used to filter WLAN communications, implement local access-control policies, or to enable remote management of the access point.
Ensure that HTTP, SNMP, and other management interfaces will be turned off after initial configuration.
Ensure that password access to the access point is enabled.
For sites with WLAN systems supporting joint operations, ensure that IPSec technology will be used to meet the FIPS 140-1/2 compliance requirement.
Ensure that only NSA-approved Type 1 cellular or satellite telephones will be used for classified voice or classified data wireless telephone transmissions. The classification level of information transmitted over the phone will not exceed the classification level approved for the phone.

10.4 Security for outsourcing and procurement

Organizations of all types may need to assist in improving security in government outsourcing and procurement by providing information as requested about contractors, equipment, software, and services. References for service providers will be essential to improving security and qualifying service providers and contractors.

In November 2001 the U.S. GAO released a report entitled "Leading Commercial Practices for Outsourcing of Services." The report focused on practices that were most critical, rather than the full set of practices that could be implemented. Commercial firms were asked to provide examples of how such critical practices are implemented. This information was used to develop an evaluation framework that could provide a basis for comparison and contrast between commercial and federal (DOD and civilian) IT acquisition practices. Among the practices included in the report were the following:

- Examine how IT will support business processes when evaluating sourcing strategies.
- Use third-party assistance with experience in a variety of sourcing arrangements when formulating a sourcing strategy.
- Incorporate lessons learned from peers who have engaged in similar sourcing decisions.
- Estimate the impact of the sourcing decision on the internal organization as well as the impact on enterprise alliances and relationships.
- Consider optimizing IT and business processes before deciding on a sourcing strategy.
- Benchmark and baseline productivity of internal services prior to making the final sourcing decision.
- Consider starting with a representative service or selective set of services to outsource balanced against economies of scale.
- Determine the business reasons for outsourcing IT. Leading organizations identified the following business reasons:
  - To expand the geographic reach of the organization without increasing internal resources for IT
  - To respond more quickly to business and industry changes by leveraging the experience of an external service provider

- To predict operating costs better by contracting for IT services using a standard unit of measure
- To reduce capital investments by shifting ownership of IT resources to external service providers
- To focus internal resources on core business competencies by transferring responsibility for IT services to external providers

In addition, it is important to clarify all of the needs of the outsourcing organization in a thorough contract. Practices identified by the GAO for contract administration include the following:

- Use performance requirements and service-level agreements (SLAs).
- Base performance requirements on business outcomes.
- Include measures that reflect end-user satisfaction as well as technical IT performance.
- Review and update performance requirements periodically.
- Require the provider to meet minimum performance in each category of service.
- Require the provider to achieve escalating performance standards at agreed-upon intervals.
- Incorporate sufficient flexibility so that minimum acceptable performance is adjusted as conditions change, as the provider becomes more adept at satisfying customer demands, and as improvement goals are achieved.
- Use SLAs to articulate clearly all aspects of performance, including management, processes, and requirements.
- Specify circumstances under which the provider is excused from performance levels mandated by master service agreements.
- Identify SLAs for which compensation is based, while additional ones may be defined to manage performance.

The contract must be flexible enough to adapt to changes in the business environment. It should include clauses for determining pricing structures, performing satisfaction surveys and using the results to redefine performance levels, terminating the contract, resolving disputes in a timely manner, and taking work away from the provider for nonperformance. The contract must also specify which laws govern security of the operation and the standards for security.

Numerous laws govern the use of government computers and networks. There are also many standards and policies that have been set by government organizations about the use of computers. In order to improve security in outsourced environments, it is essential that security policies be followed in the service organizations just as they would be in the government organization.

The Computer Security Acts of 1987 and 1988 declare that improving the security and privacy of sensitive information in federal computer systems is in the public interest and create a means for establishing minimum acceptable security practices for such systems. It assigns NIST responsibility for developing the standards and guidelines needed to assure the cost-effective security and privacy of sensitive information in federal computer systems. NIST draws on the technical advice and assistance (including work products) of the NSA, where appropriate.

Some of the more important laws, regulations, procedures, and policies are as follows:

Public Laws:

P.L. 73-416, Communications Act of 1934

P.L. 93-579, Privacy Act of 1974

P.L. 95-511, Foreign Intelligence Surveillance Act of 1978

P.L. 99-474, Computer Fraud and Abuse Act of 1986

P.L. 99-508, Electronic Communications Privacy Act of 1986

P.L. 100-235, Computer Security Act of 1987

P.L. 104-104, Telecommunications Act of 1996

P.L. 104-106, Information Technology Management Reform Act of 1996

P.L. 104-201, National Defense Authorization Act for Fiscal Year 1997

P.L. 104-231, Electronic Freedom of Information Act of 1996

P.L. 104-294, Title I, Economic Espionage Act of 1996

P.L. 104-294, Title II, National Infrastructure Protection Act of 1996

P.L. 105-220, Section 508 Accessibility, August 7, 1998

NIST FIPS:

FIPS 46-3, Data Encryption Standard (DES), 1999

FIPS 73, Guidelines for Security of Computer Applications, 1980

FIPS 87, Guidelines for Contingency Planning, 1981

FIPS 81, DES Modes of Operation, 1980/1981

FIPS 102, Guideline for Computer Security Certification and Accreditation, 1983

FIPS 112, Password Usage, 1985

FIPS 140-2, Security Requirements for Cryptographic Modules, 2001

FIPS 180-1, Secure Hash Standard (SHS), 1993

FIPS 186-2, Digital Signature Standard (DSS), 2000

NIST Special Publications:

(800) 12, *An Introduction to Computer Security: The NIST Handbook,* 1995

(800) 13, *Telecommunications Security Guidelines for Telecommunications Management Network,* 1995

(800) 14, *Generally Accepted Principles and Practices for Security Information Technology Systems,* 1996

(800) 16, *Information Technology Security Training Requirements: A Role- and Performance-Based Model,* 1998

(800) 18, *Guide for Developing Security Plans for Information Technology Systems,* 1998

(800) 21, *Guideline for Implementing Cryptography in the Federal Government,* 1999

(800) 23, *Guidelines to Federal Organizations on Security Assurance and Acquisition/Use of Tested/Evaluated Products,* 2000

(800) 24, *PBX Vulnerability Analysis: Finding Holes in Your PBX before Someone Else Does,* 2001

(800) 25, *Federal Agency Use of Public Key Technology for Digital Signatures and Authentication,* 2000

(800) 26, *Security Self-Assessment Guide for Information Technology Systems,* 2001

(800) 27, *Engineering Principles for Information Technology Security (A Baseline for Achieving Security),* 2001

(800) 31, *Intrusion Detection Systems (IDS),* 2001

(800) 32, *Introduction to Public Key Technology and the Federal PKI Infrastructure,* 2001

NSTISSC provides policies and instructions for IA for national security applications:

1, *National Policy on Application of Communications Security to U.S. Civil and Commercial Space Systems,* 1985

6, *National Policy on Certification and Accreditation of National Security Telecommunications and Information Systems,* 1994

7, *National Policy on Secure Electronic Messaging Services,* 1995

11, *National Policy Governing the Acquisition of Information Assurance (IA) and IA-Enabled IT Products,* 2000

100, *Confidential, National Policy on Application of Communications Security to Command Destruct Systems,* 1988

200, *National Policy on Controlled Access Protection,* 1987

501, *National Training Program for Information Systems Security (INFOSEC) Professionals,* 1992

502, *National Security Telecommunications and Automated Information Systems Security,* 1993

1000, *National Information Assurance Certification and Accreditation Process (NIACAP)*, 2000

4009, *National Information Systems Security Glossary,* 2000

4011, *National Training Standard for Information Systems Security (INFOSEC) Professionals,* 1994

4012, *National Training Standard for Designated Approving Authority (DAA)*, 1997

4013, *National Training Standard for System Administrators in Information Systems Security (INFOSEC)*, 1997

4014, *National Training Standard for Information Systems Security Officers (ISSO)*, 1997

4015, *National Training Standard for System Certifiers,* 2000

7000, *Confidential NOFORN, TEMPEST Countermeasures for Facilities,* 1993

10.5 Working with local government

State government support and coordination are essential for successfully implementing homeland security efforts. The list in Appendix B shows the contacts, addresses, phone numbers, and, where available, the Web sites for state-level homeland security offices. Several organizations of governments have provided research and assistance for state and local governments to work on homeland security initiatives and specifically cybersecurity.

The National Governors Association Center (NGAC) for Best Practices provides support to governors in responding to the challenges of homeland security leadership through technical assistance, policy research, and by facilitating their participation in national discussion and initiatives. Center activities focus on states' efforts to protect critical infrastructure; develop interoperable communications capabilities; and prepare for and respond to bioterrorism, agroterrorism, nuclear and radiological terrorism, and cyberterrorism impacting the government's ability to obtain, disseminate, and store essential information.

Interim Report of the Task Force on Protecting Democracy of the National Conference of State Legislatures, released in July 2002, makes several recommendations to state legislatures about cybersecurity, including the following:

- Require law-enforcement agencies to refocus security to include electronic threats as well as physical threats.
- Review and update your state laws and penalties regarding cyberterrorism.
- Conduct appropriate response exercises.
- Ensure appropriate and timely backup and maintenance of computer systems.
- Ensure that the legislature saves its electronic files outside a normal operating environment.
- Determine how classified information is shared in your state and who has access.

- Encourage universities and colleges to offer degrees or certificates in IA computer security.
- Establish computer emergency response teams (CERTs) in each state to respond to cyberattacks and assist with physical/intelligence technology vulnerability assessments.
- Establish university and college programs to supplement CERTs.
- Consider funding computer-crime units for state law-enforcement agencies, regional computer forensics labs, computer-investigative training for law-enforcement personnel, and state infrastructure protection centers.

The National Association of State Chief Information Officers (NASCIO) has established the NASCIO-DHS Interstate ISAC Information Sharing Program. All 50 states, the District of Columbia, and several of the U.S. territories are participating in the program. NASCIO also developed an enterprise architectural framework for government IS integration. The adaptive enterprise architecture is designed to support effectively the business of government, and it enables information sharing across traditional barriers, enhances governments' ability to deliver effective and timely citizen services, and supports agencies in their efforts to improve government functions.

The NASCIO Architecture Program and the Enterprise Architecture Development Tool Kit guides state and local government agencies in the definition, development, utilization, maintenance, and institutionalization of an enterprise architecture program. The NASCIO Architecture Working Group, comprising state, county, and federal CIOs and government and corporate architects, developed the NASCIO architecture framework and the explanatory document, the "Enterprise Architecture Development Tool Kit." As part of the architecture program, NASCIO continues to serve as a champion of the benefits of sound infrastructure and enterprise architecture. The NASCIO architectural framework is a nationally accepted foundation for IT architecture development.

10.6 Mobilizing organization resources for priority IV

Action Checklist Number 10 (see Table 10.2) shows which steps IT managers in all types of organizations can take to synchronize their efforts with those of the government to achieve the goals of securing governments' cyberspace. The next chapter focuses on developing greater national security and international cyberspace security cooperation.

Table 10.2 *Action Checklist Number 10*

Action Item	Status (e.g., Completed, Pending, or N/A)
Determine if the organization can or must provide direct assistance to the federal government in assessing threats and vulnerabilities.	
If the organization can or needs to work with the federal government on assessing threats and vulnerabilities, develop a plan to accomplish that work.	
Determine if the organization needs to address the goals and objectives regarding trusted individuals using government computer systems.	
If the organization needs to work on a trusted individual's program, develop a plan to implement the program, including the use of agreements to safeguard information and warning banners on computer systems.	
Determine if the organization needs to address the goals and objectives regarding wireless communications with government computer systems.	
If the organization needs to work on securing wireless communications, develop a security plan to implement the plan.	
Determine if the organization can or must provide direct assistance to the government in securing outsourcing or procurement operations.	
If the organization can or needs to work with the government on securing outsourcing or procurement operations, develop a plan to accomplish that work.	
Determine if the organization can or must provide direct or indirect assistance to the state government in assessing threats and vulnerabilities.	
If the organization can or needs to work with the state government on assessing threats and vulnerabilities, develop a plan to accomplish that work.	

Table 10.2 *Action Checklist Number 10 (continued)*

Action Item	Status (e.g., Completed, Pending, or N/A)
Determine if the organization can or must provide direct or indirect assistance to the local government in assessing threats and vulnerabilities.	
If the organization can or needs to work with the local government on assessing threats and vulnerabilities, develop a plan to accomplish that work.	

11

Global Cyberspace Security Cooperation

One aspect of the Internet that people have grasped slowly is that it reaches virtually around the world. That means people in far away places who do not like the United States for some reason or another have access to a potential means of wreaking havoc. To meet the goals of priority V and participate in developing greater national and international cyberspace security cooperation, an organization should take or be prepared to take the following steps:

- Help strengthen cyber-related counterintelligence efforts by providing the government with information about known activities that may be relevant to these efforts.
- Provide information to the government that can improve capabilities for attack attribution and coordination of response before, during, and after an incident.
- Assist the government to facilitate dialog and partnerships among international public and private sectors focused on protecting information infrastructures.
- Participate in the government's national and international watch-and-warning networks to detect and prevent cyberattacks as they emerge.
- Use influence to get other countries to accept the Council of Europe (CoE) Convention on Cybercrime.

11.1 Strengthen cyber-related counterintelligence efforts

Those organizations with offices or operations in several countries are in a unique position to provide assistance in the fight against cyberterrorism. Even though an organization's computers and networks located in the United States may not be attacked, it is entirely possible that the computers and networks located in other countries may be under attack or have been penetrated or damaged.

Organizations located in the United States that have had such experiences should strongly consider reporting this information to the FBI or other law-enforcement agencies. The following types of instances should be reported, because they may help in compiling profiles of potential hackers and terrorists:

- Systems intrusions and hacking incidents
- Theft of intellectual property or trade secrets
- Theft of computer-based business information
- Harassing e-mails
- Denial-of-service attacks
- Physical destruction of computers or networking equipment
- Theft of portable computing devices
- Repeated virus attacks that are unique to an environment or location
- Break-ins or destruction of physical facilities that house computers or network equipment

The FBI may not be able to help investigate specific crimes or even intervene with local law-enforcement authorities. However, such information can be helpful in mapping the frequency and types of incidents and can contribute to the formulation of warnings for other organizations operating in the same region or country. Reports can also be made to the FBI liaison at U.S. consulates and embassies in many locations around the world, including the following:

Europe

- Vienna, Austria

- Brussels, Belgium
- Copenhagen, Denmark
- London, England
- Tallinn, Estonia
- Paris, France
- Berlin, Germany
- Athens, Greece
- Rome, Italy
- Warsaw, Poland
- Moscow, Russia
- Madrid, Spain
- Bern, Switzerland
- Kiev, Ukraine

Africa

- Lagos, Nigeria
- Pretoria, South Africa

Asia/Pacific

- Canberra, Australia
- Hong Kong, China
- Tokyo, Japan
- Manila, Philippines
- Singapore, Singapore
- Bangkok, Thailand

Central Asia/Middle East

- Cairo, Egypt
- New Delhi, India
- Tel Aviv, Israel

- Almaty, Kazakhstan
- Islamabad, Pakistan
- Riyadh, Saudi Arabia
- Ankara, Turkey

Western Hemisphere

- Buenos Aires, Argentina
- Bridgetown, Barbados
- Brasilia, Brazil
- Ottawa, Canada
- Santiago, Chili
- Bogotá, Colombia
- Mexico City, Mexico
- Panama City, Panama
- Caracas, Venezuela

According to the FBI, it is also important to work to collect digital evidence in an organized fashion and to apply standard procedures to analyze that evidence and do so around the world. The Scientific Working Group on Digital Evidence (SWGDE) was established in February 1998 through a collaborative effort of the Federal Crime Laboratory Directors. SWGDE, as the United States–based component of standardization efforts conducted by the International Organization on Computer Evidence (IOCE), was charged with the development of crossdisciplinary guidelines and standards for the recovery, preservation, and examination of digital evidence, including audio, imaging, and electronic devices.

From a law-enforcement perspective, more of the information that serves as currency in the judicial process is being stored, transmitted, or processed in digital form. The connectivity resulting from a single world economy in which the companies providing goods and services are truly international has enabled criminals to act transjurisdictionally with ease. Consequently, a perpetrator may be brought to justice in one jurisdiction while the digital evidence required to prosecute the case successfully may reside only in other jurisdictions.

This situation requires that all countries have the ability to collect and preserve digital evidence for their own needs, as well as for the potential needs of other countries. Each jurisdiction has its own system of government and administration of justice, but in order for one country to protect itself and its citizens, it must be able to make use of evidence collected by other countries. Though it is not reasonable to expect all countries to know about and abide by the precise laws and rules of other countries, a means that will allow the exchange of evidence must be found. The following concepts and principles need to be applied in cybercrime investigations and the collection of digital evidence.

The acquisition of digital evidence begins when information or physical items are collected or stored for examination purposes. The term *evidence* implies that the collector of evidence is recognized by the courts. The process of collecting is also assumed to be a legal process and appropriate for rules of evidence in that locality. A data object or physical item only becomes evidence when so deemed by a law-enforcement official or designee.

In order to ensure that digital evidence is collected, preserved, examined, or transferred in a manner safeguarding the accuracy and reliability of the evidence, law-enforcement and forensic organizations must establish and maintain an effective quality system. Standard operating procedures (SOPs) are documented quality-control guidelines, which must be supported by proper case records and use broadly accepted procedures, equipment, and materials.

All agencies that seize or examine digital evidence must maintain an appropriate SOP document. All elements of an agency's policies and procedures concerning digital evidence must be clearly set forth in this SOP document, which must be issued under the agency's management authority. The use of SOPs is fundamental to both law enforcement and forensic science. Guidelines that are consistent with scientific and legal principles are essential to the acceptance of results and conclusions by courts and other agencies. The development and implementation of these SOPs must be under an agency's management authority.

Procedures used must be generally accepted in the field or supported by data gathered and recorded in a scientific manner. Because a variety of scientific procedures may validly be applied to a given problem, standards and criteria for assessing procedures need to remain flexible. The validity of a procedure may be established by demonstrating the accuracy and reliability of specific techniques. In the digital-evidence area, peer review of SOPs by other agencies may be useful.

The law-enforcement agency must maintain written copies of appropriate technical procedures. Procedures should set forth their purpose and appropriate application. Required elements such as hardware and software must be listed, and the proper steps for successful use should be listed or discussed. Any limitations in the use of the procedure or the use or interpretation of the results should be established. Personnel who use these procedures must be familiar with them and have them available for reference.

The law-enforcement agency must use hardware and software that is appropriate and effective for the seizure or examination procedure. Although many acceptable procedures may be used to perform a task, considerable variation among cases requires that personnel have the flexibility to exercise judgment in selecting a method appropriate to the problem. Hardware used in the seizure or examination of digital evidence should be in good operating condition and be tested to ensure that it operates correctly. Software must be tested to ensure that it produces reliable results for use in seizure or examination purposes.

All activity relating to the seizure, storage, examination, or transfer of digital evidence must be recorded in writing and be available for review and testimony. In general, documentation to support conclusions must be such that, in the absence of the originator, another competent person could evaluate what was done, interpret the data, and arrive at the same conclusions as the originator.

The requirement for evidence reliability necessitates a chain of custody for all items of evidence. Chain-of-custody documentation must be maintained for all digital evidence.

Case notes and records of observations must be of a permanent nature. Handwritten notes and observations must be in ink, not pencil, although pencil (including color) may be appropriate for diagrams or making tracings. Any corrections to notes must be made by an initialed, single strikeout; nothing in the handwritten information should be obliterated or erased. Notes and records should be authenticated by handwritten signatures, initials, digital signatures, or other marking systems.

Any action that has the potential to alter, damage, or destroy any aspect of original evidence must be performed by qualified persons in a forensically sound manner. As outlined in the preceding standards and criteria, evidence has value only if it can be shown to be accurate, reliable, and controlled. A quality forensic program consists of properly trained personnel and appropriate equipment, software, and procedures.

11.2 Improve attack attribution and response

One of the major goals of information collection and analysis is to improve capabilities for attack attribution and response before, during, and after an incident. In many cases this may require international cooperation between law-enforcement agencies, as well as government and private-sector organizations of all types. The FBI and NIPC have participated with international partners to investigate many cyberthreats during the last several years. The following examples were presented on the FBI Web site.

Evidence of the prevalence of computers as tools in crime is apparent in the case of the Phonemasters, an international ring of hackers who were able to gain access to major telephone networks, portions of the national power grid, air traffic–control systems, and numerous databases. This hacker ring provided calling card numbers, credit reports, criminal records, and other data to individuals in Canada, the United States, Switzerland, and Italy who willing to pay for the information.

The investigation of this case required the capture of Phonemasters' data communications under a Title III order and was successfully accomplished by collecting and analyzing the analog modem signals from the target phone lines. Phonemasters suspects Calvin Cantrell and Cory Lindsay were convicted in September 1999 for theft and possession of unauthorized access devices and unauthorized access to a federal-interest computer. Cantrell was sentenced to two years in prison while Lindsay received a sentence of 41 months.

Another example is the Solar Sunrise case, the code name for a multiagency investigation of intrusions into more than 500 military, civilian government, and private-sector computer systems in the United States during February and March 1998. The intrusions took place during the build-up of U.S. military personnel in the Middle East in response to tensions with Iraq over United Nations weapons inspections. The intruders penetrated at least 200 unclassified U.S. military computer systems, including seven air force bases and four navy installations; Department of Energy National Laboratories; NASA sites; and university sites. The timing of the intrusions and the fact that some activity appeared to come from an ISP in the Middle East led many U.S. military officials to suspect that this might be an instance of Iraqi information warfare.

The NIPC coordinated an extensive interagency investigation involving FBI field offices, the DOD, NASA, Defense Information Systems Agency, Air Force Office of Special Investigations, the DOJ, and the intelligence community. Internationally, NIPC worked closely with the Israeli law-enforcement authorities. Within several days, the investigation determined that two juveniles in Cloverdale, California, and individuals in Israel were the perpetrators. This case demonstrated the critical need for an interagency center to coordinate our investigative efforts to determine the source of such intrusions and the need for strong international cooperation. Israeli authorities are preparing to prosecute the chief defendant in their case in the summer of 2000.

Other cases demonstrate how much international cooperation has improved in this area. In February 2000, the NIPC received reports that CNN, Yahoo!, Amazon.com, eBay, and other e-commerce sites had been subject to distributed denial-of-service (DDOS) attacks. The NIPC had issued warnings in December 1999 about the possibility of such attacks and even created and released a tool that victims could use to detect whether their systems had been infiltrated by an attacker for use against other systems. When attacks did occur in February, companies cooperated with the NIPC and our National Infrastructure Protection and Computer Intrusion Squads in several FBI field offices (including Los Angeles and Atlanta) and provided critical logs and other information.

Within days, the FBI and NIPC had traced some of the attacks to Canada and subsequently worked with the Royal Canadian Mounted Police (RCMP) to identify the suspect. The RCMP arrested a juvenile subject in April 2000, and charges are expected to be brought shortly for at least some of the attacks. The unprecedented speed and scope of this investigation was evidence of the great improvement made in our ability to conduct large-scale, complex international investigations.

Another example involves the compromise between January and March 2000 of multiple e-commerce Web sites in the United States, Canada, Thailand, Japan, and the United Kingdom by a hacker known as Curador. Curador broke into the sites and apparently stole as many as 28,000 credit card numbers with losses estimated to be at least $3.5 million. Thousands of credit card numbers and expiration dates were posted to various Internet Web sites. After an extensive investigation, on March 23, 2000, the FBI assisted the Dyfed Powys (Wales, United Kingdom) Police Service in a search at the residence of Curador, whose real name is Raphael Gray. Mr. Gray, age 18, was arrested in the United Kingdom, along with a coconspirator, under the United Kingdom's Computer Misuse Act of 1990.

11.3 Partnerships among international public and private sectors

The IOCE was established in 1995 to provide international law-enforcement agencies a forum for the exchange of information concerning computer crime investigation and other computer-related forensic issues. Comprised of accredited government agencies involved in computer-forensic investigations, IOCE identifies and discusses issues of interest to its constituents, facilitates the international dissemination of information, and develops recommendations for consideration by its member agencies.

In addition to formulating computer evidence standards, IOCE develops communications services between member agencies and holds conferences geared toward the establishment of working relationships.

In response to the G-8 Communiqué and Action plans of 1997, IOCE was tasked with the development of international standards for the exchange and recovery of electronic evidence. Working groups in Canada, Europe, the United Kingdom, and the United States have been formed to address this standardization of computer evidence.

During the International Hi-Tech Crime and Forensics Conference (IHCFC) of October 1999, the IOCE held meetings and a workshop that reviewed the United Kingdom Good Practice Guide and the SWGDE draft standards. The working group proposed the following principles, which were voted upon by the IOCE delegates present with unanimous approval.

The international principles developed by IOCE for the standardized recovery of computer-based evidence are governed by the following attributes:

- Consistency with all legal systems
- Allowance for the use of a common language
- Durability
- Ability to cross international boundaries
- Ability to instill confidence in the integrity of evidence
- Applicability to all forensic evidence
- Applicability at every level, including that of individual, agency, and country

These principles were presented and approved at the IHCFC in October 1999. They are as follows:

- Upon the seizure of digital evidence, actions taken should not change that evidence.
- When it is necessary for a person to access original digital evidence, that person must be forensically competent.
- All activity relating to the seizure, access, storage, or transfer of digital evidence must be fully documented, preserved, and available for review.
- An individual is responsible for all actions taken with respect to digital evidence while the digital evidence is in that person's possession.
- Any agency that is responsible for seizing, accessing, storing, or transferring digital evidence is responsible for compliance with these principles.

Other items recommended by IOCE for further debate or facilitation include the following:

- Forensic competency and the need to generate agreement on international accreditation and the validation of tools, techniques, and training
- Issues relating to practices and procedures for the examination of digital evidence
- The sharing of information relating to hi-tech crime and forensic computing, such as events, tools, and techniques

During the last three years, the NIPC worked with its international partners on several fronts to address computer crime and cyberterrorism issues. This included outreach activities designed to raise awareness about the cyberthreat, encouraging countries to address the threat through substantive legislation and provide advice on how to organize to deal with the threat most effectively. Almost weekly the NIPC hosted a foreign delegation to discuss topics ranging from current cases to the establishment of NIPC-like entities in other countries. Since the NIPC was founded, Japan, the United Kingdom, Canada, Germany, and Sweden have formed or are in the process of forming interagency entities similar to the NIPC. The NIPC has briefed visitors from the United Kingdom, Germany, France, Norway, Canada, Japan, Denmark, Sweden, Israel, and other nations over the past year.

In order to help make foreign partners more capable to assist international investigations and to address cybercrime within their own countries, the NIPC also provided training to investigators from several countries. Much of this training took place at the International Law Enforcement Academies in Budapest, Hungary, and Bangkok, Thailand. In addition, a small number of select international investigators received training in NIPC-sponsored classes in the United States. The NIPC also held workshops with other countries to share information on techniques and trends in cyberintrusions. In September 1999 the NIPC sponsored an International Cyber Crime Conference in New Orleans, Louisiana, to provide training to international law-enforcement officers and forge links between foreign law-enforcement officers and personnel.

11.4 Watch-and-warning networks

It is important that all organizations that are part of the critical infrastructure participate in the government's national and international watch-and-warning networks to detect and prevent cyberattacks as they emerge. The federal government, particularly the intelligence and law-enforcement communities, play a significant role in providing, coordinating, and ensuring that threat information is understood across all levels of government.

In addition, it is recognized that state and local law enforcement, as well as private-sector security entities, are valuable sources of localized threat information. These organizations possess a better understanding of the vulnerabilities impacting their facilities, systems, and functions than does the federal government. Development of accepted and efficient processes and systems for communication and the exchange of crucial security-related information is critical to improve homeland security.

Information sharing and warning systems are discussed in Chapter 1 and Chapter 4, along with steps that IT managers should take to participate in those systems. Chapter 7 covers participation in a national response system.

11.5 CoE Convention on Cybercrime

It is an important aspect of international law and the ability to address computer crime and computer terrorism that a wide range of countries accept the CoE Convention on Cybercrime. It is advisable that each organization that has operations in any country that is a signatory of the convention become familiar with the articles of the convention and analyze how they impact IT policies, procedures, and operations.

The CoE (www.coe.int) consists of 41 member states, including all of the members of the European Union. Since the late 1980s, the CoE has been working to address growing international concern over the threats posed by hacking and other computer-related crimes. In 1989, it published a study and recommendations addressing the need for new substantive laws criminalizing certain conduct committed through computer networks. This was followed by a second study, published in 1995, which contained principles concerning the adequacy of criminal procedural laws in this area. Starting with the principles developed in the 1989 and 1995 reports, in 1997 the CoE established a Committee of Experts on Crime in Cyberspace (PC-CY) to begin drafting a binding convention to facilitate international cooperation in the investigation and prosecution of computer crimes.

The United States was invited to participate as an observer in both the 1989 and 1995 recommendations, as well as in the development of the Convention on Cyber Crime. The United States, represented by the DOJ and the DOS, in close consultation with other government agencies, has actively participated in the negotiations in both the drafting and plenary sessions, working closely with both CoE and non-CoE member states.

The convention breaks new ground by being the first multilateral agreement drafted specifically to address the problems posed by the international nature of computer crime. Although we believe the vast bulk of the obligations and powers contemplated by the draft convention are already provided for under U.S. law, the convention makes progress in this area by:

- Requiring signatory countries to establish certain substantive offenses in the area of computer crime
- Requiring parties to adopt domestic procedural laws to investigate computer crimes
- Providing a solid basis for international law-enforcement cooperation in combating crime committed through computer systems

The articles of the CoE Convention on Cybercrime read as follows:

Article 1: Definitions

For the purposes of this Convention:

a. “computer system” means any device or a group of interconnected or related devices, one or more of which, pursuant to a program, performs automatic processing of data;

b. “computer data” means any representation of facts, information, or concepts in a form suitable for processing in a computer system, including a program suitable to cause a computer system to perform a function;

c. “service provider” means:

i. any public or private entity that provides to users of its service the ability to communicate by means of a computer system, and

ii. any other entity that processes or stores computer data on behalf of such communication service or users of such service.

d. “traffic data” means any computer data relating to a communication by means of a computer system, generated by a computer system that formed a part in the chain of communication, indicating the communication’s origin, destination, route, time, date, size, duration, or type of underlying service.

Article 2: Illegal access

Each Party shall adopt such legislative and other measures as may be necessary to establish as criminal offenses under its domestic law, when committed intentionally, the access to the whole or any part of a computer system without right. A Party may require that the offense be committed by infringing security measures, with the intent of obtaining computer data or other dishonest intent, or in relation to a computer system that is connected to another computer system.

Article 3: Illegal interception

Each Party shall adopt such legislative and other measures as may be necessary to establish as criminal offenses under its domestic law, when committed intentionally, the interception without right, made by technical means, of nonpublic transmissions of computer data to, from, or within a computer system, including electromagnetic emissions from a computer system carrying such computer data. A Party may require that the offense be committed with dishonest intent, or in relation to a computer system that is connected to another computer system.

Article 4: Data interference

1. Each Party shall adopt such legislative and other measures as may be necessary to establish as criminal offenses under its domestic law, when committed intentionally, the damaging, deletion, deterioration, alteration, or suppression of computer data without right.

2. A Party may reserve the right to require that the conduct described in paragraph 1 result in serious harm.

Article 5: System interference

Each Party shall adopt such legislative and other measures as may be necessary to establish as criminal offenses under its domestic law, when committed intentionally, the serious hindering without right of the functioning of a computer system by inputting, transmitting, damaging, deleting, deteriorating, altering, or suppressing computer data.

Article 6: Misuse of devices

1. Each Party shall adopt such legislative and other measures as may be necessary to establish as criminal offenses under its domestic law, when committed intentionally and without right:

a. the production, sale, procurement for use, import, distribution, or otherwise making available of:

i. a device, including a computer program, designed or adapted primarily for the purpose of committing any of the offenses established in accordance with Articles 2–5;

ii. a computer password, access code, or similar data by which the whole or any part of a computer system is capable of being accessed with intent that it be used for the purpose of committing any of the offenses established in Articles 2–5; and

b. the possession of an item referred to in paragraphs (a)(1) or (2) above, with intent that it be used for the purpose of committing any of the offences established in Articles 2–5. A Party may require by law that a number of such items be possessed before criminal liability attaches.

2. This article shall not be interpreted as imposing criminal liability where the production, sale, procurement for use, import, distribution, or otherwise making available or possession referred to in paragraph 1 of this Article is not for the purpose of committing an offense established in accordance with Articles 2–5 of this Convention, such as for the authorized testing or protection of a computer system.

3. Each Party may reserve the right not to apply paragraph 1 of this Article, provided that the reservation does not concern the sale, distribution, or otherwise making available of the items referred to in paragraphs 1(a) or (2).

Article 7: Computer-related forgery

Each Party shall adopt such legislative and other measures as may be necessary to establish as criminal offenses under its domestic law, when committed intentionally and without right, the input, alteration, deletion, or suppression of computer data, resulting in inauthentic data with the intent that it be considered or acted upon for legal purposes as if it were authentic, regardless of whether or not the data is directly readable and intelligible. A Party may require an intent to defraud, or similar dishonest intent, before criminal liability attaches.

Article 8: Computer-related fraud

Each Party shall adopt such legislative and other measures as may be necessary to establish as criminal offenses under its domestic law, when committed intentionally and without right, the causing of a loss of property to another by:

a. any input, alteration, deletion, or suppression of computer data,

b. any interference with the functioning of a computer system, with fraudulent or dishonest intent of procuring, without right, an economic benefit for oneself or for another.

Article 9: Offenses related to child pornography

1. Each Party shall adopt such legislative and other measures as may be necessary to establish as criminal offenses under its domestic law, when committed intentionally and without right, the following conduct:

a. producing child pornography for the purpose of its distribution through a computer system;

b. offering or making available child pornography through a computer system;

c. distributing or transmitting child pornography through a computer system;

d. procuring child pornography through a computer system for oneself or for another;

e. possessing child pornography in a computer system or on a computer-data storage medium.

2. For the purpose of paragraph 1 above "child pornography" shall include pornographic material that visually depicts:

a. a minor engaged in sexually explicit conduct;

b. a person appearing to be a minor engaged in sexually explicit conduct;

c. realistic images representing a minor engaged in sexually explicit conduct.

3. For the purpose of paragraph 2 above, the term "minor" shall include all persons under 18 years of age. A Party may, however, require a lower age limit, which shall be not less than 16 years.

4. Each Party may reserve the right not to apply, in whole or in part, paragraphs 1(d) and 1(e), and 2(b) and 2(c).

Article 10: Offenses related to infringements of copyright and related rights

1. Each Party shall adopt such legislative and other measures as may be necessary to establish as criminal offenses under its domestic law the infringement of copyright, as defined under the law of that Party pursuant to the obligations it has undertaken under the Paris Act of 24 July 1971 of the Bern Convention for the Protection of Literary and Artistic Works, the Agreement on Trade-Related Aspects of Intellectual Property Rights and the WIPO Copyright Treaty, with the exception of any moral rights conferred by such Conventions, where such acts are committed willfully, on a commercial scale and by means of a computer system.

2. Each Party shall adopt such legislative and other measures as may be necessary to establish as criminal offenses under its domestic law the infringement of related rights, as defined under the law of that Party, pursuant to the obligations it has undertaken under the International Convention for the Protection of Performers, Producers of Phonograms

and Broadcasting Organizations done in Rome (Rome Convention), the Agreement on Trade-Related Aspects of Intellectual Property Rights and the WIPO Performances and Phonograms Treaty, with the exception of any moral rights conferred by such Conventions, where such acts are committed willfully, on a commercial scale and by means of a computer system.

3. A Party may reserve the right not to impose criminal liability under paragraphs 1 and 2 of this Article in limited circumstances, provided that other effective remedies are available and that such reservation does not derogate from the Party's international obligations set forth in the international instruments referred to in paragraphs 1 and 2 of this Article.

Article 11: Attempt and aiding or abetting

1. Each Party shall adopt such legislative and other measures as may be necessary to establish as criminal offences under its domestic law, when committed intentionally, aiding or abetting the commission of any of the offenses established in accordance with Articles 2–10 of the present Convention with intent that such offence be committed.

2. Each Party shall adopt such legislative and other measures as may be necessary to establish as criminal offenses under its domestic law, when committed intentionally, an attempt to commit any of the offenses established in accordance with Articles 3 through 5, 7, 8, 9 (1)a, and 9 (1)c of this Convention.

3. Each Party may reserve the right not to apply, in whole or in part, paragraph 2 of this Article.

Article 12: Corporate liability

1. Each Party shall adopt such legislative and other measures as may be necessary to ensure that a legal person can be held liable for a criminal offense established in accordance with this Convention, committed for its benefit by any natural person, acting either individually or as part of an organ of the legal person, who has a leading position within the legal person, based on:

a. a power of representation of the legal person;

b. an authority to take decisions on behalf of the legal person;

c. an authority to exercise control within the legal person.

2. Apart from the cases already provided for in paragraph 1, each Party shall take the measures necessary to ensure that a legal person can be held liable where the lack of supervision or control by a natural person referred to in paragraph 1 has made possible the commission of a criminal offence established in accordance with this Convention for the benefit of that legal person by a natural person acting under its authority.

3. Subject to the legal principles of the Party, the liability of a legal person may be criminal, civil, or administrative.

4. Such liability shall be without prejudice to the criminal liability of the natural persons who have committed the offense.

Article 13: Sanctions and measures

1. Each Party shall adopt such legislative and other measures as may be necessary to ensure that the criminal offenses established in accordance with Articles 2–11 are punishable by effective, proportionate, and dissuasive sanctions, which include deprivation of liberty.

2. Each Party shall ensure that legal persons held liable in accordance with Article 12 shall be subject to effective, proportionate and dissuasive criminal or noncriminal sanctions or measures, including monetary sanctions.

Article 14: Scope of procedural provisions

1. Each Party shall adopt such legislative and other measures as may be necessary to establish the powers and procedures provided for in this Section for the purpose of specific criminal investigations or proceedings.

2. Except as specifically otherwise provided in Article 21, each Party shall apply the powers and procedures referred to in paragraph 1 to:

a. the criminal offenses established in accordance with Articles 2–11 of this Convention;

b. other criminal offenses committed by means of a computer system; and

c. the collection of evidence in electronic form of a criminal offense.

3. a. Each Party may reserve the right to apply the measures referred to in Article 20 only to offenses or categories of offenses specified in the reservation, provided that the range of such offenses or categories of offenses is not more restricted than the range of offenses to which it applies the measures referred to in Article 21. Each Party shall consider restricting

such a reservation to enable the broadest application of the measure referred to in Article 20.

b. Where a Party, due to limitations in its legislation in force at the time of the adoption of the present Convention, is not able to apply the measures referred to in Articles 20 and 21 to communications being transmitted within a computer system of a service provider, which system

i. is being operated for the benefit of a closed group of users, and

ii. does not employ public communications networks and is not connected with another computer system, whether public or private, that Party may reserve the right not to apply these measures to such communications. Each Party shall consider restricting such a reservation to enable the broadest application of the measures referred to in Articles 20 and 21.

Article 15: Conditions and safeguards

1. Each Party shall ensure that the establishment, implementation, and application of the powers and procedures provided for in this Section are subject to conditions and safeguards provided for under its domestic law, which shall provide for the adequate protection of human rights and liberties, including rights arising pursuant to obligations it has undertaken under the 1950 Council of Europe Convention for the Protection of Human Rights and Fundamental Freedoms, the 1966 United Nations International Covenant on Civil and Political Rights, and other applicable international human rights instruments, and which shall incorporate the principle of proportionality.

2. Such conditions and safeguards shall, as appropriate in view of the nature of the power or procedure concerned, inter alia, include judicial or other independent supervision, grounds justifying application, and limitation on the scope and the duration of such power or procedure.

3. To the extent that it is consistent with the public interest, in particular the sound administration of justice, a Party shall consider the impact of the powers and procedures in this Section upon the rights, responsibilities, and legitimate interests of third parties.

Article 16: Expedited preservation of stored computer data

1. Each Party shall adopt such legislative and other measures as may be necessary to enable its competent authorities to order or similarly obtain

the expeditious preservation of specified computer data, including traffic data, that has been stored by means of a computer system, in particular where there are grounds to believe that the computer data is particularly vulnerable to loss or modification.

2. Where a Party gives effect to paragraph 1 above by means of an order to a person to preserve specified stored computer data in the person's possession or control, the Party shall adopt such legislative and other measures as may be necessary to oblige that person to preserve and maintain the integrity of that computer data for a period of time as long as necessary, up to a maximum of 90 days, to enable the competent authorities to seek its disclosure. A Party may provide for such an order to be subsequently renewed.

3. Each Party shall adopt such legislative or other measures as may be necessary to oblige the custodian or other person who is to preserve the computer data to keep confidential the undertaking of such procedures for the period of time provided for by its domestic law.

4. The powers and procedures referred to in this Article shall be subject to Articles 14 and 15.

Article 17: Expedited preservation and partial disclosure of traffic data

1. Each Party shall adopt, in respect of traffic data that is to be preserved under Article 16, such legislative and other measures as may be necessary to:

a. ensure that such expeditious preservation of traffic data is available regardless of whether one or more service providers were involved in the transmission of that communication; and

b. ensure the expeditious disclosure to the Party's competent authority, or a person designated by that authority, of a sufficient amount of traffic data to enable the Party to identify the service providers and the path through which the communication was transmitted.

2. The powers and procedures referred to in this Article shall be subject to Articles 14 and 15.

Article 18: Production order

1. Each Party shall adopt such legislative and other measures as may be necessary to empower its competent authorities to order:

a. a person in its territory to submit specified computer data in that person's possession or control, which is stored in a computer system or a computer-data storage medium; and

b. a service provider offering its services in the territory of the Party to submit subscriber information relating to such services in that service provider's possession or control;

2. The powers and procedures referred to in this Article shall be subject to Articles 14 and 15.

3. For the purpose of this Article, "subscriber information" means any information, contained in the form of computer data or any other form, that is held by a service provider, relating to subscribers of its services, other than traffic or content data, by which can be established:

a. the type of the communication service used, the technical provisions taken thereto, and the period of service;

b. the subscriber's identity, postal or geographic address, telephone and other access number, billing and payment information, available on the basis of the service agreement or arrangement;

c. any other information on the site of the installation of communication equipment available on the basis of the service agreement or arrangement.

Article 19: Search and seizure of stored computer data

1. Each Party shall adopt such legislative and other measures as may be necessary to empower its competent authorities to search or similarly access:

a. a computer system or part of it and computer data stored therein; and

b. computer-data storage medium in which computer data may be stored in its territory.

2. Each Party shall adopt such legislative and other measures as may be necessary to ensure that where its authorities search or similarly access a specific computer system or part of it, pursuant to paragraph 1(a), and have grounds to believe that the data sought is stored in another computer system or part of it in its territory, and such data is lawfully accessible from or available to the initial system, such authorities shall be able to expeditiously extend the search or similar accessing to the other system.

3. Each Party shall adopt such legislative and other measures as may be necessary to empower its competent authorities to seize or similarly secure

computer data accessed according to paragraphs 1 or 2. These measures shall include the power to :

a. seize or similarly secure a computer system or part of it or a computer-data storage medium;

b. make and retain a copy of those computer data;

c. maintain the integrity of the relevant stored computer data; and

d. render inaccessible or remove those computer data in the accessed computer system.

4. Each Party shall adopt such legislative and other measures as may be necessary to empower its competent authorities to order any person who has knowledge about the functioning of the computer system or measures applied to protect the computer data therein to provide, as is reasonable, the necessary information to enable the undertaking of the measures referred to in paragraphs 1 and 2.

5. The powers and procedures referred to in this Article shall be subject to Articles 14 and 15.

Article 20: Real-time collection of traffic data

1. Each Party shall adopt such legislative and other measures as may be necessary to empower its competent authorities to:

a. collect or record through application of technical means on the territory of that Party, and

b. compel a service provider, within its existing technical capability, to:

i. collect or record through application of technical means on the territory of that Party, or

ii. cooperate and assist the competent authorities in the collection or recording of, traffic data, in real-time, associated with specified communications in its territory transmitted by means of a computer system.

2. Where a Party, due to the established principles of its domestic legal system, cannot adopt the measures referred to in paragraph 1(a), it may instead adopt legislative and other measures as may be necessary to ensure the real-time collection or recording of traffic data associated with specified communications in its territory through application of technical means on that territory.

3. Each Party shall adopt such legislative and other measures as may be necessary to oblige a service provider to keep confidential the fact of and any information about the execution of any power provided for in this Article.

4. The powers and procedures referred to in this Article shall be subject to Articles 14 and 15.

Article 21: Interception of content data

1. Each Party shall adopt such legislative and other measures as may be necessary, in relation to a range of serious offenses to be determined by domestic law, to empower its competent authorities to:

a. collect or record through application of technical means on the territory of that Party, and

b. compel a service provider, within its existing technical capability, to:

i. collect or record through application of technical means on the territory of that Party, or

ii. cooperate and assist the competent authorities in the collection or recording of content data, in real time, of specified communications in its territory transmitted by means of a computer system.

2. Where a Party, due to the established principles of its domestic legal system, cannot adopt the measures referred to in paragraph 1(a), it may instead adopt legislative and other measures as may be necessary to ensure the real-time collection or recording of content data of specified communications in its territory through application of technical means on that territory.

3. Each Party shall adopt such legislative and other measures as may be necessary to oblige a service provider to keep confidential the fact of and any information about the execution of any power provided for in this Article.

4. The powers and procedures referred to in this Article shall be subject to Articles 14 and 15.

Article 22: Jurisdiction

1. Each Party shall adopt such legislative and other measures as may be necessary to establish jurisdiction over any offense established in accordance with Articles 2–11 of this Convention, when the offense is committed :

a. in its territory; or

b. on board a ship flying the flag of that Party; or

c. on board an aircraft registered under the laws of that Party; or

d. by one of its nationals, if the offense is punishable under criminal law where it was committed or if the offense is committed outside the territorial jurisdiction of any State.

2. Each Party may reserve the right not to apply or to apply only in specific cases or conditions the jurisdiction rules laid down in paragraphs (1)b–(1)d of this Article or any part thereof.

3. Each Party shall adopt such measures as may be necessary to establish jurisdiction over the offenses referred to in Article 24, paragraph (1) of this Convention, in cases where an alleged offender is present in its territory and it does not extradite him/her to another Party, solely on the basis of his/her nationality, after a request for extradition.

4. This Convention does not exclude any criminal jurisdiction exercised in accordance with domestic law.

5. When more than one Party claims jurisdiction over an alleged offense established in accordance with this Convention, the Parties involved shall, where appropriate, consult with a view to determining the most appropriate jurisdiction for prosecution.

Article 23: General principles relating to international cooperation

The Parties shall cooperate with each other, in accordance with the provisions of this chapter, and through application of relevant international instruments on international cooperation in criminal matters, arrangements agreed on the basis of uniform or reciprocal legislation, and domestic laws, to the widest extent possible for the purposes of investigations or proceedings concerning criminal offenses related to computer systems and data, or for the collection of evidence in electronic form of a criminal offense.

Article 24: Extradition

1. a. This article applies to extradition between Parties for the criminal offenses established in accordance with Articles 2–11 of this Convention, provided that they are punishable under the laws of both Parties concerned

by deprivation of liberty for a maximum period of at least one year, or by a more severe penalty.

b. Where a different minimum penalty is to be applied under an arrangement agreed on the basis of uniform or reciprocal legislation or an extradition treaty, including the European Convention on Extradition (ETS No. 24), applicable between two or more parties, the minimum penalty provided for under such arrangement or treaty shall apply.

2. The criminal offenses described in paragraph 1 of this Article shall be deemed to be included as extraditable offences in any extradition treaty existing between or among the Parties. The Parties undertake to include such offenses as extraditable offenses in any extradition treaty to be concluded between or among them.

3. If a Party that makes extradition conditional on the existence of a treaty receives a request for extradition from another Party with which it does not have an extradition treaty, it may consider this Convention as the legal basis for extradition with respect to any criminal offence referred to in paragraph 1 of this Article.

4. Parties that do not make extradition conditional on the existence of a treaty shall recognize the criminal offences referred to in paragraph 1 of this Article as extraditable offenses between themselves.

5. Extradition shall be subject to the conditions provided for by the law of the requested Party or by applicable extradition treaties, including the grounds on which the requested Party may refuse extradition.

6. If extradition for a criminal offence referred to in paragraph 1 of this Article is refused solely on the basis of the nationality of the person sought, or because the requested Party deems that it has jurisdiction over the offense, the requested Party shall submit the case at the request of the requesting Party to its competent authorities for the purpose of prosecution and shall report the final outcome to the requesting Party in due course. Those authorities shall take their decision and conduct their investigations and proceedings in the same manner as in the case of any other offense of a comparable nature under the law of that Party.

7. a. Each Party shall, at the time of signature or when depositing its instrument of ratification, acceptance, approval, or accession, communicate to the Secretary General of the Council of Europe the name and addresses of each authority responsible for the making to or receipt of a request for extradition or provisional arrest in the absence of a treaty.

b. The Secretary General of the Council of Europe shall set up and keep updated a register of authorities so designated by the Parties. Each Party shall ensure that the details held on the register are correct at all times.

Article 25: General principles relating to mutual assistance

1. The Parties shall afford one another mutual assistance to the widest extent possible for the purpose of investigations or proceedings concerning criminal offenses related to computer systems and data, or for the collection of evidence in electronic form of a criminal offense.

2. Each Party shall also adopt such legislative and other measures as may be necessary to carry out the obligations set forth in Articles 27–35.

3. Each Party may, in urgent circumstances, make requests for mutual assistance or communications related thereto by expedited means of communications, including fax or e-mail, to the extent that such means provide appropriate levels of security and authentication (including the use of encryption, where necessary), with formal confirmation to follow, where required by the requested Party. The requested Party shall accept and respond to the request by any such expedited means of communication.

4. Except as otherwise specifically provided in Articles in this Chapter, mutual assistance shall be subject to the conditions provided for by the law of the requested Party or by applicable mutual assistance treaties, including the grounds on which the requested Party may refuse cooperation. The requested Party shall not exercise the right to refuse mutual assistance in relation to the offenses referred to in Articles 2–11 solely on the ground that the request concerns an offense which it considers a fiscal offense.

5. Where, in accordance with the provisions of this chapter, the requested Party is permitted to make mutual assistance conditional upon the existence of dual criminality, that condition shall be deemed fulfilled, irrespective of whether its laws place the offense within the same category of offence or denominates the offense by the same terminology as the requesting Party, if the conduct underlying the offense for which assistance is sought is a criminal offense under its laws.

Article 26: Spontaneous information

1. A Party may, within the limits of its domestic law, without prior request, forward to another Party information obtained within the framework of its own investigations when it considers that the disclosure of such

information might assist the receiving Party in initiating or carrying out investigations or proceedings concerning criminal offenses established in accordance with this Convention or might lead to a request for co-operation by that Party under this chapter.

2. Prior to providing such information, the providing Party may request that it be kept confidential or used subject to conditions. If the receiving Party cannot comply with such request, it shall notify the providing Party, which shall then determine whether the information should nevertheless be provided. If the receiving Party accepts the information subject to the conditions, it shall be bound by them.

Article 27: Procedures pertaining to mutual assistance requests in the absence of applicable international agreements

1. Where there is no mutual assistance treaty or arrangement on the basis of uniform or reciprocal legislation in force between the requesting and requested Parties, the provisions of paragraphs 2–9 of this Article shall apply. The provisions of this article shall not apply where such treaty, arrangement, or legislation is available, unless the Parties concerned agree to apply any or all of the remainder of this Article in lieu thereof.

2. a. Each Party shall designate a central authority or authorities that shall be responsible for sending and answering requests for mutual assistance, the execution of such requests, or the transmission of them to the authorities competent for their execution.

b. The central authorities shall communicate directly with each other.

c. Each Party shall, at the time of signature or when depositing its instrument of ratification, acceptance, approval, or accession, communicate to the Secretary General of the Council of Europe the names and addresses of the authorities designated in pursuance of this paragraph.

d. The Secretary General of the Council of Europe shall set up and keep updated a register of central authorities so designated by the Parties. Each Party shall ensure that the details held on the register are correct at all times.

3. Mutual assistance requests under this Article shall be executed in accordance with the procedures specified by the requesting Party except where incompatible with the law of the requested Party.

4. The requested Party may, in addition to grounds for refusal available under Article 25, paragraph (4), refuse assistance if:

a. the request concerns an offense which the requested Party considers a political offense or an offense connected with a political offense; or

b. it considers that execution of the request is likely to prejudice its sovereignty, security, ordre public, or other essential interests.

5. The requested Party may postpone action on a request if such action would prejudice criminal investigations or proceedings conducted by its authorities.

6. Before refusing or postponing assistance, the requested Party shall, where appropriate after having consulted with the requesting Party, consider whether the request may be granted partially or subject to such conditions as it deems necessary.

7. The requested Party shall promptly inform the requesting Party of the outcome of the execution of a request for assistance. If the request is refused or postponed, reasons shall be given for the refusal or postponement. The requested Party shall also inform the requesting Party of any reasons that render impossible the execution of the request or are likely to delay it significantly.

8. The requesting Party may request that the requested Party keep confidential the fact and substance of any request made under this Chapter except to the extent necessary to execute the request. If the requested Party cannot comply with the request for confidentiality, it shall promptly inform the requesting Party, which shall then determine whether the request should nevertheless be executed.

9. a. In the event of urgency, requests for mutual assistance or communications related thereto may be sent directly by judicial authorities of the requesting Party to such authorities of the requested Party. In any such cases a copy shall be sent at the same time to the central authority of the requested Party through the central authority of the requesting Party.

b. Any request or communication under this paragraph may be made through the International Criminal Police Organization (Interpol).

c. Where a request is made pursuant to subparagraph (a) and the authority is not competent to deal with the request, it shall refer the request to the competent national authority and inform directly the requesting Party that it has done so.

d. Requests or communications made under this paragraph that do not involve coercive action may be directly transmitted by the competent authorities of the requesting Party to the competent authorities of the requested Party.

e. Each Party may, at the time of signature or when depositing its instrument of ratification, acceptance, approval or accession inform the Secretary General of the Council of Europe that, for reasons of efficiency, requests made under this paragraph are to be addressed to its central authority.

Article 28: Confidentiality and limitation on use

1. When there is no mutual assistance treaty or arrangement on the basis of uniform or reciprocal legislation in force between the requesting and the requested Parties, the provisions of this Article shall apply. The provisions of this article shall not apply where such treaty, arrangement, or legislation is available unless the Parties concerned agree to apply any or all of the remainder of this Article in lieu thereof.

2. The requested Party may make the furnishing of information or material in response to a request dependent on the condition that it is:

a. kept confidential where the request for mutual legal assistance could not be complied with in the absence of such condition, or

b. not used for investigations or proceedings other than those stated in the request.

3. If the requesting Party cannot comply with a condition referred to in paragraph 2, it shall promptly inform the other Party, which shall then determine whether the information is nevertheless provided. When the requesting Party accepts the condition, it shall be bound by it.

4. Any Party that furnishes information or material subject to a condition referred to in paragraph 2 may require the other Party to explain, in relation to that condition, the use made of such information or material.

Article 29: Expedited preservation of stored computer data

1. A Party may request another Party to order or otherwise obtain the expeditious preservation of data stored by means of a computer system, which is located within the territory of that other Party and in respect of which the requesting Party intends to submit a request for mutual assistance for the search or similar access, seizure or similar securing, or disclosure of the data.

2. A request for preservation made under paragraph 1 shall specify:

a. the authority that is seeking the preservation;

b. the offense that is the subject of a criminal investigation or proceeding and a brief summary of related facts;

c. the stored computer data to be preserved and its relationship to the offense;

d. any available information to identify the custodian of the stored computer data or the location of the computer system;

e. the necessity of the preservation; and

f. that the Party intends to submit a request for mutual assistance for the search or similar access, seizure or similar securing, or disclosure of the stored computer data.

3. Upon receiving the request from another Party, the requested Party shall take all appropriate measures to preserve expeditiously the specified data in accordance with its domestic law. For the purposes of responding to a request, dual criminality shall not be required as a condition to providing such preservation.

4. A Party that requires dual criminality as a condition for responding to a request for mutual assistance for the search or similar access, seizure or similar securing, or disclosure of the data may, in respect of offenses other than those established in accordance with Articles 2–11 of this Convention, reserve the right to refuse the request for preservation under this Article in cases where it has reason to believe that at the time of disclosure the condition of dual criminality cannot be fulfilled.

5. In addition, a request for preservation may only be refused if :

a. the request concerns an offense which the requested Party considers a political offense or an offense connected with a political offense; or

b. the requested Party considers that execution of the request is likely to prejudice its sovereignty, security, ordre public, or other essential interests.

6. Where the requested Party believes that preservation will not ensure the future availability of the data or will threaten the confidentiality of, or otherwise prejudice the requesting Party's investigation, it shall promptly so inform the requesting Party, which shall then determine whether the request should nevertheless be executed.

7. Any preservation effected in response to the request referred to in paragraph 1 shall be for a period not less than 60 days in order to enable the requesting Party to submit a request for the search or similar access, seizure or similar securing, or disclosure of the data. Following the receipt of such

request, the data shall continue to be preserved pending a decision on that request.

Article 30: Expedited disclosure of preserved traffic data

1. Where, in the course of the execution of a request made under Article 29 to preserve traffic data concerning a specific communication, the requested Party discovers that a service provider in another State was involved in the transmission of the communication, the requested Party shall expeditiously disclose to the requesting Party a sufficient amount of traffic data in order to identify that service provider and the path through which the communication was transmitted.

2. Disclosure of traffic data under paragraph 1 may only be withheld if :

a. the request concerns an offense which the requested Party considers a political offense or an offense connected with a political offense; or

b. the requested Party considers that execution of the request is likely to prejudice its sovereignty, security, ordre public, or other essential interests.

Article 31: Mutual assistance regarding accessing of stored computer data

1. A Party may request another Party to search or similarly access, seize or similarly secure, and disclose data stored by means of a computer system located within the territory of the requested Party, including data that has been preserved pursuant to Article 29.

2. The requested Party shall respond to the request through application of international instruments, arrangements, and laws referred to in Article 23, and in accordance with other relevant provisions of this Chapter.

3. The request shall be responded to on an expedited basis where:

a. there are grounds to believe that relevant data is particularly vulnerable to loss or modification; or

b. the instruments, arrangements, and laws referred to in paragraph 2 otherwise provide for expedited cooperation.

Article 32: Transborder access to stored computer data with consent or where publicly available

A Party may, without obtaining the authorization of another Party:

a. access publicly available (open source) stored computer data, regardless of where the data is located geographically; or

b. access or receive, through a computer system in its territory, stored computer data located in another Party, if the Party obtains the lawful and voluntary consent of the person who has the lawful authority to disclose the data to the Party through that computer system.

Article 33: Mutual assistance regarding the real-time collection of traffic data

1. The Parties shall provide mutual assistance to each other with respect to the real-time collection of traffic data associated with specified communications in its territory transmitted by means of a computer system. Subject to paragraph 2, assistance shall be governed by the conditions and procedures provided for under domestic law.

2. Each Party shall provide such assistance at least with respect to criminal offenses for which real-time collection of traffic data would be available in a similar domestic case.

Article 34: Mutual assistance regarding the interception of content data

The Parties shall provide mutual assistance to each other with respect to the real-time collection or recording of content data of specified communications transmitted by means of a computer system to the extent permitted by their applicable treaties and domestic laws.

Article 35: 24/7 Network

1. Each Party shall designate a point of contact available on a 24 hour, 7 day per week basis in order to ensure the provision of immediate assistance for the purpose of investigations or proceedings concerning criminal offenses related to computer systems and data, or for the collection of evidence in electronic form of a criminal offense. Such assistance shall include facilitating, or, if permitted by its domestic law and practice, directly carrying out:

a. provision of technical advice;

b. preservation of data pursuant to Articles 29 and 30; and

c. collection of evidence, giving of legal information, and locating of suspects.

2. a. A Party's point of contact shall have the capacity to carry out communications with the point of contact of another Party on an expedited basis.

b. If the point of contact designated by a Party is not part of that Party's authority or authorities responsible for international mutual assistance or extradition, the point of contact shall ensure that it is able to co-ordinate with such authority or authorities on an expedited basis.

3. Each Party shall ensure that trained and equipped personnel are available in order to facilitate the operation of the network.

Article 36: Signature and entry into force

1. This Convention shall be open for signature by the member States of the Council of Europe and by nonmember States which have participated in its elaboration.

2. This Convention is subject to ratification, acceptance, or approval. Instruments of ratification, acceptance, or approval shall be deposited with the Secretary General of the Council of Europe.

3. This Convention shall enter into force on the first day of the month following the expiration of a period of three months after the date on which five States, including at least three member States of the Council of Europe, have expressed their consent to be bound by the Convention in accordance with the provisions of paragraphs 1 and 2.

4. In respect of any signatory State which subsequently expresses its consent to be bound by it, the Convention shall enter into force on the first day of the month following the expiration of a period of three months after the date of the expression of its consent to be bound by the Convention in accordance with the provisions of paragraphs 1 and 2.

Article 37: Accession to the Convention

1. After the entry into force of this Convention, the Committee of Ministers of the Council of Europe, after consulting with and obtaining the unanimous consent of the Contracting States to the Convention, may invite any State not a member of the Council and which has not participated in its elaboration to accede to this Convention. The decision shall be taken by the majority provided for in Article 20(d) of the Statute of the Council of Europe and by the unanimous vote of the representatives of the Contracting States entitled to sit on the Committee of Ministers.

2. In respect of any State acceding to the Convention under paragraph 1 above, the Convention shall enter into force on the first day of the month following the expiration of a period of three months after the date of deposit of the instrument of accession with the Secretary General of the Council of Europe.

Article 38: Territorial application

1. Any State may, at the time of signature or when depositing its instrument of ratification, acceptance, approval, or accession, specify the territory or territories to which this Convention shall apply.

2. Any State may, at any later date, by a declaration addressed to the Secretary General of the Council of Europe, extend the application of this Convention to any other territory specified in the declaration. In respect of such territory the Convention shall enter into force on the first day of the month following the expiration of a period of three months after the date of receipt of the declaration by the Secretary General.

3. Any declaration made under the two preceding paragraphs may, in respect of any territory specified in such declaration, be withdrawn by a notification addressed to the Secretary General of the Council of Europe. The withdrawal shall become effective on the first day of the month following the expiration of a period of three months after the date of receipt of such notification by the Secretary General.

Article 39: Effects of the Convention

1. The purpose of the present Convention is to supplement applicable multilateral or bilateral treaties or arrangements as between the Parties, including the provisions of:

- the European Convention on Extradition opened for signature in Paris on 13 December 1957 (ETS No. 24);
- the European Convention on Mutual Assistance in Criminal Matters opened for signature in Strasbourg on 20 April 1959 (ETS No. 30);
- the Additional Protocol to the European Convention on Mutual Assistance in Criminal Matters opened for signature in Strasbourg on 17 March 1978 (ETS No. 99).

2. If two or more Parties have already concluded an agreement or treaty on the matters dealt with in this Convention or otherwise have established their relations on such matters, or should they in future do so, they shall

also be entitled to apply that agreement or treaty or to regulate those relations accordingly. However, where Parties establish their relations in respect of the matters dealt with in the present convention other than as regulated therein, they shall do so in a manner that is not inconsistent with the Convention's objectives and principles.

3. Nothing in this Convention shall affect other rights, restrictions, obligations, and responsibilities of a Party.

Article 40: Declarations

By a written notification addressed to the Secretary General of the Council of Europe, any State may, at the time of signature or when depositing its instrument of ratification, acceptance, approval, or accession, declare that it avails itself of the possibility of requiring additional elements as provided for under Article 2, Article 3, Article 6, paragraph 1(b), Article 7, Article 9, paragraph 3, and Article 27, paragraph 9(e).

Article 41: Federal clause

1. A federal State may reserve the right to assume obligations under Chapter II of this Convention consistent with its fundamental principles governing the relationship between its central government and constituent States or other similar territorial entities provided that it is still able to co-operate under Chapter III.

2. When making a reservation under paragraph 1, a federal State may not apply the terms of such reservation to exclude or substantially diminish its obligations to provide for measures set forth in Chapter II. Overall, it shall provide for a broad and effective law-enforcement capability with respect to those measures.

3. With regard to the provisions of this Convention, the application of which comes under the jurisdiction of constituent States or other similar territorial entities, that are not obliged by the constitutional system of the federation to take legislative measures, the federal government shall inform the competent authorities of such States of the said provisions with its favorable opinion, encouraging them to take appropriate action to give them effect.

Article 42: Reservations

By a written notification addressed to the Secretary General of the Council of Europe, any State may, at the time of signature or when depositing its instrument of ratification, acceptance, approval, or accession, declare that it avails itself of the reservation(s) provided for in Article 4, paragraph 2, Article 6, paragraph 3, Article 9, paragraph 4, Article 10, paragraph 3, Article 11, paragraph 3, Article 14, paragraph 3, Article 22, paragraph 2, Article 29, paragraph 4, and Article 41, paragraph 1. No other reservation may be made.

Article 43: Status and withdrawal of reservations

1. A Party that has made a reservation in accordance with Article 42 may wholly or partially withdraw it by means of a notification addressed to the Secretary General. Such withdrawal shall take effect on the date of receipt of such notification by the Secretary General. If the notification states that the withdrawal of a reservation is to take effect on a date specified therein, and such date is later than the date on which the notification is received by the Secretary General, the withdrawal shall take effect on such a later date.

2. A Party that has made a reservation as referred to in Article 42 shall withdraw such reservation, in whole or in part, as soon as circumstances so permit.

3. The Secretary General of the Council of Europe may periodically enquire with Parties that have made one or more reservations as referred to in Article 42 as to the prospects for withdrawing such reservation(s).

Article 44: Amendments

1. Amendments to this Convention may be proposed by any Party, and shall be communicated by the Secretary General of the Council of Europe to the member States of the Council of Europe, to the nonmember States which have participated in the elaboration of this Convention as well as to any State which has acceded to, or has been invited to accede to, this Convention in accordance with the provisions of Article 37.

2. Any amendment proposed by a Party shall be communicated to the European Committee on Crime Problems (CDPC), which shall submit to the Committee of Ministers its opinion on that proposed amendment.

3. The Committee of Ministers shall consider the proposed amendment and the opinion submitted by the European Committee on Crime

Problems (CDPC) and, following consultation with the nonmember State Parties to this Convention, may adopt the amendment.

4. The text of any amendment adopted by the Committee of Ministers in accordance with paragraph 3 of this Article shall be forwarded to the Parties for acceptance.

5. Any amendment adopted in accordance with paragraph 3 of this Article shall come into force on the thirtieth day after all Parties have informed the Secretary General of their acceptance thereof.

Article 45: Settlement of disputes

1. The European Committee on Crime Problems (CDPC) shall be kept informed regarding the interpretation and application of this Convention.

2. In case of a dispute between Parties as to the interpretation or application of this Convention, they shall seek a settlement of the dispute through negotiation or any other peaceful means of their choice, including submission of the dispute to the European Committee on Crime Problems (CDPC), to an arbitral tribunal whose decisions shall be binding upon the Parties, or to the International Court of Justice, as agreed upon by the Parties concerned.

Article 46: Consultations of the Parties

1. The Parties shall, as appropriate, consult periodically with a view to facilitating:

a. the effective use and implementation of this Convention, including the identification of any problems thereof, as well as the effects of any declaration or reservation made under this Convention;

b. the exchange of information on significant legal, policy, or technological developments pertaining to cybercrime and the collection of evidence in electronic form;

c. consideration of possible supplementation or amendment of the Convention.

2. The European Committee on Crime Problems (CDPC) shall be kept periodically informed regarding the result of consultations referred to in paragraph 1.

3. The European Committee on Crime Problems (CDPC) shall, as appropriate, facilitate the consultations referred to in paragraph 1 and take

the measures necessary to assist the Parties in their efforts to supplement or amend the Convention. At the latest three years after the present Convention enters into force, the European Committee on Crime Problems (CDPC) shall, in cooperation with the Parties, conduct a review of all of the Convention's provisions and, if necessary, recommend any appropriate amendments.

4. Except where assumed by the Council of Europe, expenses incurred in carrying out the provisions of paragraph 1 shall be borne by the Parties in the manner to be determined by them.

5. The Parties shall be assisted by the Secretariat of the Council of Europe in carrying out their functions pursuant to this Article.

Article 47: Denunciation

1. Any Party may, at any time, denounce this Convention by means of a notification addressed to the Secretary General of the Council of Europe.

2. Such denunciation shall become effective on the first day of the month following the expiration of a period of three months after the date of receipt of the notification by the Secretary General.

Article 48: Notification

The Secretary General of the Council of Europe shall notify the member States of the Council of Europe, the nonmember States which have participated in the elaboration of this Convention, as well as any State which has acceded to, or has been invited to accede to, this Convention of:

a. any signature;

b. the deposit of any instrument of ratification, acceptance, approval or accession;

c. any date of entry into force of this Convention in accordance with Articles 36 and 37;

d. any declaration made under Article 40 or reservation made in accordance with Article 42;

e. any other act, notification or communication relating to this Convention.

11.6 Mobilizing organization resources for priority V

Action Checklist Number 11 (see Table 11.1) shows which steps IT managers in all types of organizations can take to synchronize their efforts with those of the government to develop greater national security and international cyberspace-security cooperation. The next chapter focuses on the future of homeland security.

Table 11.1 *Action Checklist Number 11*

Action Item	Status (e.g., Completed, Pending, or N/A)
Determine if computers or networks that are owned or operated by the organization located in other countries are or have been under attack.	
If computers or networks that are owned or operated by the organization located in other countries are or have been under attack, develop a reporting mechanism to alert authorities in the United States of these occurrences.	
Develop a policy and procedure, to assist in attack attribution and response and modify the computer-incident response plan accordingly.	
Determine if the organization has operations in any country that is a signatory of the CoE Convention on Cybercrime and analyze how that may impact IT policies, procedures, and operations.	
Devise plans to influence countries in which the organization has operations and that are not signatories of the CoE Convention on Cybercrime to become signatories.	

12

Moving into the Future

The future of homeland security initiatives remains uncertain. As presidents come and go and the perspectives of the U.S. Congress sway back and forth, so will the approach to homeland security. It is doubtful that terrorism will cease. It has yet to be seen how active terrorists will become in the United States and how often they will strike. If historic patterns hold true, then a major incident can be expected every three to five years.

This chapter examines what law-enforcement agencies have been asked to do by the Joint Intelligence Committee of the U.S. Congress, as well as some of the successes that the government has had in the fight against terrorism. This will help provide insight into the direction that the U.S. government will be taking in dealing with terrorism.

In addition, a road map for implementing homeland security initiatives for enterprise IT is provided. The projects and tasks from the action checklists in each chapter are broken out into three groups. The first concerns what needs to be accomplished at the enterprise level, the second what needs to be accomplished in the IT department, and the third, those things that specifically need to be accomplished by the IT and network security units.

12.1 The perspective of law enforcement

On July 24, 2003, the final report of the Joint Intelligence Committee investigation into the September 11, 2001, terrorist attacks was released. The committee recommended that the FBI, as well as other law-enforcement agencies, should:

- Consider prevention of terrorist attacks as the FBI's number one priority.

- Improve information sharing within the intelligence community through the TTIC.
- Improve coordination between the NSA, FBI, and CIA.
- Improve technology to target terrorists and identify terrorist threats better.
- Establish an Office of Intelligence.
- Increase the number of resources allocated to counterterrorism analysis.
- Improve information sharing with state and local law enforcement
- Establish the national JTTF.
- Expand recruitment of vital language skills.
- Increase efforts to infiltrate terrorist organizations operating in the United States.
- Improve counterterrorism training.
- Have stronger accountability.

The Counter-Terrorism Training Coordination Working Group convened by the U.S. DOJ's Office of Justice Programs works to examine the counterterrorism tools available to law enforcement and first-responder communities. Recognizing that sharing information is essential to the coordination of efforts to support state and local counterterrorism training, the Counter-Terrorism Training and Resources for Law Enforcement Web site was created.

The Web site serves as a single point of access to counterterrorism training opportunities and related materials available across the federal government and from private and nonprofit organizations. Working group participants include the following:

- Bureau of Justice Assistance
- Executive Office for U.S. Attorneys
- FBI
- Federal Emergency Management Agency (FEMA)
- Federal Law Enforcement Training Center
- National Institute of Justice

- Office for Domestic Preparedness
- Office of Community-Oriented Policing Services
- Department of Homeland Security
- Office of Justice Programs
- Office of the Police Corps and Law Enforcement Education
- U.S. Army Military Police School
- U.S. Customs Service
- U.S. Department of Labor

On July 31, 2003, John S. Pistole, deputy assistant director of the Counterterrorism Division of the FBI testified before the Senate Committee on Governmental Affairs. Pistole stated that identifying, tracking, and dismantling the financial structure supporting terrorist groups is critical to dismantling the organizations successfully and preventing future terrorist attacks. As is the case in most investigations, locating and following the money plays a critical role in identifying those involved in the criminal activity, establishing links among them, and developing evidence of their involvement in the activity.

The Terrorist Financing Operations Section (TFOS) of the FBI is both an operational and coordinating entity with proactive and reactive responsibilities. As a coordinating entity, the TFOS is responsible for ensuring that a unified approach is pursued in investigating terrorist financing networks. The TFOS achieves this directive by:

- Coordinating the financial aspects of FBI field office and Legat terrorism investigation
- Establishing overall initiatives, policy, and guidance on terrorist-financing matters
- Participating in the National Security Council's Policy Coordinating Committee (PCC) on Terrorist Financing
- Coordinating national liaison with the financial services sector
- Cooperating in and coordinating criminal terrorist-financing investigations with the DOJ
- Providing support and training to field offices to include the designated terrorism financing coordinator (TFC)

The FBI, working in coordination with other agencies of the U.S. government, has participated in numerous cases involving the funding of terrorism, including the following:

- An FBI joint terrorism task force in Charlotte, North Carolina, used racketeering statutes to obtain convictions that disrupted and dismantled a Hizballah procurement and fundraising cell. Twenty-six individuals were arrested for crimes including immigration fraud, visa fraud, cigarette smuggling, interstate transportation of stolen property, fraud, bank fraud, bribery, money laundering, racketeering, and providing material support to a terrorist organization.
- The FBI coordinated with the Office of Foreign Asset Control (OFAC) to justify the blocking of Holy Land Foundation for Relief and Development (HLF) assets and the closing of its U.S. offices, shutting down HAMAS's largest fundraising entity in the United States. The HLF had been linked to the funding of HAMAS terrorist activities, and in 2000, HLF raised $13 million.
- Offices of the Benevolence International Foundation (BIF), a U.S.-based charity, were shut down and its assets and records blocked following an OFAC and FBI investigation that determined that the charity was being used to funnel money to al Qaida. In February 2003, Enaam Arnaout, the head of BIF, pled guilty to racketeering conspiracy, admitting he fraudulently obtained charitable donations in order to provide financial assistance to persons engaged in violent activities overseas.

As a result of information developed by the FBI, a foreign security service, in conjunction with U.S. intelligence community agencies, apprehended one of the most significant money launderers associated with Osama bin Laden for funneling $67 million through international accounts to al Qaida and the Taliban.

A criminal case against Sami Al-Arian, the alleged U.S. leader of the Palestinian Islamic Jihad (PIJ), and the World Islamic Studies Enterprise has forced the closure of several front companies suspected of funneling money to support PIJ operations against Israel. In August 2002, the investigation led to the deportation of Mazen Al-Najjar, the brother-in-law of Sami Al-Arian and a known PIJ member. In February, following a 50-count indictment for RICO and material support of terrorism violations, the FBI arrested Al-Arian and three other U.S.-based members of the PIJ, including

Sameeh Hammoudeh, Hatim Naji Fariz, and Ghassan Ballout. The FBI also executed seven search warrants associated with this action.

TFOS has provided this operational support in the al Qaida sleeper cell cases in Buffalo, New York, and Portland, Oregon, as well as in the Richard Reid, John Walker Lindh, Jose Padilla, Al Haramain, PIJ, and Mohamed Almoayad cases, among many others. This type of operational support has also been provided to divisions investigating NGOs, such as the HLF, BIF, and the Global Relief Foundation.

TFOS has engaged in extensive coordination with authorities of numerous foreign governments in terrorist-financing matters, leading to joint investigative efforts throughout the world. These joint investigations have successfully targeted the financing of several overseas al Qaida cells, including those located in Indonesia, Malaysia, Singapore, Spain, and Italy. Furthermore, with the assistance of relationships established with the central banks of several strategic countries, successful disruptions of al Qaida financing have been accomplished in counties such as the United Arab Emirates, Pakistan, Afghanistan, and Indonesia.

The FBI conducted a detailed financial investigation/analysis of the 19 hijackers and their support network following the September 11, 2001, attacks. This investigation initially identified the al Qaida funding sources of the 19 hijackers in the United Arab Emirates and Germany. The financial investigation also provided the first links between Ramzi Binalshibh and the 9/11 operation.

A continuing investigation, in coordination with the PENTTBOMB Team, has traced the origin of the funding of 9/11 back to financial accounts in Pakistan, where high-ranking and well-known al Qaida operatives played a major role in moving the money forward, eventually into the hands of the hijackers located in the United States.

As part of the 9/11 financial investigation, thousands of individuals and organizations were investigated in the United States and abroad to determine whether they played any part in supporting the hijackers or the operation. Although the vast majority of these individuals and organizations was cleared, this process of elimination resulted in numerous other quality terrorism investigations being initiated, as well as criminal charges against hundreds of individuals for fraud and other criminal activity.

At the request of a foreign liaison service, TFOS traced financial transactions in a near real-time manner that led to the location of a terrorist cell and prevention of a terrorist act.

Since 9/11, the United States has frozen $36.3 million in terrorist assets, while other countries have frozen an estimated $97 million, for a total of over $133 million.

U.S. authorities issued blocking orders on the assets of 281 terrorists, terrorist organizations, and terrorist supporters, effectively denying them access to the U.S. financial system.

Federal law-enforcement officials have arrested over 61 individuals, indicted 43, and convicted 12 in connection with terrorist-financing investigations.

U.S. government agencies, which include the FBI's TFOS, deployed trainers and advisors on missions to countries around the world to assist with the drafting of legislation to combat terrorist financing, strengthen bank supervision in identifying suspicious transactions, and address other financial crimes and corruption.

Since 9/11, over 120 countries have introduced new terrorist-related legislation, and approximately 80 countries established Financial Investigation Units.

12.2 The homeland security road map for IT

The way organizations approach implementing homeland security initiatives in enterprise IT varies by both the size of the organization and the industry sector in which the organization operates. As a guide for managers responsible for implementation, the action checklists from each chapter have been compiled into the following three lists (see Tables 12.1–12.3):

1. The Enterprise Action Checklist shows those action items that are of enterprisewide concern. The IT department or function will need to participate in executing most of those actions items but will work in conjunction with many other departments or corporate officers. The departments involved are indicated for each action item. When the term *security* is used, it means the corporate or enterprise security department, rather than the IT security function, unless they are within the same functional unit.
2. The IT Management Action Checklist shows those action items that are of primary concern or are the primary responsibility of the IT department. It is probable that the IT department will take the lead role in the activity, but when appropriate, the

involvement of other departments is indicated. When the term *security* is used it means the corporate or enterprise security department, rather than the IT security function, unless they are within the same functional unit.

3. The IT Security Action Checklist shows those action items that are of primary concern or are the primary responsibility of the IT security unit. It is probable that the IT security unit will take the lead role in the activity, but, when appropriate, the involvement of other departments is indicated. When the term *security* is used, it means the corporate or enterprise security department, rather than the IT security function, unless they are within the same functional unit.

Table 12.1 *Enterprise Action Checklist*

Action Item	Chapter and Item	Departments Involved
Determine if the organization has taken a position on homeland security.	1-1	CEO, IT, legal counsel, business units
Evaluate what actions the organization needs to take if the threat level is raised by the government.	1-5	CEO, security, IT, business units
Determine the status of implementation of DRPs and what related training has been achieved.	2-5	CEO, HR, IT, disaster recovery, contingency management, business units
Determine the status of implementation of plans for the management of data privacy and what related training has been achieved.	2-8	CEO, HR, business units, privacy management
Conduct a structured threat assessment to determine if the organization is a component of the critical national infrastructure.	3-1	CEO, security, IT, legal counsel, business units
Conduct a structured threat assessment to determine the level of dependency on components of the critical national infrastructure.	3-2	CEO, security, IT, business units
Conduct a structured threat assessment to determine the proximity of the organization's facilities to facilities or structures that are components of the critical national infrastructure.	3-3	CEO, security, IT, business units
Initiate a security improvement process.	3-4	CEO, HR, security, business units
Develop procedures for reporting computer-related incidents.	4-2	CEO, IT, legal counsel

Table 12.1 *Enterprise Action Checklist (continued)*

Action Item	Chapter and Item	Departments Involved
Assign staff responsibilities for reporting computer-related incidents.	4-3	CEO, IT, legal counsel
Evaluate security initiatives for sectors in which the organization has operations.	5-1	CEO, IT, security, business units
Assess organizational plans to meet security needs.	5-2	CEO, IT, security, business units
Evaluate the methods by which the organization communicates and conducts business transactions with suppliers.	6-1	CFO, IT, business units
Determine the vulnerabilities in the systems used to work with suppliers and develop an action plan to improve security in those systems.	6-2	CFO, IT, business units, security
Evaluate the methods by which the organization communicates and conducts business transactions with customers.	6-3	CFO, IT, business units
Determine the vulnerabilities in the systems used to work with customers and develop an action plan to improve security in those systems.	6-4	CFO, IT, business units, security
Evaluate the methods by which the organization communicates and conducts business transactions with service providers.	6-5	CFO, IT, business units
Determine the vulnerabilities in the systems used to work with service providers and develop an action plan to improve security in those systems.	6-6	CFO, IT, business units, security
Determine if the organization's view of the health of cyberspace is influenced by political, economic, or business issues that could impact IT policies and computer-incident response plans.	7-5	CFO, IT, business units, security
Determine if DRPs are up-to-date and if any changes or updates need to be made to the plans.	7-7	IT, disaster recovery, contingency management, business units
Determine if there are opportunities to work with local law-enforcement agencies on joint training exercises.	8-2	CEO, PR, disaster recovery, business units
Evaluate the physical security of computer and network facilities to determine if it meets minimum standards or customary standards for the industry sector; modify physical security procedures as necessary.	8-9	IT, business units, security

Table 12.1 *Enterprise Action Checklist (continued)*

Action Item	Chapter and Item	Departments Involved
Determine if the organization wants to make recommendations for priorities in cybersecurity research.	8-10	CEO, IT, legal counsel
Determine if the organization can or must provide direct assistance to the federal government in assessing threats and vulnerabilities.	10-1	IT, business units, security, legal counsel
If the organization can or needs to work with the federal government on assessing threats and vulnerabilities, develop a plan to accomplish that work.	10-2	IT, business units, security,
Determine if the organization needs to address the goals and objectives regarding trusted individuals using government computer systems.	10-3	IT, business units, security, legal counsel
If the organization needs to work on a trusted individual's program, develop a plan to implement the program, including the use of agreements to safeguard information and warning banners on computer systems.	10-4	IT, business units, security, legal counsel
Determine if the organization can or must provide direct assistance to the government in securing outsourcing or procurement operations.	10-7	IT, business units, security, legal counsel
If the organization can or needs to work with the government on securing outsourcing or procurement operations, develop a plan to accomplish that work.	10-8	IT, business units, security
Determine if the organization can or must provide direct or indirect assistance to the state government in assessing threats and vulnerabilities.	10-9	IT, business units, security, legal counsel
If the organization can or needs to work with the state government on assessing threats and vulnerabilities, develop a plan to accomplish that work.	10-10	IT, business units, security
Determine if the organization can or must provide direct or indirect assistance to the local government in assessing threats and vulnerabilities.	10-11	IT, business units, security, legal counsel
If the organization can or needs to work with the local government on assessing threats and vulnerabilities, develop a plan to accomplish that work.	10-12	IT, business units, security
Determine if the organization has operations in any country that is a signatory of the CoE Convention on Cybercrime and analyze how that may impact IT policies, procedures, and operations.	11-4	CEO, IT, legal counsel, business units

Table 12.1 *Enterprise Action Checklist (continued)*

Action Item	Chapter and Item	Departments Involved
Devise plans to influence countries in which the organization has operations and that are not signatories of the CoE Convention on Cybercrime to become signatories.	11-5	CEO, IT, legal counsel, business units

Table 12.2 *IT Management Action Checklist*

Action Item	Chapter and Item	Departments Involved
Evaluate how the organization's position on homeland security impacts IT.	1-2	CEO, IT, legal counsel
Assess how the USA Patriot Act impacts IT support requirements.	1-3	CEO, IT, legal counsel
Assess if the formation of DHS impacts IT support requirements.	1-4	CEO, IT, legal counsel
Evaluate what actions the IT department needs to take if the threat level is raised by the government.	1-6	CEO, IT, legal counsel, business units
Evaluate changes in IT management practices that were made as a result of terrorist attacks of September 11, 2001, to determine if new procedures are still adequate to address current security conditions or needs.	2-1	IT, business units
Evaluate changes in IT management practices that were made as a result of the establishment of DHS to determine if new procedures are still adequate to address current security conditions or needs.	2-2	IT, business units
Assess the level of training within the IT department to determine if the skill base necessary to evaluate, test, maintain, and improve policies, plans, and procedures exists.	2-3	IT, HR
Evaluate IT staffing to determine if the staffing level and staffing mix are adequate to address current needs.	2-4	IT, HR, business units
Assess the level of training of IT users to determine what security-related training should be implemented.	2-9	IT, HR, business units
Establish an internal organization process to monitor technology development, standards for technology use, and technologies that have been tested and proven effective.	3-5	IT, security, business units

Table 12.2 *IT Management Action Checklist (continued)*

Action Item	Chapter and Item	Departments Involved
Establish policies for reporting computer-related incidents.	4-1	CEO, IT, legal counsel
Determine how IT security staff are trained and develop a program to improve training.	8-1	IT, HR
Determine if the technology used by the organization meets the Common Criteria standards and make plans to migrate away from technologies that do not meet the standards.	8-5	IT, business units
Determine if the technology acquisition process used by the organization requires that products meet Common Criteria standards and modify procedures as necessary.	8-6	IT, purchasing, business units
Evaluate the configuration management processes and procedures of the organizations to determine if they provide sufficient levels of control to improve security; modify procedures as necessary.	8-7	IT, business units
Evaluate the process and procedures for installing patches to eliminate vulnerabilities; modify procedures as necessary.	8-8	IT
Determine if the organization needs to address the goals and objectives regarding wireless communications with government computer systems.	10-5	CEO, IT, security, business units
Determine if computers or networks that are owned or operated by the organization located in other countries are or have been under attack.	11-1	CEO, IT, security, business units
If computers or networks that are owned or operated by the organization located in other countries are or have been under attack, develop a reporting mechanism to alert authorities in the United States of these occurrences.	11-2	CEO, IT, security, business units

Table 12.3 *IT Security Action Checklist*

Action Item	Chapter and Item	Departments Involved
Determine the status of implementation of IS security plans and what related training has been achieved.	2-6	IT security, business units
Determine the status of implementation of computer-incident response plans and what related training has been achieved.	2-7	IT security, business units, HR, security

Table 12.3 *IT Security Action Checklist (continued)*

Action Item	Chapter and Item	Departments Involved
Assign staff responsibilities for participating InfraGard or professional organizations.	4-4	IT security
Evaluate IT solutions that address security needs or support new security requirements.	5-3	IT security, business units
Compare IT solutions that address security needs or support new security requirements for effectiveness, usability, and return on investment.	5-4	IT security, business units
Select and acquire IT products or services.	5-5	IT security, business units
Deploy and test applicable IT solutions.	5-6	IT security, business units
Monitor performance of IT solutions and tune, enhance, or migrate product sets.	5-7	IT security, business units
Evaluate the organization's ability to participate in and benefit from a national cyberincident response system.	7-1	IT security, business units, security
Develop processes and procedures to utilize information provided by the national cyberincident response system.	7-2	IT security, business units, security
Determine if the organization is using reports, analyses, standards, and recommendations provided by researching agencies such as the NSA and the NIST to improve IS security.	7-3	IT security, business units
Evaluate how security standards and procedures are set in the organization.	7-4	IT security, business units, security
Evaluate the sources of cybersecurity information that the organization has, including vendors, service providers, and other organizations that can be used to maintain security during threat situations.	7-6	IT security, business units, security
Determine how the organization obtains information on vulnerabilities and develop steps to obtain more timely information on vulnerabilities.	8-3	IT security, business units, security
Determine if the organization actually uses information on vulnerabilities to keep security methods updated, and make changes in the approach if necessary.	8-4	IT security, business units
Develop and launch a technology-focused cybersecurity training program for various types of employees, including executives, managers, supervisors, project leaders, and end users in all capacities.	9-1	IT security, HR, business units

Table 12.3 *IT Security Action Checklist (continued)*

Action Item	Chapter and Item	Departments Involved
Develop and launch an information security–focused training program for different types of employees based on their levels and areas of responsibilities.	9-2	IT security, HR, business units
Evaluate the need for certified computer-security professionals in the organization, and determine a course of action to increase the level of certification of in-house staff.	9-3	IT security, HR, business units
If the organization needs to work on securing wireless communications, develop a security plan to implement the plan.	10-6	IT security, business units
Develop a policy and procedure to assist in attack attribution and response, and modify the computer-incident response plan accordingly.	11-3	IT security, business units, legal counsel

Homeland Security Acronyms

Acronym	Definition
AAA	Anti-Aircraft Artillery
AAAS	American Association for the Advancement of Science
AAM	Air-to-Air Missile
ACC	Air Combat Command
ACCINTNET	ACC Intelligence Network
ACIC	Army Counter Intelligence Center
ACIS	Arms Control Intelligence Staff
ACM	Assistant Chief of Mission
ACS	Aerospace Medicine Consultation Service
ACTD	Advanced Concept Technology Demonstration
ACTIVE	Advanced Controls Technology for Integrated Vehicles
ADCI/A&P	Assistant Director of Central Intelligence for Analysis and Production
ADCI/C	Assistant Director of Central Intelligence for Collection
ADM	Advanced Development Model
ADM	Administrative Section
ADS	Advanced Distributed Simulation
ADT	Active Denial Technology
AEOS	Advanced Electro-Optical System
AES	Advanced Encryption Standard
AETC	Air Education and Training Command

Acronym	Definition
AFC4A	Air Force C4 Agency
AFCERT	Air Force Computer Emergency Response Team
AFCS	Automatic Flight Control System
AFEWES	Air Force Electronic Warfare Effectiveness Simulator
AFGIHS	Air Force Geographic Information Handling System
AFIT	Air Force Institute of Technology
AFIWC	Air Force Information Warfare Center
AFMC	Air Force Materiel Command
AFMSS	Air Force Mission Support System
AFOSI	Air Force Office of Special Investigations
AFOSR	Air Force Office of Scientific Research
AFPD	Air Force Policy Directive
AFRES	Air Force Reserves
AFRL	Air Force Research Laboratory
AFSAA	Air Force Studies and Analysis Agency
AFSFC	Air Force Space Forecasting Center
AFSOC	Air Force Special Operations Command
AFSPC	Air Force Space Command
AGARD	Advisory Group for Aerospace Research and Development
AGILE	Advanced Generation of Interoperability for Law Enforcement
AGRF	Advanced Guidance Research Facility
AHDL	Analog Hardware Descriptive Language
AI	Artificial Intelligence
AIA	Air Intelligence Agency
AID	Agency for International Development
AIM	Air Intercept Missile
AIMS	Automated Infrastructure Management System
AIRST	Advanced Infrared Search and Track
AIS	Automated Information Systems

Acronym	Definition
AIT	Active Imaging Test Bed
ALC	Air Logistics Center
AMB SEC	Ambassador's Secretary
AMB	Ambassador
AMC	Air Mobility Command
ANG	Air National Guard
ANSI	American National Standards Institute
AOA	Analysis of Alternatives (formerly: COEA)
AOA	Angle of Attack
APHIS	Animal and Plant Health Inspection Service Office
APT	Advanced Personnel Testing
ARGOS	Advanced Research and Global Observation Satellite
ARSO	Assistant Regional Security Officer
ASAT	Antisatellite
ASC	Aeronautical Systems Center
ASIMS	Automated Security Incident Measuring System
ASP	Aircraft Self-Protection
ASSIST	Automated Systems Security Incident Support Team
ASTREX	Advanced Space Structures Technology Research Experiment
ATAC	Anti Terrorism Alert Center
ATAF	Allied Tactical Air Forces
ATAGS	Advanced Technology Anti-G Suit
ATARR	Advanced Turbine Aerothermal Research Rig
ATC	Applied Technology Center
ATD	Advanced Technology Demonstration
ATEGG	Advanced Turbine Engine Gas Generator
ATF	Alcohol, Tobacco, and Firearms
ATIRCM	Advanced Threat Infrared Countermeasures
ATO	Advanced Technology Office

Acronym	Definition
ATO	Agricultural Trade Office (USDA/FAS)
ATR	Automatic Target Recognition
AWACS	Airborne Warning and Control System
BCAO	Branch Cultural Affairs Officer
BDA	Bomb Damage Assessment
BIST	Built-in-Self-Test
BLU	Bomb, Live Unit
BO	Branch Office (of Embassy)
BUREC	Bureau of Reclamation
BVR	Beyond Visual Range
BW	Biological Weapons
C2	Command and Control
C2W	Command and Control Warfare
C3	Command, Control, and Communications
C3I	Command, Control, Communications and Intelligence
C4	Command, Control, Communication, and Computers
CA	Cooperative Agreement
CAO	Cultural Affairs Officer
CAP	Combat Air Patrol
CATT	Computer-Assisted Technology Transfer
CBW	Chemical and Biological Warfare
CCM	Counter-Countermeasure
CCP	Consolidated Cryptologic Program
CCRP	Continuously Computed Release Point
CDC	Centers for Disease Control
CDFS	Core Driven Fan Stage
CEO	Cultural Exchange Officer
CEP	Circular Error Probable
CERT	Computer Emergency Response Team

Acronym	Definition
CERT/CC	Computer Emergency Response Team/Coordination Center
CFIT	Controlled Flight into Terrain
CG	Consul General, Consulate General
C-HFET	Complementary Heterostructure Field Effect Transistor
CHG	Charge d'Affaires
CI	Counterintelligence
CI&SCM	Counterintelligence and Security Countermeasures
CI/LI	Corrosion Inhibitor/Lubricity Improver (MIL-I-25017)
CIA	Central Intelligence Agency
CIAP	Central Intelligence Agency Program
CIARDS	Central Intelligence Agency Retirement and Disability System
CICA	Competition in Contracting Act
CINC	Commander in Chief
CINC	Combined Intelligence Center
CINCAFSOUTH	Commander in Chief Allied Forces Southern Europe
CINCEUR	Commander in Chief U.S. European Command
CINCPAC	Commander in Chief U.S. Pacific Command
CINCU.S.AFE	Commander in Chief U.S. Air Forces Europe
CINCU.S.AREUR	Commander in Chief U.S. Army Europe
CISO	Counterintelligence Support Officer at Unified Commands
CITAC	Computer Investigations and Infrastructure Threat Assessment Center
CLANSIG	Clandestine Signals Intelligence
CM	Countermeasure
CM	Chief of Mission
CMAWS	Common Missile Approach Warning System
CMO	Central MASINT Organization
CNA	Computer Network Attack
CNC	Crime and Narcotics Center
CNI	Communications, Navigation, and Identification

Acronym	Definition
COE	Common Operating Environment
COEA	Cost and Operational Effectiveness Analysis
COM	Commercial Section (FCS)
COMSEC	Communications Security
CON	Consul, Consular Section
CONOPS	Concept of Operations
COSPO	Community Open Source Program Office
COVCOM	Covert Communications
CPCC	Community Personnel Coordinating Committee
CRADA	Cooperative Research and Development Agreement
CSA	Computer Security Act
CSAR	Combat Search and Rescue
CSAT	Crew System Associate Technology
CSG	The Council of State Governments
CSIR	Computer (and Network) Security Incident Response
CSIRC	Computer Security Incident Response Capability
CSRC	Computer Security Response Center
CSSO	Computer Systems Security Officers
CT	Counterterrorism
CTAPS	Contingency Tactical Air Combat System Automated Planning System
CTC	Counterterrorism Center
CU.S.	Customs Service (Treasury)
CW	Chemical Weapons
CWC	Chemical Weapons Convention
D2	Degrade and Destroy
D3	Degrade, Disrupt, Deny
D4	Degrade, Disrupt, Deny, Destroy
DAD	Distributed Architecture Decoy
DAO	Defense Attaché Office

Acronym	Definition
DAO	Office of the Defense Attaché
DARO	Defense Airborne Reconnaissance Office
DARPA	Defense Advanced Research Projects Agency
DARTS	Dynamic Avionics Real-Time Scheduling
DATT	Defense Attaché
DAWS	Defense Automated Warning System
DCI	Director of Central Intelligence
DCIIS	Defense Counterintelligence Integrated Information System
DCM	Deputy Chief of Mission
DC-X	Delta Clipper Experimental
DDCI/CM	Deputy Director of Central Intelligence for Community Management
DDR&E	Director, Defense Research and Engineering
DDS	Defense Dissemination System
DEA	Data Exchange Agreement
DEA	Drug Enforcement Administration
DEECS	Digital Electronic Engine Control System
DEF ADV	Defense Adviser
DEL	Delegation
DEM/VAL	Demonstration and Validation
DEP DIR	Deputy Director
DEP	Deputy
DEPSECDEF	Deputy Secretary of Defense
DEVEL	Development
DEW	Directed Energy Weapon
DIA	Defense Intelligence Agency
DIAC	Defense Intelligence Analysis Center
DIACCS	Defense IA Command and Control System
DIAMOND	Defense Intrusion Analysis and Monitoring Desk
DIAP	Defense Information Assurance Program

Acronym	Definition
DICE	Data Integration and Collection Environment
DIDS	Distributed Intrusions Detection System
DII	Defense Information Infrastructure
DIR	Director
DIRCM	Directed Infrared Countermeasures
DIRNSA	Director, National Security Agency
DIS	Distributed Interactive Simulation
DISA	Defense Information Systems Agency
DISN	Defense Information System Network
DITSCAP	DoD IT Security Certification and Accreditation Process
DITSWG	Defense Information Technology Security Working Group
DJ	Deceptive Jamming
DLA	Defense Logistics Agency
DMA	Defense Mapping Agency
DMC	Defense MegaCenter
DMD	Digital Micromirror Device
DME	Distance Measuring Equipment
DMR	Dual-Mode Ramjet
DMS	Defense Message System
DMSP	Defense Meteorological Satellite Program
DNA	Defense Nuclear Agency
DO	Directorate of Operations
DOD	Department of Defense
DOD/FCIP	Department of Defense Foreign Counterintelligence Program
DODD	Department of Defense Directive
DODIIS	Department of Defense Intelligence Information System
DOE	Department of Energy
DOJ	Department of Justice
DoN	Department of the Navy

Acronym	Definition
DP	Development Prototype
DPAO	Deputy Public Affairs Officer
DPG	Defense Planning Guidance
DSA	Defense Supply Adviser
DSB	Defense Science Board
DSCS	Defense Satellite Communication System
DSN	Defense Switched Network
DSO	Defensive System Operator
DSS	Defense Security Service
DT&E	Development, Test, and Evaluation
DUSD	Deputy Undersecretary of Defense
E	Embassy
EA	Electronic Attack
EBRD	Economic Board for Reconstruction and Development
ECM	Electronic Countermeasures
ECO	Economic Section
ECO/COM	Economic/Commercial Section
ECOSOC	Economic and Social Council
EDO	Export Development Officer
EDRB	Expanded Defense Resources Board
EELV	Evolved Expendable Launch Vehicle
EFOIA	Electronic Freedom of Information Act
EFS-M	Enhanced Flight Screening-Medical
EIA	Electronic Industry Alliance
EIS	Environmental Impact Statement
ELINT	Electronic Intelligence Technical and Operational Intelligence Information
ELINT	Electronic Intelligence
ELMC	Electrical Load Management Centers
ELO	Extremely Low Observable

Acronym	Definition
EO	Electro-Optical
EO/IR	Electro-Optical/Infrared
EOP	Executive Office of the President
EP	Electronic Protection
EPA	Environmental Protection Agency
EPAD	Electrically Powered Actuation Device
EPU	Emergency Power Unit
ESM	Electronic Support Measures
EST	Environment, Science, and Technology
ETA	Education, Training, and Awareness
ETF	Environmental Task Force
EXDIR/ICA	Executive Director/Intelligence Community Affairs
EXEC	Executive
EX-IM	Export-Import
EXLITE	Extended Life Tire
FAA	Federal Aviation Administration
FAA/CASLO	Federal Aviation Administration Civil Aviation Security Liaison Officer
FAA/FSIDO	Federal Aviation Administration Flight Standards International District Office
FAO	Foreign Agricultural Office
FAS	Foreign Agricultural Service
FBI	Federal Bureau of Investigation
FBI/FCI	Federal Bureau of Investigation Foreign Counterintelligence Program
FBI/SCM	Federal Bureau of Investigation Security Countermeasures Program
FBIS	Foreign Broadcast Information Service
FBO	Foreign Buildings Office
FCC	Federal Communications Commission
FCI	Foreign Counterintelligence
FCS	Foreign Commercial Service
FCT	Foreign Comparative Test

Acronym	Definition
FEMA	Federal Emergency Management Agency
FFRDC	Federally Funded Research and Development Center
FIN	Financial Attaché (Treasury)
FIS	Foreign Intelligence Service
FISA	Foreign Intelligence Surveillance Act
FLC	Foreign Language Committee
FLC	Federal Laboratory Consortium
FLEX	Force Level Execution
FOC	Full Operational Capability
FOD	Foreign Object Damage
FODAG	Food and Agriculture Organizations
FOIA	Freedom of Information Act
FSI	Foreign Service Institute
FSU	Former Soviet Union
FTS	Fourier Transform Spectrometer
GAO	General Accounting Office
GATT	General Agreement on Trade and Tariffs
GDIP	General Defense Intelligence Program
GPS	Global Positioning System
HQ	Headquarters
HUMINT	Human Source Intelligence
I&W	Indications and Warning
IA	Information Assurance
IACP	International Association of Chiefs of Police
IADS	Integrated Air Defense System
IAEA	International Atomic Energy Agency
IAFC	International Association of Fire Chiefs
IAG	Information Assurance Group
IAGS	Inter-American Geodetic Survey

Acronym	Definition
IAPWG	Information Assurance Policy Working Group
IATAC	Information Assurance Technology Analysis Center
IAVA	Information Assurance Vulnerability Alert
IC	Intelligence Community
IC CIO	Intelligence Community Chief Information Officer
ICAO	International Civil Aviation Organization
ICMA	International City/County Management Association
IDHS	Intelligence Data Handling System
IG	Inspector General
IHT	Incident Handling Team
IIR	Imaging Infrared
IMINT	Imagery Intelligence and Geospatial Information
IMIS	Integrated Maintenance Information System
INFOSEC	Information Security
INR	Department of State Bureau of Intelligence and Research
INS	Immigration and Naturalization Service
IO	Information Operations
IPO	Information Program Officer
IPRG	Intelligence Program Review Group
IPT	Integrated Product Team
IPTF	Infrastructure Protection Task Force
IPU	Integrated Power Unit
IRC	INFOSEC Research Council
IRM	Information Resources Management
IRMA	Infrared Modeling and Analysis
IRS	Incident Reporting Structure
IRS	Internal Revenue Service
IRT	Incident Response Team
ISA	Instrumentation Society of America

Acronym	Definition
ISM	Information Systems Manager
ISO	International Organization for Standardization
ISSM	Information System Security Manager
ISSO	Information System Security Officer
IT	Information Technology
IW	Information Warfare
JCCC	Joint Communications Control Center
JCS	Joint Chiefs of Staff
JIC	Joint Intelligence Center
JID	Joint Intrusion Detection
JIEO	Joint Interoperability Engineering Organization
JR	Jam Resistance
KMI	Key Management Infrastructure
LaRC	Langley Research Center
LASE	Large Aperture Speckle Experiment
LCC	Life Cycle Cost
LE	Law Enforcement
LEGATT	Legal Attaché
LO	Liaison Officer
M	Mission
M&S	Modeling and Simulation
MAA	Mission Area Assessment
MAAG	Military Assistance Advisory Group
MAP	Mission Area Plan
MBB	Mission Based Budgeting
MCC	Major Cities Chiefs Association
MCD	Minimum Cost Design
MCDES	Malicious Code Detection and Eradication System
MCSA	Major County Sheriffs' Association

Acronym	Definition
MGT & RFM	Management and Reform
MIG AFF	Migration Affairs
MIL	Military
MILGP	Military Group
MILSATCOM	Military Satellite Communications
MLO	Military Liaison Office
MLS WG	Multilevel Security Working Group
MNS	Mission Needs Statement
MOA	Memorandum of Agreement
MOOTW	Military Operations Other Than War
MSC	Military Staff Committee
MSO	Mission Support Officer
MTBF	Mean Time Between Failure
MTI	Moving Target Indicator
NAAG	National Association of Attorneys General
NACIC	National Counterintelligence Center
NACO	National Association of Counties
NAFTA	North American Free Trade Agreement
NAIC	National Air Intelligence Center
NARC	Narcotics Officer
NAS	Narcotics Affairs Section
NASA	National Aeronautics and Space Administration
NATO	North Atlantic Treaty Organization
NAVAIRSYSCOM	Naval Air Systems Command
NAVCIRT	Naval Computer Incident Response Team
NBC	Nuclear, Biological, Chemical weapons
NCIOB	National Counterintelligence Operations Board
NCIPB	National Counterintelligence Policy Board
NCIS	Naval Criminal Investigative Service

Acronym	Definition
NCJA	National Criminal Justice Association
NCSC	National Computer Security Center
NCSL	National Conference of State Legislatures
NDIC	National Drug Intelligence Center
NDU	National Defense University
NEMA	National Emergency Management Association
NENA	National Emergency Number Association
NFIP	National Foreign Intelligence Program
NGA	National Governors Association
NIAC	National Infrastructure Assurance Council
NIC	National Intelligence Council
NICB	National Intelligence Collection Board
NID	Network Intrusion Detector
NIFTR	Near Isothermal Flowing Test Rig
NII	National Information Infrastructure
NIJ	National Institute of Justice
NIMA	National Imagery and Mapping Agency
NIPB	National Intelligence Producers Board
NIPC	National Infrastructure Protection Center
NISP	National Industrial Security Program
NIST	National Institute of Standards and Technology
NITB	National INFOSEC Technical Baseline
NIV	Nonimmigrant Visas
NLC	National League of Cities
NLECTC	National Law Enforcement and Corrections Technology Center
NLETS	National Law Enforcement Telecommunications System
NLO	Naval Liaison Officer
NOC	Network Operating Centers
NOSC	Network Operation Security Center

Acronym	Definition
NPSTC	National Public Safety Telecommunications Council
NRC	National Research Council
NRO	National Reconnaissance Office
NRP	National Reconnaissance Program
NS/EP	National Security and Emergency Preparedness
NSA	National Security Agency
NSA	National Sheriffs' Association
NSA/CSS	National Security Agency/Central Security Service
NSD	National Security Directive
NSIRC	National Security Incident Response Center
NSOC	National Security Operations Center
NSTAC	National Security Telecommunications Advisory Committee
NSTISSC	National Security Telecommunications and Information Systems Security Committee
NSTISSI	National Security Telecommunications and Information Systems Security Instruction
NTIA	National Telecommunications and Information Administration
O&M	Operations and Maintenance
OAS	Organization of American States
ODC	Office of Defense Cooperation
ODP	Office for State and Local Domestic Preparedness Support
OHS	Office of Homeland Security
OIC	Officer in Charge
OJP	Office of Justice Programs
OMC	Office of Military Cooperation
OMS	Office Management Specialist
ONR	Office of Naval Research
OPM	Office of Personnel Management
OPO	Optical Parametric Oscillator

Acronym	Definition
OPSEC	Operations Security
ORA	Office of Regional Affairs
ORD	Office of Research and Development
ORTA	Office of Research and Technology Applications
OSD	Office of the Secretary of Defense
OSD/JS	Office of the Secretary of Defense/Joint Staff
OSINT	Open Source Intelligence
OSO	Offensive System Operator
P3I	Preplanned Product Improvement
PA&E	Program Assessment and Evaluation
PA&EO	Program Assessment and Evaluation Office, Community Management Staff
PCCIP	President's Commission on Critical Infrastructure Protection
PCS	Personal Communications Services
PD	Pulse Doppler (Radar)
PDD	Presidential Decision Directive
PGP	Pretty Good Privacy
PKI	Public Key Infrastructure
PLAID	Precision Location and Identification
PMAD	Power Management and Distribution
PMD	Program Management Directive
PO	Principal Officer
POL	Political Section
POL/ECO	Political/Economic Section
POL/LAB	Political and Labor Section
POLAD	Political Adviser
POM	Program Objective Memorandum
PPBS	Planning, Program, and Budgeting System
PRG	Program Review Group
R&M	Reliability and Maintainability

Acronym	Definition
RAMTIP	Reliability and Maintainability Technology Insertion Program
RCERTs	Regional Computer Emergency Response Teams
RCON	Regional Consular Affairs Officer
RCS	Radar Cross Section
RDT&E	Research, Development, Test, and Evaluation
REDSO	Regional Economic Development Services Office
REF	Refugee Coordinator
RELO	Regional English Language Officer
REP	Representative
RM&S	Reliability, Maintainability, and Supportability
RMO	Regional Medical Officer
RSO	Regional Security Officer
S/V/L	Survivability/Vulnerability/Lethality
SAB	Scientific Advisory Board
SAO	Security Assistance Office
SAR	Suspicious Activity Report
SAR	Search and Rescue
SAR	Special Access Required
SAWS	Silent Attack Warning System
SCI	Scientific Attaché
SCO	Senior Commercial Office
SERE	Survival, Evasion, Resistance, Escape
SERT	Security Emergency Response Team
SET	Secure Encrypted Transaction
SIO	Special Information Operations
SLG	State and Local Government
SOC	Special Operations Command
SOF	Special Operations Forces
SOI	Space Object Identification

Acronym	Definition
SPA	Special Assistant
SPACECOM	Space Command
SPAWAR	Space and Naval Warfare Systems Command
SPB	Security Policy Board
SPO	Single Point of Failure
SPO	System Program Office
SSAA	Systems Security Authorization Agreement
SSN	Space Surveillance Network
SSO	Special Security Office/Officer
SSRT	Software Security Response Team
STC	Security Trade Control
STRATCOM	Strategic Command
STTR	Small Business Technology Transfer Program
SWC	Space Warfare Center
SWIM	Solar Wind Interplanetary Measurements
T&E	Test and Evaluation
TAT	Tactical Analysis Team
TCT	Time Critical Target
TDA	Technology Development Approach
TEO	Technology Executive Officer
TestPAES	Test Planning, Analysis and Evaluation System
THREATCON	Threat Condition
TIA	Telecommunications Industry Association
TIP	Technology Investment Plan
TIP	Technology Insertion Program
TIPP	Test Instrument Planning and Programming
TRANSEC	Transmission Security
TTO	Technology Transition Office
UAV	Unmanned Aerial Vehicle

Acronym	Definition
UAV	Unmanned Aerospace Vehicle
UNEP	United Nations Environment Program
UNESCO	United Nations Educational, Scientific, and Cultural Organization
UNIDO	United Nations Industrial Development Organization
URI	University Research Initiative
USA	United States Army
USACOM	U.S. Atlantic Command
USCENTCOM	U.S. Central Command
USCG	U.S. Coast Guard
USCM	The United State Conference of Mayors
USCS	U.S. Cryptologic System
USDOC	U.S. Department of Commerce
USEU	U.S. Mission to the European Union
USEUCOM	U.S. European Command
USGS	U.S. Geological Survey
USMTM	U.S. Military Training Mission
USNATO	U.S. Mission to the North Atlantic Treaty Organization
USOAS	U.S. Mission to the Organization of American States
USOECD	U.S. Mission to the Organization for Economic Cooperation and Development
USTTA	U.S. Travel and Tourism Agency
USUN	U.S. Mission to the United Nations
VAAP	Vulnerability-and-Assessment Program
VAS	Vulnerability Assessment System
VOC	Volatile Organic Compounds
WMD	Weapon of Mass Destruction

B

Homeland Security Resources

State government support and coordination is essential for successfully implementing homeland security efforts. The following list shows the contacts, addresses, phone numbers, and, where available, the Web sites for state-level homeland security offices.

Alabama

James Walker

Homeland Security Director

Alabama Office of Homeland Security

401 Adams Ave., Suite 560

Montgomery, AL 36103-5690

(334) 353-0242

Fax: (334) 353-0606

Alaska

BG Craig Campbell

P.O. Box 5800

Ft. Richardson, AK 99505-0800

(907) 428-6003

www.ak-prepared.com/homelandsecurity

Arizona

Chuck Blanchard

Director of Homeland Security

1700 West Washington Street, 3rd Floor
Phoenix, AZ 85007

Arkansas
Bud Harper
Director, Emergency Management
P.O. Box 758
Conway, AR 72033
(501) 730-9750
www.adem.state.ar.us

California
George Vinson
Special Advisor on State Security
State Capitol, 1st Floor
Sacramento, CA 95814
(916) 324-8908

Colorado
Sue Mencer
Executive Director, Colorado Deptartment of Public Safety
700 Kipling Street
Denver, CO 80215
(303) 273-1770

Connecticut
Vincent DeRosa
Deputy Commissioner, Division of Protective Services
55 West Main St., Suite 500
Waterbury, CT 06702
(203) 805-6600
www.state.ct.us/dps/PS/index.htm

DPS.Feedback@po.state.ct.us

Delaware

Phil Cabaud
Homeland Security Director
Office of the Governor
Tatnall Building, 2nd Floor
William Penn Street
Dover, DE 19901
(302) 744-4242

District of Columbia

Margret Nedelkoff Kellems
Deputy Mayor for Public Safety and Justice
(202) 727-4036
http://washingtondc.gov

Florida

Tim Moore
Commissioner, Florida Deptartment of Law Enforcement
P.O. Box 1489
Tallahassee, FL 32302-1489
(850) 410-7233
www.fdle.state.fl.us

Georgia

Bill Hitchens
Director of Homeland Security
P.O. Box 1456
Atlanta, GA 30371
(404) 624-7030
www.gahomelandsecurity.com

Hawaii

BG Robert Lee
Adjutant General
3949 Diamond Head Rd.
Honolulu, HI 96816-4495
(808) 733-4246
www.scd.state.hi.us

Idaho

MG Jack Kane
Adjutant General
4040 West Guard Street
Boise, ID 83705-5004
(208) 422-5242
www.state.id.us/government/executive.html

Illinois

Carl Hawkinson
Homeland Security Advisor
207 State House
Springfield, IL 62706
(217) 524-1486

Indiana

Clifford Ong
Director, Indiana Counterterrorism and Security Council
100 North Senate Avenue
Indianapolis, IN 46204
(317) 232-8303
www.in.gov/c-tasc

Iowa

Ellen Gordon
Administrator, Emergency Management
Hoover State Office Building
1305 E. Walnut
Des Moines, IA 50319
(515) 281-3231
www.iowahomelandsecurity.org

Kansas

MG Gregory Gardner
Adjutant General
2800 SW Topeka
Topeka, KS, 66611-1287
(785) 274-1121/1109

Kentucky

BG D. Allen Youngman
Adjutant General
100 Minuteman Parkway
Frankfurt, KY 40601-6168
(502) 607-1257
http://homeland.state.ky.us

Louisiana

MG Bennett C. Landreneau
Adjutant General and Director
Louisiana Office of Emergency Preparedness
7667 Independence Blvd.
Baton Rouge, LA 70806
(225) 925-7333

Maine

MG Joseph Tinkham, II
Adjutant General
Homeland Security
1 State House Station
Augusta, ME 04333-0001
Normal working hours: (207) 626-4440

Maryland

Thomas J. Lockwood
Homeland Security Director
State House, 100 State Circle
Annapolis, MD 21401
(410) 974-3901
www.mema.state.md.us

Massachusetts

Richard Swensen
Office of Commonwealth Security
Executive Office of Public Safety
1 Ashburton Place, Room 2133
Boston, MA 02108
(617) 727-3600 ext. 556

Michigan

COL Tadarial Sturdivant
Director of State Police
Contact: CPT John Ort
713 South Harrison Rd.
E. Lansing, MI 48823
(517) 336-6198
www.msp.state.mi.us

Minnesota

Rich Stanek

Commissioner of Public Safety and Homeland Security Director

DPS, North Central Life Tower

445 Minnesota St., Suite 1000

St. Paul, MN 55101

dps.state.mn.us/homelandsecurity/index.htm

Mississippi

Robert Latham

Executive Director, Mississippi Emergency Management Agency

P.O. Box 4501

Jackson, MS 39296-4501

(601) 960-9999

www.homelandsecurity.ms.gov

Missouri

COL Tim Daniel

Special Adviser for Homeland Security

P.O. Box 809

Jefferson City, MO 65102

(573) 522-3007

www.homelandsecurity.state.mo.us

Montana

Jim Greene

Administrator, Disaster and Emergency Services

Department of Military Affairs—HAFRC

Montana Disaster and Emergency Services

1900 Williams Street

P.O. Box 4789

Helena, MT 59604-4789

(406) 841-3911
www.discoveringmontana.com/css/default.asp

Nebraska
Lieutenant Governor Dave Heineman
P.O. Box 94848
Lincoln, NE 68509-4848
(402) 471-2256
dave.heineman@email.state.ne.us

Nevada
Jerry Bussell
Homeland Security Director
2525 S. Carson St
Carson City, NV 89710
(775) 687-7320

New Hampshire
Donald Bliss
Director, Emergency Management and State Fire Marshal
10 Hazen Drive
Concord, NH 03305
(603) 271-3294

New Jersey
Sidney Caspersen, Director
N.J. Office of Counterterrorism
P.O. Box 091
Trenton, NJ 08625
(609) 341-3434
www.njcounterterrorism.org

New Mexico
R. L. Stockard
Homeland Security Director
New Mexico Office of Public Safety
P.O. Box 1628
Santa Fe, NM 87507-1628
(505) 827-3370

New York
John Scanlon
Director, Office of Public Security
Executive Chamber
633 3rd Ave, 38th Floor
New York, NY 10017
(212) 867-7060
info@security.state.ny.us

North Carolina
Bryan Beatty
Secretary, Deptartment of Crime Control and Public Safety
4701 Mail Service Center
Raleigh, NC 27699
(919) 733-2126
www.ncgov.com/asp/subpages/safety_security.asp

North Dakota
Doug Friez
Homeland Security Coordinator/Emergency Management Director
Fraine Barracks Lane, Building 35
Fraine Barracks
Bismarck, ND 58504
(701) 328-8100

www.state.nd.us/dem/homesec.html

Ohio

Kenneth L. Morckel
Director of Public Safety
1970 W. Broad St.
Columbus, OH 43223-1102
(614) 466-4344
www.state.oh.us/odps/sos/ohshome.htm

Oklahoma

Bob A. Ricks
Director
Oklahoma Office of Homeland Security
P.O. Box 11415
Oklahoma City, OK 73136-0415
(405) 425-2001
Fax: (405) 425-2324
okohs@dps.state.ok.us
www.youroklahoma.com/homelandsecurity

Oregon

Ronald C. Ruecker
Superintendent of Oregon State Police
400 Public Service Building
Salem, OR 97310
(503) 378-3725

Pennsylvania

Keith Martin
Director, Pennsylvania Office of Homeland Security
2605 Interstate Drive

Harrisburg, PA 17110
(717) 651-2715
www.homelandsecurity.state.pa.us

Puerto Rico
Annabelle Rodriguez
Attorney General
La Fortaleza
P.O. Box 9020082
San Juan, PR 00902-0082
(787) 721-7700

Rhode Island
MG Reginald Centracchio
Adjutant General
222 State House
Providence, RI 02903
(401) 275-4102

South Carolina
Robert M. Stewart
Chief, S.C. Law Enforcement Division (SLED)
P.O. Box 21398
Columbia, SC 29221-1398
(803) 737-9000

South Dakota
Deb Bowman
Chief of Homeland Security
500 East Capitol Avenue
Pierre, SD 57501
1-866-homland

Tennessee
MG (Ret.) Jerry Humble
215 Eighth Avenue, North
Nashville, TN 37203
(615) 532-7825

Texas
Jay Kimbrough
Deputy Attorney General for Criminal Justice
P.O. Box 12428
Austin, TX 78711
(512) 936-1882

Utah
Scott Behunin
Division Director, Comprehensive Emergency Management
210 State Capitol
Salt Lake City, UT 84114
(801) 538-3400
www.cem.utah.gov

Vermont
Kerry Sleeper
Commissioner, VT State Police
103 South Main Street
Waterbury, VT 05671-2101
(802) 244-8775

Virginia
Assistant to the Governor for Commonwealth Preparedness
John Hager
202 N. 9th Street, 5th Floor

Richmond, VA 23219
(804) 225-3826
www.commonwealthpreparedness.state.va.us

Washington
MG Timothy J. Lowenberg
Adjutant General and Director
State Military Department
Washington Military Department, Building 1
Camp Murray, WA 98430-5000
(253) 512-8201

West Virginia
Joe Martin
Secretary, Department of Military Affairs and Public Safety
State Capitol Complex, Building 6, Room B-122
Charleston, WV 25305
(304) 558-2930

Wisconsin
Ed Gleason
Administrator, Emergency Management
P.O. Box 7865
Madison, WI 53707-7865
(608) 242-3210
www.wisconsin.gov/state/core/domestic_prep.html

Wyoming
MG Ed Boenisch
Adjutant General
TAG Office, 5500 Bishop Blvd.
Cheyenne, WY 82009-3320

(307) 772-5234

Guam

Frank Blas
Homeland Security Advisor
P.O. Box 2950
Hagatna, GU 96932
(671) 475-9600/9602

Northern Mariana Islands

Jerry Crisostomo
Special Advisor for Homeland Security
Caller Box 10007
Saipan, MP 96950
(670) 664-2280

Virgin Islands

MG Cleave A. McBean
Adjutant General
21-22 Kongens Gade
St. Thomas, VI 00802
(340) 712-7711

American Samoa

Leiataua Birdsall V. Ala'ilima
Special Assistant to the Governor
Office of Territory Emergency Mgmt
American Somoa Government
Pago Pago, AS 96799
(011) 684-633-4116

There have also been numerous organizations that can provide some assistance for counterterrorism training and improvement of homeland security, including the following:

American Biological Safety Association (ABSA)

ABSA promotes the continued and timely exchange of information related to biosafety. ABSA's Web site contains links to conferences and upcoming events, announcements, scientific publications, e-mail lists, and more.

American College for Preventative Medicine (ACPM)

ACPM is the national professional society for physicians committed to disease prevention and health promotion. The Web site offers numerous resources, including the comprehensive, online educational program Recognizing Waterborne Disease and the Health Effects of Water Pollution, which prepares health-care providers to deal with outbreaks of waterborne disease from naturally occurring and intentional acts of water contamination. This online program, for which physicians can receive up to 22 hours of continuing medical education credit, can be viewed at ACPM's Online CME Center.

American Institute of Homeland Defense

The American Institute of Homeland Defense provides law enforcement, military, and corporate personnel in the homeland security field with certified training and accredited education.

American Public University System (APUS)

APUS is a learning community of faculty, students, staff, and graduates aligned in three private, degree-granting member institutions: American Public University (APU), American Military University (AMU), and American Community College (ACC). APUS offers a nontraditional, distance-education system using the most current technology to deliver personal, individualized instruction. ACC offers associate degree concentrations in counterterrorism fundamentals and weapons of mass destruction. APU and AMU bachelor's degree programs include majors in intelligence studies, homeland security studies, and emergency and disaster management. APU and AMU offer graduate programs in strategic intelligence and military studies.

American Radio Relay League (ARRL)—The National Association for Amateur Radio

ARRL is a national membership association for amateur radio operators that promotes interest in amateur radio communications and experimentation, represents U.S. radio amateurs in legislative matters, and maintains fraternalism and a high standard of conduct among amateur radio operators. With more than 160,000 members, ARRL is the largest organization of radio amateurs in the United States. In 2003, ARRL will offer a free Amateur Radio Emergency Communications Course to 5,200 volunteers nationwide.

Association of Former Intelligence Officers (AFIO)

AFIO is a nonprofit, politically unaffiliated, educational organization of former intelligence professionals and supporters. Its Web site features archives of course syllabi for college-level intelligence courses, reviews of intelligence-related publications, and a list of governmental, military, and legislative search engines or Web sites pertaining to intelligence matters. AFIO maintains chapters throughout the United States, offering opportunities for peer contact through regular meetings and periodic training events.

Association of Schools of Public Health

The Association of Schools of Public Health is the only national organization that represents the deans, faculty, and students of the accredited member schools of public health and other programs seeking accreditation. The Web site provides a Public Health Preparedness Resource Center, which offers a searchable online catalog of courses and training opportunities and other information developed by the member schools.

ATF Online—Training

The Bureau of Alcohol, Tobacco, Firearms, and Explosives offers firearms-related and arson and explosives training for federal, state, and local law-enforcement agencies.

Bioterrorism Learning Center

Visitors to this Web site can view lectures on the latest bioterrorism issues in a variety of formats, including streaming audio, video, and PowerPoint presentations. The unedited presentations, recorded from conferences across the country, are presented by leading regional and national experts. More than 20 lectures are available for viewing.

BombSecurity.com Consulting and Training Resources

This Web site provides links to consultants, trainers, and school personnel with bomb security and counterterrorism expertise. Program topics include blast-mitigation engineering, bomb countermeasures, executive protection, terrorism counteraction, and weapons of mass destruction preparedness.

Bureau of Explosives

A subsidiary of the American Association of Railroads, the Bureau of Explosives is a proactive, customer-oriented information and service group dedicated to enhancing and maintaining safe transportation in the railroad industry.

Casualty Care Research Center (CCRC)

CCRC is a national center for research on all aspects of injury control and combat casualty care. CCRC is staffed by military and civilian personnel and experts from the Department of Military and Emergency Medicine.

The Center for National Response

The Center for National Response, located at the West Virginia Memorial Tunnel, is a U.S. DOD facility that provides a training space for first responders. The two-lane, 2,800-foot-long highway tunnel comprises more than 79,000 square feet of training space. The tunnel provides a realistic environment where emergency teams can practice techniques designed to mitigate the effects of a weapons of mass destruction incident in an underground space.

The Center for Counterterrorism Studies (CT Studies)

CT Studies offers security and counterterrorism training on such topics as clandestine communication techniques, countersurveillance training, domestic terrorism, international terrorism, investigative techniques, terror tactics around the globe, and terrorism issues for law-enforcement officers. See also training courses offered by the sister center, Center for Counterintelligence and Security Studies.

Center for Public Safety, Northwestern University

Established as the Traffic Institute in 1936, the center is a nonprofit organization that provides programs of specialized training, continuing education, research and development, publications, and direct assistance to public agencies responsible for law enforcement, criminal justice, public safety, and highway transportation systems.

Center for Terrorism Preparedness, University of Findlay

The Center for Terrorism Preparedness offers education, training, and consulting services to law-enforcement personnel and other first responders, public health and medical personnel, corporate safety and security personnel, and city and county officials.

Centers for the Study of Bioterrorism and Emerging Infections

The Centers for the Study of Bioterrorism and Emerging Infections provide publications on the U.S. DHS, potential biological threats, and possible international terrorism outlets.

CERT Coordination Center (CERT/CC)

CERT/CC is a major reporting center for Internet-security problems. CERT provides technical advice to administrators whose sites may have been compromised, coordinates and develops solutions to security breaches, identifies intruder trends, analyzes product vulnerabilities, issues e-mail advisories, presents training courses, and publishes technical documents.

Children, Terrorism, and Disasters—American Academy of Pediatrics

The American Academy of Pediatrics Task Force on Terrorism prepared this Web site in response to the events of September 11, 2001. Composed of pediatric experts in fields such as infectious diseases, emergency medicine, disaster planning, and mental health, this task force seeks to ensure that pediatricians and other pediatric providers have the information they need about terrorism and disasters.

Computer-Aided Management of Emergency Operations (CAMEO)

CAMEO is a system of software applications used to plan for and respond to chemical emergencies. Developed by the Environmental Protection Agency's Chemical Emergency Preparedness and Prevention Office and the National Oceanic and Atmospheric Administration, Office of Response and Restoration, CAMEO helps frontline chemical emergency planners and responders access, store, and evaluate information critical to developing emergency plans.

Defense Security Service (DSS) Academy

The DSS Academy provides security professionals with instruction on information security, risk management, and professional development. In-person training, videoteletraining, independent study, and computer-based training formats are all available.

Energetic Materials Research and Testing Center (EMRTC)

EMRTC specializes in the research, development, and analysis of energetic materials for both corporate and government clients. Affiliated with New Mexico Tech, EMRTC conducts incident-response training related to terrorist bombings, bomb threats, rural border operations, hostage negotiations, and laboratory safety.

Explosive Ordnance Technologies, Inc. (EOTI)

EOTI provides agencies and organizations with specialized training and technical assistance to mitigate, prepare, respond, and recover from attacks by weapons of mass destruction.

Extension Disaster Education Network (EDEN)

EDEN is a multistate effort designed to improve the delivery of services to citizens affected by disasters. To enhance short- and long-term programming efforts, EDEN's Web site offers resources on disaster preparedness, recovery, and mitigation. Planners and first responders can benefit from a searchable disaster-information database, a page featuring state and federal homeland security resources, and the results of USDA-sponsored surveys concerning bioterrorism.

Federal Emergency Management Agency (FEMA)

FEMA provides communities with access to services through their regional offices and regional tribal liaisons. FEMA's Web site offers essentials on education, training, grants, and funding. It also features a library of FEMA-specific disaster information. The Web site presents links to virtual resources, including DisasterHelp.gov and HazardMaps.gov, FEMA's site for public access to online hazard advisory maps. Online training from the National Emergency Training Center's Virtual Campus can be accessed via FEMA's Training Resources Portal Page, which links to training at the Emergency Management Institute (EMI) and the U.S. Fire Administration's National Fire Academy (NFA). FEMA.gov En Español provides the Spanish-speaking community with information about FEMA, disaster resources, preparedness articles, children's books, and links to other disaster-related sites in Spanish.

Federal Learning Exchange (FLX)

FLX provides a database of training and education resources for federal employees, agencies, and departments. Visitors can search for courses, programs, and seminars on topics of interest, including basic skills, IT and telecommunication, and public safety and security.

Fort Sherman Institute: An Institute for Human Protection

The Fort Sherman Institute, a branch of North Idaho College in Post Falls, Idaho, was established to train, educate, and support government, military, and corporate organizations in antiterrorism and hostage survival. Interested individuals or groups should contact the school for eligibility information and course details.

The Humane Society of the United States (HSUS)

The HSUS Disaster Center, which features disaster planning and response resources for natural and manmade emergencies, offers information on the Disaster Animal Response Team (DART) program. DART team members, who are trained in community disaster response and preparedness, specialize in response techniques for rescuing animals caught in disasters. People with skills and experience in animal handling, emergency/public services, or disaster work who are interested in joining DART should e-mail disaster@hsus.org for additional information. HSUS also provides direct financial support to the volunteer canine teams of the Federal Emergency Management Agency Urban Search and Rescue Response Task Forces through the Disaster Dog Program.

InfraGard

InfraGard is a cooperative endeavor of the FBI and a membership that includes businesses, academic institutions, and state and local law-enforcement agencies. InfraGard's objective is to increase the security of national infrastructures through continuing exchanges of information relevant to infrastructure protection and through education, outreach, and similar efforts to increase awareness of infrastructure protection issues. InfraGard disseminates important information by hosting an annual national convention and regional summits, publishing articles, sponsoring state and local chapters, and furnishing members with various methods to report computer intrusions.

Interagency Operations Security Support Staff (IOSS)

The National Operations Security Program (OPSEC) was established in 1988 as a means to identify, control, and protect unclassified information and evidence associated with U.S. national-security programs and activities. The IOSS unit consults with other U.S. government departments and agencies, providing technical guidance and assistance to make OPSEC programs throughout government self-sufficient and to protect U.S. operations. IOSS staff is available to assist organizations and individuals with OPSEC materials, training, operations analysis, and implementation of OPSEC practices.

International Association of Bomb Technicians and Investigators (IABTI)

As a freestanding, nonprofit organization, the IABTI seeks to combat the illegal use of explosives through information and education exchange among professionals in law enforcement, emergency services, the military, forensic science, and related disciplines.

International Association of Chiefs of Police (IACP)

The IACP offers regularly scheduled law-enforcement training nationwide, including terrorism-related classes. In coordination with the Office for Domestic Preparedness and the School of Criminal Justice, Michigan State University, IACP is developing a 16-hour executive-level weapons of mass destruction preparedness course for police chiefs and executives. The course will focus on activities that are critical for effective leadership at the scene of a weapons of mass destruction incident.

International Association of Fire Fighters (IAFF) Virtual Academy

IAFF's Virtual Academy provides its members with high-quality, timely educational opportunities. Online training modules cover topics such as hazardous materials, decontamination, and equipment.

International Money Laundering Information Network (IMoLIN)

The United Nations Global Program against Money Laundering developed this online reference tool for investigators interested in money laundering related to drugs, terrorism, and other criminal activities. The site features a calendar of international training events, full texts of money laundering legislation, updates on United Nations Action against Terrorism documents, and password-protected access to the Anti–Money Laundering International Database. For more information about this network, law-enforcement officers may send an e-mail message to the United Nations Office of Drugs and Crime or write to the postal address provided on the Web site.

International Tactical EMS Association (TEMS)

TEMS maintains an organized network of tactical officers, tactical medical providers, law-enforcement agencies, and other interested parties within the critical-incident resolution community. TEMS works to reduce morbidity and mortality associated with tactical training and special operations.

Law Enforcement Agency Resource Network (LEARN)

The Anti-Defamation League's resource outlet for law enforcement contains links to publications, news, training opportunities, terrorism working groups and task forces, a database of terrorist organizations, maps, and an events calendar concerning extremism in America. LEARN provides access to the public Militia Watchdog Archives and a form for subscribing to the Militia Watchdog mailing list, a restricted, electronic forum "open to persons who have a verifiable professional interest in keeping track of the extreme right, anti-government extremists, domestic terrorism, and similar subjects."

Law Enforcement, Emergency Management, and Corrections Training Resources (LECTR)

LECTR provides a central repository of professional training announcements, Internet-based training opportunities, instructional media, and other training media pertaining to law enforcement, emergency management, and corrections.

Management Development Centers

Sponsored by the U.S. Office of Personnel Management, the Management Development Centers serve government leaders and organizations by improving performance and enhancing leadership through interagency residential training, customized courses and consulting, and innovative customer-focused service. The centers offer several courses related to homeland defense, national security, and counterterrorism.

Multistate Anti-Terrorism Information Exchange (MATRIX)

MATRIX is a pilot program funded by the Bureau of Justice Assistance to increase and enhance the exchange of sensitive information about terrorism and other criminal activity between local, state, and federal law-enforcement agencies. Information about how to contact MATRIX is available at www.iir.com/matrix/contact_matrix.htm.

National Cybercrime Training Partnership

The National Cybercrime Training Partnership provides local, state, and federal law-enforcement agencies with guidance and assistance in an effort to ensure that the law-enforcement community is properly trained to address electronic and high-technology crime.

National Environmental Health Association (NEHA)

NEHA is a member-based association with interests in food protection, hazardous waste, air and water quality, epidemiology, and bioterrorism preparedness in the public and private sectors. Members enjoy access to online courses for first responders and the *Journal of Environmental Health*. The NEHA Web site offers an online bookstore, chemical and bioterrorism preparedness information and resources, conference links, a calendar of events, and links to related sources.

National Fire Academy (NFA) Training Resources

NFA partners with state fire-training agencies to provide training for first responders to manage the consequences of acts of terrorism. Other NFA training topics include emergency response to terrorism, incident command systems, public fire education planning, and response to hazardous materials incidents.

National Fire Protection Association (NFPA)

NFPA is an international nonprofit organization that advocates scientifically based codes and standards and provides research and public and professional education on fire and related hazards. Its Web site presents numerous links, free tutorials, a training catalog, and an interactive joint project, Target Safety NFPA Safety Training. NFPA offers a variety of training opportunities in diverse areas, such as hazard communications, bloodborne pathogens for firefighters, electrical safety, and safety for the aviation industry. To help first responders recognize the signs of terrorist activity, NFPA has developed a three-hour Online Terrorist Awareness Course.

National Institute for Occupational Training and Health (NIOSH)

The Centers for Disease Control's NIOSH conducts research and makes recommendations for the prevention of work-related injuries and illnesses. The NIOSH Web site presents information about chemical safety, emergency response, traumatic injuries, respirators, and health-care worker safety. Training and funding updates are also available. A "Spotlights" section offers resources on specialized topics such as emergency preparedness for business.

National Interagency Civil-Military Institute (NICI)

NICI provides free training, information, and research services on domestic military support capabilities in public safety and disaster preparedness. Course topics include emerging technologies and their application to emergency-management systems, preparing for and managing the consequences of terrorism, roles and capabilities of emergency responders, and threat analysis.

National Law Enforcement and Corrections Technology Centers (NLECTC), National Institute of Justice

NLECTC provides technology and technical assistance to state and local public-safety professionals in such areas as evidence analysis, IS, communications systems, sensors and surveillance, and emerging technologies.

National Law Enforcement Trainers Association (NLETA)

NLETA is a professional association comprising qualified and experienced law-enforcement trainers, performance consultants, and other experts. NLETA's mission is to support these professionals directly by providing them with benefits and services. Membership is restricted to qualified instructors with at least two years of experience.

National Ocean Service, Office of Response and Restoration

This Web site offers tools and information for emergency responders, planners, and others working to understand and mitigate the effects of oil and hazardous materials in the nation's waters and on its coastlines.

National Personal Protective Technology Laboratory (NPPTL)

The National Institute for Occupational Safety and Health's (NIOSH) NPPTL focuses expertise from many scientific disciplines to advance federal research on respirators and other personal protective technologies for workers. NPPTL's strategic research program ensures that the development of new personal protective equipment keeps pace with employer and worker needs.

National Sheriffs' Association (NSA)

The NSA seeks to help sheriffs, their deputies, chiefs of police, and others in the field of criminal justice perform their jobs in the best possible manner and better serve the people of their jurisdictions. In partnership with the Office for Domestic Preparedness, NSA offers Managing Weapons of Mass Destruction Incidents: An Executive-Level Program for Sheriffs, a course that offers a broad overview of the terrorist threat and addresses response strategies and safety. NSA also produces the bimonthly magazine *Sheriff*, which addresses the current concerns of law enforcement.

National Tactical Officers Association (NTOA)

The NTOA is a nonprofit association dedicated to the advancement of the special weapons and tactics profession throughout the world. NTOA provides a clearinghouse for tactical information and cost-effective tactical training.

National Terrorism Preparedness Institute (NTPI), Southeastern Public Safety Institute, St. Petersburg College

NTPI curricula prepare first responders to respond to terrorism incidents involving weapons of mass destruction. Trainings are designed to be interactive, current, and cost effective and include onsite instruction as well as satellite television and Web cast programs.

Office for Domestic Preparedness (ODP)

ODP develops, validates, delivers, and evaluates comprehensive training on responding to incidents of terrorism involving weapons of mass destruction. ODP offers specialized courses that range from basic awareness to hands-on technical and command courses. Technical assistance is available from ODP under three categories: general technical assistance, information management, and Statewide Domestic Preparedness Strategy development. See the ODP Weapons of Mass Destruction Training Program Course Catalog (PDF), or a list of ODP's specialized training courses.

Office of Community-Oriented Policing Services (COPS)

Police-community collaboration is a key element of any emergency response plan. COPS supplies training and technical assistance to agencies receiving COPS grants and resources to the field to support community policing.

Public Health Emergency Preparedness and Response Centers for Disease Control and Prevention (CDC)

The Public Health Emergency Preparedness and Response page on the CDC's Web site offers the latest medical data on chemical, radiological, and biological threats and agents, including anthrax and smallpox. Comprehensive information for first responders and emergency medical personnel is provided regarding preparation and planning; response; mass trauma; medical surveillance; laboratory safety, testing, and procedures; training; resources and links; and related news.

Radiation Emergency Assistance Center/Training Site (REAC/TS)

REAC/TS provides the U.S. Department of Energy, the World Health Organization, and the International Atomic Energy Agency with management support during radiation accidents. REAC/TS is a 24-hour emergency-response program offering training, consultation, and assistance related to responding to all types of radiation accidents or incidents. The center's team of physicians, nurses, health physicists, radiobiologists, and emergency coordinators offers around-the-clock assistance at the local, national, and international levels.

RAND Center for Domestic and International Health Security

The Center for Domestic and International Health Security is a multidisciplinary research collaboration housed at RAND. The center's mission is to make health a key component of U.S. foreign policy and to protect the health of the American homeland by preparing it for potential terrorist attacks.

SEARCH, the National Consortium for Justice Information and Statistics

SEARCH, the National Consortium for Justice Information and Statistics, is a nonprofit membership organization created by and for the states. Dedicated to improving the criminal justice system through the effective application of information and identification technology, SEARCH provides justice agencies with products, services, and resources. It offers technical assistance to local and state justice agencies to help them develop, manage, and improve their automated information systems. The SEARCH National Technical Assistance and Training Program provides local, state, and federal agencies with comprehensive, hands-on training on computer technology issues with criminal-justice applications.

State and Local Anti-Terrorism Training (SLATT) Program, Bureau of Justice Assistance

The SLATT Program provides preincident awareness, preincident preparation, prevention, and interdiction training and information for state and local law-enforcement personnel in the areas of domestic counterterrorism and extremist criminal activity.

State Domestic Preparedness, National Emergency Management Association (NEMA)

NEMA's State Domestic Preparedness Web pages include "best practice" reviews of local- and state-level strategies, a catalog of state training programs for domestic terrorism preparedness, and summaries of congressional activity on relevant topics.

Substance Abuse and Mental Health Services Administration's National Mental Health Information Center—U.S. Department of Health and Human Services

The Center for Mental Health Services supports immediate, short-term crisis counseling and ongoing support for the victims of disasters. Qualifying federal disasters include severe storms, forest fires, and incidents of mass criminal victimization. Support is provided in the form of grants to states for counseling outreach within federal disaster areas and grants for the delivery of training to crisis counselors who provide crisis assistance after federal relief workers return home.

Transportation Emergency Preparedness Program

The U.S. Department of Energy's Transportation Emergency Preparedness Program integrates transportation emergency preparedness activities under a single program to address the emergency response concerns of state, tribal, and local officials regarding the shipment of radioactive materials.

Transportation Technology Center, Inc.

Transportation Technology Center, Inc., manages a research and test center for transportation and nontransportation systems. The center offers a wide range of services, including research, development, and evaluation testing. With more than 48 miles of railroad track, the center is able to test vehicle performance and railway components such as signal and safety devices.

United States Army Medical Research Institute of Chemical Defense, Chemical Casualty Care Division (USAMRICD-CCCD)

USAMRICD-CCCD trains medical professionals and first responders in the management of chemical casualties and provides military and civilian authorities with consultation services. CCCD also organizes and implements a postgraduate education program for medical professionals and training for first responders. For specific information concerning classes available to civilian personnel, refer to the Upcoming Events, Computer-Based Training, and Satellite Broadcast pages of the CCCD Web site.

United States Army Medical Research Institute of Infectious Diseases (USAMRIID)

USAMRIID is the U.S. DOD's lead research laboratory for developing medical countermeasures, vaccines, drugs, and diagnostic tools to protect

U.S. military personnel from biological warfare agents and naturally occurring infectious diseases. USAMRIID offers specialized training to military and civilian health-care providers to enhance their capability to diagnose and treat casualties of biological warfare and terrorism. The education component offers in-house and satellite courses and provides an online repository of current U.S. DOD reference materials and related Web links.

U.S. Department of Homeland Security (DHS)

The U.S. DHS's first priority is to protect the nation against terrorist attacks. Component agencies analyze threats and intelligence, guard the nation's borders and airports, protect its critical infrastructure, and coordinate the national response to future emergencies.

U.S. Food and Drug Administration's Bioterrorism Home Page

This Web page serves as a gateway to the latest bioterrorism information posted to the Food and Drug Administration's Web site, including news, articles, studies, guidelines, health initiatives, and funding announcements.

U.S. Geological Survey (USGS)

The USGS is a bureau of the U.S. Department of the Interior. USGS seeks to minimize loss of life and property from natural disasters, manage natural resources, and enhance and protect the quality of life by providing reliable scientific information about the Earth. Maps and other geologic information are available by state. Through the EarthExplorer section of this Web site, viewers may access or order aerial photographs, cartographic products, and satellite images, including declassified intelligence satellite photographs.

U.S. National Response Center (NRC), U.S. National Response Team (NRT)

Federal reporting requirements mandate that parties responsible for an oil or chemical discharge immediately contact NRC, the sole national point of contact for reporting oil, chemical, radiological, and biological discharges. NRT comprises 16 federal agencies with expertise in emergency response to pollution incidents, including those resulting from terrorist acts. NRT provides preincident policy guidance and postincident technical advice and access to response resources.

U.S. Northern Command—Defending the Homeland

As provided by U.S. law and as directed by the president or secretary of defense, the U.S. Northern Command provides civil authorities with military assistance. This help is always in support of a lead federal agency, such as the Federal Emergency Management Agency. Military civil support includes domestic disaster-relief operations that occur during fires, hurricanes, floods, and earthquakes. Support also includes counterdrug operations and consequent management assistance, such as aid that would occur after a terrorist event involving a weapon of mass destruction. Generally, an emergency must exceed the management capabilities of local, state, and federal agencies before U.S. Northern Command becomes involved.

Weapons of Mass Destruction Civil Support Teams (WMD-CST)

These U.S. DOD units, staffed by the Army and the Air National Guard, support local and state authorities at domestic WMD and nuclear, biological, and chemical incident sites. CSTs are able to deploy rapidly, help local first responders determine the nature of an attack, provide medical and technical advice, and assist with requests for additional military support. CSTs will normally be the first National Guard units to arrive at a WMD incident. Requests for assistance during an emergency from the local level must be initiated by an official government agency, passed to the state emergency manager through emergency management channels, and be directed to the adjutant general.

World Health Organization (WHO)

WHO is a United Nations agency dedicated to helping people from across the globe attain the highest possible level of health by promoting healthy lifestyles, reducing mortality, developing health systems that equitably improve health outcomes, and framing and enabling health-related policies. WHO tracks and verifies infectious-disease outbreaks worldwide, offers current alert and response information, and provides links to health topics covering WHO's projects and activities, publications, and research tools, including WHO's library database.

Index